IZAAK WALTON

IZAAK WALTON

Selected Writings

Edited with an Introduction by
Jessica Martin

Fyfield*Books*

First published in Great Britain in 1997 by
Carcanet Press Limited
4th Floor, Conavon Court
12-16 Blackfriars Street
Manchester M3 5BQ

A CIP catalogue record for this book
is available from the British Library.
ISBN 1 85754 307 6

The publisher acknowledges financial assistance
from the Arts Council of England.

Set in 10pt Palatino by Bryan Williamson, Frome
Printed and bound in England by SRP Ltd, Exeter

Contents

Introduction

In Winchester, on 9 August 1683, Izaak Walton wrote his last piece of prose – his Will. He was ninety years old. On 24 October he had it witnessed and sealed with the bloodstone seal John Donne had given him, which he habitually used. Some weeks later, on 15 December, he died in Winchester, when the weather was exceptionally cold.

From this once private document, which now makes the final piece in this selection, Walton speaks directly as he does not in any public work of prose. The best-known of these, the *Compleat Angler*, built as it is around two or three characterised voices, shows him clothed in genial *personae*. His biographical works, the *Lives* (for which he was so much more esteemed than for the *Angler* in his own lifetime) see him interpreted through more or less subjective narrations of the actions of men he admired – via the priest-poets Herbert and Donne, the apparently irenic theologian Richard Hooker, Walton's patron and acquaintance Sir Henry Wotton, and the casuist and Restoration bishop Robert Sanderson. His single overtly political work, *Love and Truth*, written and published when he was in his eighties, is self-consciously anonymous.

These other 'masked' – but always apparently confiding – Waltons invite personal speculation, character assessment, moral judgement; they set before us a pious lay voice, theologically diffident, politically loyal without analysis or detachment, rejoicing in qualities labelled 'simplicity' or 'sincerity', praising charity. They have actually provoked an enormous range of reactions, from the near-veneration the 'good old man' has inspired in anglers and Anglicans, through the barely controlled disappointment of academics and editors complaining 'where Walton fails is in truth', to Byron's mysterious condemnation of Walton as a 'quaint, old, cruel coxcomb'.

It is reassuring to find, then, that the direct voice speaking from the Will bears a kind of family resemblance to the masks assumed in the printed prose; it *is* pious, it is theologically decided while declining to be involved in nice points; and it is precisely, practically kind. He finishes the longish codicil bequeathing mourning rings with the words 'Mrs Dalbin must not be forgotten'. He asks to hand on the responsibility for his 'A[u]nte Beacham' to his son Izaak, accompanying this with exact funds and instructions: 'about fiftie shilling a year in or for bacon and cheise'. He leaves his Staffordshire farm, given certain family conditions, which were fulfilled, 'to the towne or corperation of Stafford (in which I was born)' stipulating to what ends the rent they collect should be put: some to buy apprenticeships for two local boys each year, some to be paid yearly to a local maidservant or 'som honest poor man's daughter . . . to [be] paide her, on or at the day of her marriage.' A little he offers to the town as a fee for administering the other bequests, and the remainder he leaves to 'be imployed to buie coles for some pore people, that shall most neide them in the saide towne; the saide coles to be delivered in the last weike of Janewary, or in every first weike in Febrewary; I say then, because I take that time to be the hardest and most pinching times with pore people'.

It seems that Walton's kindness, the one quality every reader (except Byron) agreed on, was quite real. Beyond that, though, the ground starts to shift confusingly; 'more than most authors' suggests his *DNB* entry 'he lives in his writings, which are the pure expression of a kind, humorous and pious soul in love with nature' – words which imply an unusual transparency of self, a kind of naïvety about what is involved in writing a book which *incidentally* results in works of art. Distilled virtue: pure prose. It looks tempting, with its barely tacit suggestion that the goodness of his life guaranteed that his books must be good too, and plenty of Walton's readers have been happy to leave it at that. (On its own it also, as it happens, belittles his abilities.) But it's not true, and Andrew Lang, the *DNB* biographer, knows it's not true, because he finishes his sentence by affirming that 'the expression itself is unique for its apparent simplicity which is really elaborately studied art.' The country we survey is pastoral, not rural: a *trompe l'oeil* landscape.

Walton himself was quick to exploit its possibilities. His was an 'artlesse Pensil', he said in his 1640 Introduction to the *Life of Donne*; yet the phrase implies a paradox where the possibilities of revision, of reconsideration and redrawing surrounding 'Pensil' crowd the word 'artlesse' into a corner so that it becomes a code word for a *style*. Unversed spontaneity was certainly the aim, but it was an effect which needed a lot of fiddling. In fact he revised constantly, almost obsessively, and since his handwriting was vile and his spelling eccentric even by early modern standards, he could be a menace to his publisher. (The 'artlesse Pensil' was itself revised into a 'pen' in 1658, but reinstated in 1670. Perhaps Walton was loathe to lose the versatility of the original; pictorial yet provisional, a sketch claiming the vivid 'truth' of rough lines while modestly – and prudently – avoiding committing itself.)

Studied diffidence of this kind is in part a feature of the commemorative – what we would now call the biographical – genre in which Walton first made his name. It was, primarily, a celebratory form; and it was a matter of decorum for its narrator routinely to declare the inadequacy with which he had celebrated the virtues of the dead. (Usually, the reluctant author was persuaded to it by anxious choruses of importunate 'friends' and so could decline any personal responsibility for the result.) At its most conventional it was a technique of compliment which magnified your best praise *en bloc* as well as covering you against mistakes and infelicities. In Walton, though, there was more to his humility than a cliché of form. When he brought his first signed piece of prose into print in 1640, the *Life of Dr. John Donne*, he was doing something surprising, even audacious, and he knew it.

The narrated life as Walton practised it had strong roots in the learned tribute – the sermon preached by a divine at the dead man's funeral, using him perhaps as Christian exemplar, or perhaps shaping the narrative into an oration which lauded him in ways more self-consciously classical. Often what actually came out was a bit of both. As these funeral set-pieces were committed to print, they were transmuted by its different pressures and expectations, sometimes into free-standing but more obviously reader-friendly versions of themselves, and sometimes doubling as, or edited into, prefaces to the dead man's own writings. They might at this point become a form which called itself a 'Life', as Walton called his first three posthumous tributes-cum-prefaces *Lives*. But their origins – exhortatory and epideictic – shaped the conventions Walton inherited, as well as highlighting how far his lay status made him a usurper in what until now had been an almost exclusively clerical authorship. And it wasn't simply that Walton was not a priest. He wasn't anything else prominent either – whereas, for instance, the layman George Paule, whose *Life of Archbishop Whitgift* first appeared in 1609, was a knight and Comptroller of the Archbishop's household, partly writing up Whitgift as a way of justifying his regime and partly playing at being Tacitus. Paule was Walton's only lay model of the century so far, but his authorial stance is unlikely to have been very helpful.

In the 1630s Walton was a middle-class, middle-aged citizen, owning 'half a shop' near Chancery Lane, and a member of the Ironmongers' Company; he appears as an 'ironmonger' on his marriage certificate in 1626. He knew Donne because he was his parishioner and verger in the City church St Dunstan's-in-the-West, where Donne held a living in conjunction with the Deanery of St Paul's from 1621 until his death ten years later. Probably through Donne, he became acquainted with a number of well-connected men, in and out of the Church; Sir Henry Wotton (whose Life he was to write in 1651), the Bishop of Chichester Dr Henry King, Dr John Hales of Eton. But he wasn't himself a graduate, or a clergyman, or aristocratically related in any way (though his first wife, Rachel Floud, had the distant ecclesiastical distinction of being granddaughter to Cranmer's great-nephew); he was a grammar school boy from Stafford with a yeoman background, a tendency to literary dabbling and a weakness for high-church divines. In fact, jumped-up – which perhaps goes some way to explain Byron's later dislike, and the tone in which Leslie Stephen was to call him a 'worthy tradesman' or Edmund Gosse (himself dismissed as a 'little dapper grocer' by Stephen's daughter Virginia) more affectionately 'that immortal piscatory linen draper'. The rising middle-class cannot be likeable. They are fawning, or they are low, depending on your perspective.

Walton himself, though fairly serene about it, was also careful; indeed tactful. Though there is evidence that he was known as something of a poet as early as 1613, and while his Elegy on Donne had been esteemed enough to appear with other selected tributes in the posthumous edition of Donne's *Poems* in 1633

(Walton may have helped edit the second edition), he was content simply to be researcher for the *Life* of Donne which Sir Henry Wotton planned to write. But Wotton died in 1639 with the *Life* unwritten, and Walton, noticing that an edition of eighty sermons by Donne was therefore due to appear without a prefatory notice of its author, 'reviewed my forsaken collections' and wrote Donne up in time for a proper commemoration of his extraordinary qualities to appear at the front of the *Sermons* in 1640. It took him six weeks. Running through his Introduction is his sense of himself, Donne's 'meanest friend' as an odd choice of funeral orator; but, deftly, he turns his protestations of humility, of fortunate proximity, into claims for a particularly intimate truth of impression which might contain a greater authority than the most learned eloquence could:

> If I be demanded, as once *Pompeys* poore Bondman was, (whilest he was alone on the Sea shore gathering the pieces of an old Boat to burne the body of his dead Master) What art thou that preparest the funeralls of Pompey the Great? Who I am, that so officiously set the Authors memorie on fire? I hope the question hath in it more of wonder then disdaine.
>
> Wonder indeed the Reader may, that I (who professe my selfe artlesse) should presume with my faint light to show forth his life, whose very name makes it illustrious; but be this to the disadvantage to the person represented, certaine I am, it is much to the advantage of the beholder; who shall see the Authors picture in a natural dresse, which ought to beget faith in what is spoken, for he that wants skill to deceive, may safely be trusted.

It's a passage which at its close actually shows an extraordinary confidence in its author's powers of re-creation, using rhetoric which seems to foreshadow Boswell more than it recalls the medieval hagiographers with whom Walton is usually compared. *You will know him as I knew him*, Walton is saying, *that is, intimately, and absolutely as he was; because I am less than he was and I lack the skill to mislead*. The virtuoso neatness with which Walton manages his stance declares the untruth of its final assurance. But while what we see *is* sleight of hand it is still, I think, evidently being used in Donne's (and in our) service. Walton will give himself and Donne these appropriate and complementary *personae*, and he will tailor all he reports to fit them, because for him they do not conceal but reveal. His assumed identity of humble parishioner – one of the things he was to Donne – is a true seeing of a true stance, even though it also *selects*, as Walton will include the mourning seal Donne sent to George Herbert and never mention his own. Such decisions, within the terms of Walton's laudatory form, go to make the biography an act of decorum and pious respect.

The *Life* itself does one other unusual and intimate thing. Donne's own words – mostly lifted from wrought documents, poems and sermons – are built into the narrative, used in direct conversations and in Walton's own descriptions. Donne preached, says Walton, 'like an Angel from a Cloud, though in none'; 'Preachers', wrote Donne, 'As Angels out of clouds, from Pulpits speake'. Walton was to deploy this technique in his *Life of Mr. George Herbert* thirty years later, with curious results. Walton's Herbert paraphrases his poems whenever he speaks, translating the contemplations of the spirit into commentaries on, even movers of, the actions of his life narrative. Indeed this conversion from thought to pious act is even more explicit in the way Walton translates the idealities of Herbert's manual of advice for rural priests, *The Country Parson*, into the daily usage of Bemerton, Herbert's last parish. While Walton's intention is clearly responsible – how can you have a source more direct than your subject's *own words*? – yet the effect can be a strange distortion of observable fact, of a kind which later readers of Walton found hard to bear. A.B. Grosart, editing Herbert's works in 1876, found himself driven to despair by Walton's idiosyncrasies, and said so:

> the truth must at long last be told and this mingle-mangle of unhistoric statement and mendacious zeal exposed. There are nearly as many blunders as sentences in the narrative and the *animus* is as base as the supercilious ignorance is discreditable. Alas that I must say these 'hard things' of anything from the pen of one I so revere (substantially!) Alas that they should be true!

Perhaps part of poor Grosart's problem was that Walton was not in the business of 'objective' narration of a kind we might find familiar, but was concerned instead to represent the qualities he found admirable in exemplary ways. That was, after all, what a celebratory genre was *for*. In that sense 'hagiography' describes rather than criticises Walton's practice. And if we consider the extraordinary self-presentation (not to say presence of mind) Donne shows in his bizarrely iconic deathbed preparations, it must be acknowledged that Walton is here much aided by his subjects. According to Walton, Donne spent his dying energies posing on an urn wrapped in his shroud in order that the painter he commissioned could give him an image of his own death to contemplate. This might be argued to have been an exemplary invention of Walton's in the *ars moriendi* tradition: but no one (including the others present during Donne's last illness) complained at its falsity or exclaimed at its unlikelihood; and no one, then or since, found its pious solipsism atypical of Donne. Walton's preferred images of piety were in any case less fierce, and Herbert's devotional singing to his own lute accompaniment 'the *Sunday* before his death' was (perhaps) more his style.

Walton's *Life of Donne* made his name as a writer. John Hales and Henry King praised it. Charles I liked it – not that this indicates nationwide approbation so much as it points the polarisation of Walton's own sympathies in the 1640s as the Civil War got under way. And in fact some time in 1643-4 Walton felt it necessary to resign his verger's position and leave London. London was the Parliamentary capital after 1642 and Walton, whose royalism was as unquestioned as it was unquestioning, may well have been uncomfortably situated. Besides these public reasons, his wife Rachel died; and all the children from that marriage were dead: Walton may not have cared to stay on alone in the London house.

According to the waspish seventeenth-century gossip Anthony à Wood, Walton retired to Stafford, and the impression one is left with is that he stayed there and fished until the Restoration. He does seem to have spent a bit of time in Stafford, and to have fished there, but his war was more adventurous than that implies. We know he was in London for Archbishop Laud's execution, because he tells us so in the *Life of Sanderson*, expressing his out-rage that 'the malicious Citizens fearing his pardon, shut up their Shops, professing not to open them till Justice was executed. This malice and madness is scarce credible, but I saw it.' In 1646 he married Anne Ken, younger half-sister of Thomas Ken (later the non-juring Bishop of Bath and Wells) and their first child was born in 1647-8. At this time he seems to have been living in Clerkenwell, and the following year, as well as publishing his second biography, he also (according to Elias Ashmole) had the single adventure of his life. After the battle of Worcester – at which time he was probably in Stafford – he was entrusted with Charles II's Garter jewel, the 'lesser George', carrying it up to London and delivering it to Colonel Blague, who was then in the Tower. The Colonel escaped and was able to deliver the jewel to Charles in exile. Walton at this time was approaching sixty.

The biography he brought out was his *Life of Sir Henry Wotton*, which introduced the *Reliquiae Wottonianae* of 1651. Like the ear-lier *Life*, it was functioning as a celebratory preface to the imme-diately posthumous works of a man he had known and admired – though Wotton's collected miscellanea were very much less *opera* than the *LXXX Sermons* had been, and consequently Wal-ton's biographical introduction became a much weightier contri-bution to the volume as it were by default. Perhaps because of this, and because the *Life of Donne* had been liked, the *Life of Wotton* is presented with much more confidence. Walton offers no rea-sons or excuses for his authorship, cheerfully tracing the glories of Wotton's family in terms which recall Quintilian's advice on commemorative oration rather than clutching at conventional humilities to justify himself. He allows himself to be more expan-sive, even a little experimental – as in the passage included here, where the supernatural dreaming of Wotton's great-uncle Nich-olas prefigures Aubrey's *Brief Lives* both in the self-containedness of the anecdote and in its dramatic credulity. The *Reliquiae* went into two more editions in Walton's lifetime and a third two years after his death; and the *Life* which accompanied it was also to appear in its own right as the second of Walton's collected biogra-phies in 1670 and again in 1675.

At this point, though, Walton turned his hand to an entirely different form. In 1653 there appeared the first edition of *The Compleat Angler; or, the Contemplative Man's Recreation*. The dual message of this main title is plain: yes, it is a 'How to' book, offering itself as the repository of all knowledge to do with freshwater fishing, and firmly within a tradition of advice manuals on practical subjects which predated printing. At the same time it declares the activity it describes to have a spiritual usefulness, refreshing the thoughtful soul. And the text itself is structured with an artistry of presentation much beyond the needs of any manual (although this was not an unusual feature of a 'How to' book). As it first appeared it was couched as a dialogue between two men, Piscator and Viator, as they set out on a May morning, and in the second edition of 1655 the two men were changed to three, and the functions of Piscator's interlocutors stressed more precisely. Viator, the traveller, was changed to Venator ('hunter') and a third character, Auceps ('falconer') added. Now Walton could set up discussions which assessed and celebrated their different recreations – situated in the three elements water, earth and air – as an elegant framing device for a disquisition on angling as the most contemplative, the most spiritual of the three. Its strong precedent was in the fishermen-apostles of the New Testament, as well as (shakily) in a claim that the prophet Amos was an angler because the fish-hooks 'but twice mentioned' in all the Old Testament were once mentioned by him.

A device of this kind does far more than merely set opportunities to describe how to bait for, catch and cook different kinds of fish. It considers what it might mean to *live well*: that is, to live harmoniously with yourself and the social order in which you find yourself. Walton's version proclaims its quietism – '*Study to be quiet*' he reminds us famously at the close of the later editions – but the book's form, and Walton's own rhetoric, each conceal muted political protest, as the tag he has lifted from Paul's first letter to the Thessalonians is, in context, an exhortation to the tiny minority of persecuted faithful pitted against a hostile world. And the biblical overtones have, in seventeenth-century fashion, a classical echo too: this new departure of Walton's is in part the pastoral idyll claimed by the politically unpopular. Marginalised, and perceiving exile (or execution) to be the condition of the just,

Walton seizes a post-Senecan perception of rural purity as the safeguard against the centralised corruption of the City and its politics. At the same time he seizes the brief moment when a once State-sanctioned Church crosses into political non-existence and so is enabled to use all the images of passive suffering and persecution central to its sacred story without (much) embarrassment.

This is a lot to claim for a fishing manual – which was presumably what Walton hoped people would think – but his message is unmistakable. In all editions but the first, he quotes the poet Christopher Harvey, whose metaphysical collection *The Synagogue*, a heavy imitation of Herbert's *The Temple*, was clear about its conformist allegiances at the expense of grace and subtlety. Harvey uses the form to pose rhetorical questions, on the whole; and Walton's selection, 'Common Prayer', is typical:

> What! pray'r by th'book? and common? Yes, Why not?
> > The Spirit of grace,
> > And supplication,
> > Is not left free alone
> > For time and place,
> But manner too: to read or speak by rote,
> Is all alike to him, that prayes
> In 's heart, what with his mouth he says.

Dreadful poetry, but in reiterating the sentiment Walton sticks his neck out. The other poets he chooses to quote, and the 'good men' he mentions are equally clearly aligned: Peter Heylyn, who reported Laud's final sermon as a martyr's dying words, and was to produce an exhausting account of his life-and-times called *Cyprianus Anglicanus* 'the English Cyprian'; Henry Wotton, that loyal servant of James I; Alexander Nowell, the Elizabethan Dean who had 'made that good, plain, unperplext Catechism which is printed with our good old Service book'. And so on. It is not really surprising that our one contemporary critic of the *Angler*, Richard Franck, who had served with Cromwell in Scotland, was sour about it. Not that he mentioned politics, confining himself to complaining, in rather clumsy prose, about Walton's fishing expertise, his tendency to plagiarise, and the fantastic 'facts' he lifted without comment from Gesner:

[He] lays the stress of his arguments upon other men's obser-vations, wherewith he stuffs his indigested octavo; so brings himself under the angler's censure and the common calamity of plagiary, to be pitied (poor man) for his loss of time, in scribling and transcribing other men's notions. These are the drones that rob the hive, yet flatter the bees they bring them honey . . . I remember in Stafford, I urged his own argument upon him, that pickerel weed of itself breeds pickerel *[pike]*. Which question was no sooner stated, but he transmits him-self to his authority, viz. Gesner, Dubravius, and Androvanus. Which I readily opposed, and offer'd my reasons to prove the contrary . . . which my Compleat Angler no sooner deliberated, but dropped his argument, and leaves Gesner to defend it; so huffed away: which rendred him rather an formal opinionist, than a reformed and practical artist, because to celebrate such antiquated records, whereby to maintain such an improbable assertion.

The book this appeared in, *Northern Memoirs*, was also a sporting manual, and in a sense this judgement reveals the extent to which Walton was not very interested in giving *practical* fishing tips for real fishers or in verifying his natural history in the real world. It might be helpful, in fact, to think of him as a deliberate archaiser, his ideal pastoral built on antiquation at the same time as his advice promises to issue from experience. When he borrows chunks of information and even phraseology from the fifteenth-century *Treatyse of Fysshing wyth an Angle*, or narrates the sponta-neous generation of pike from weed, or of eels from dew, he is enchanting an unstable present with views into the magical cer-tainties of the past.

Charles Kingsley, as admirer of Walton, was to imitate his archaised mixture when he combined nineteenth-century natural science and religiously driven fantasy in *The Water Babies*. Like Walton, Kingsley was to make his otherworld of clear stream and waving weeds a moral microcosm, inhabited by creatures of wonderful construction reflecting one passion or idea for our consideration. Walton seems to do this partly for fun, and largely by implication, but Kingsley takes Walton's hints and turns them into loud lessons: the self-adorning caddis fly – in Walton subtly moralised by an unusual feminine pronoun – is transformed by Kingsley into a narrated miracle of vain passivity. Kingsley did not believe, of course, that the streams of England were filled with minute babies with gills. And Walton's readiness to report moralised or plain fantastic details from other authors does not mean (as Franck evidently thought) that Walton is necessarily credulous of his authorities, because he always shields himself with that careful 'some say . . . others say' formula that lets you narrate what charms without committing yourself. It means that the charm is what matters most.

In the *Lives*, Walton's vision of the 'primitive virtues' his clerical subjects possessed has something of the same antique, or as it were original quality. His Herbert in many ways inhabits a similarly idealised landscape: a pre-Reformation world where the ploughman stops his plough to listen to the *angelus* (thinly disguised as a *'Saints-Bell'*) as 'Mr. *Herbert*' calls him to prayer in the fields. In *those* visions, though, Walton truly believed – perhaps the more strongly for the fragmented definitions of piety with which he and his contemporaries were assailed. Walton built prose walls and painted landscapes against the complex present – very popular they were, then and later – and a component of his activity was a rhetoric which claimed to embrace diverse versions of holiness. We find Walton describing the Puritan Richard Sibbes as a 'blest man' in whom 'Heaven was' (he leaves two books by Sibbes as edifying bequests to relatives) as well as declaring a 'long and very trew friendship with some of the Roman Church'. But then Sibbes' stress on the importance of the Sacrament made his kind of 'puritanism' much more sympathetic to Walton than other kinds could be, and Roman Catholicism also, of course, values the Sacraments. Walton's apparently inclusive gestures are carefully discriminated.

It is true to say, though, that the need to appear inclusive betrays a consciousness of the dangers of fragmentation. In a way, you could say that Walton's conformism, and the idealising patina with which it was covered, was in reaction to uncertainties too plainly visible. No wonder Dr Johnson – who took a comparable route – admired him so much.

With the Restoration, Walton traditionally leaves exile and goes back to the City – now no longer corrupt but again glorious, its purity restored with its monarch. Actually it seems likely that he was already there. He had a house in Clerkenwell; and we know at any rate that he was wandering around Westminster Abbey in 1658, because he defaced (or inscribed) Isaac Casaubon's monument with his signature. Besides which, the inhabitants of the glorious City in 1660 were just as much at odds as to what a 'restored purity' consisted in as the story of English Protestantism so far might lead you to expect.

She was a Church with no unvexed history, no non-factional myths. Even Foxe's *Book of Martyrs*, which seemed to command a unity of Protestant response by largely being about the Catholic persecutions of Mary I, was increasingly claimed by Nonconformists as the seventeenth century progressed – while the Church's role became for them too obviously parallel to the persecutors of the 1550s. Walton never mentions Foxe. Nor did the Church have that inevitable attendant of a unified myth: habit. Every custom, however peripheral, was already a long-established battleground. What should the congregation sing? How much should they sing? Should there be a skilled choir as well? How much, and what, should they sing? Where should the altar be put? Should it be called an altar, or the Lord's Table? What should the priest wear? Could he make up his own prayers? Walton's 'good old Service Book' was barely a century old, and had already been revised twice, in a way that betrayed, as it embedded, a radical uncertainty as to how its central Sacrament – the Eucharist – should be defined. Or *was* it a central Sacrament? How often should it be celebrated? The English Church had been examining herself to bits for a hundred and thirty odd years and was in danger of finding her only definition, at this point of 'restoration', in the fact of her own dissensions.

Faced with such diversity, it was becoming very clear that someone – some figure that might embody consensus – needed to be chosen to hold up the whole fragile edifice. But who should choose that figure, and to what end? The Restoration was everyone's opportunity to make new definitions of a national Church – for which also read imposing your 'improved' version of what the old one had or should have been doing. Everyone took the opportunity. They all shaded one into the other, and yet they all disagreed – the ceremonial-minded supporters of episcopacy, with and without Laudian sympathies, the moderate conformists with Calvinist consciences, the moderate Nonconformists who nevertheless hoped that the new Church would climb down just enough about things like having to wear surplices and kneeling in church for them to be able to re-conform, and so on – all set to appropriate, re-appropriate. On top of this, Charles II was attempting to institute limited religious toleration; and enough of the new episcopate opposed this plan for another old problem to re-surface. The whole never-very-satisfactorily-solved issue of whether the monarch, titular Head of the Church, could actually *give the Bishops orders*, became urgent again.

Walton's next book, the *Life of Mr. Richard Hooker*, was the text which recorded, or invented, that unifying figure. It was the first book Walton had written which explicitly served a political end. It also incidentally created a myth, a series of habits, which we call 'Anglicanism'. His instigators were a couple of bishops whose allegiances, though they differed in certain respects, were united in supporting the retention of church ceremonies: George Morley of Worcester and Gilbert Sheldon of London, later Archbishop of Canterbury.

It is easy to see why they chose Walton. What was wanted was someone to clothe history, or to make myth, with acceptably rich scraps of the various past. In Walton this was not merely a talent but a need. It was his own patchwork he was invited to piece together, already designed for his own spirit's comfort. When Morley and Sheldon approached him for the biographical preface to a new edition of Hooker's *Works* they were, as it happens, selecting a figure Walton had already chosen. On the flyleaf of Walton's copy of Eusebius, there are autograph notes on Hooker's character: 'make his discription . . . that he was like the dove w^{t}h out gall'. They almost certainly date from around 1658, four years before Sheldon and Morley offered Walton the lease of a house on Paternoster Row as an extra persuasion to write up Hooker according to their specifications. Walton accepted the house, but it is doubtful that he would have seen it as a bribe. He was already thinking about Hooker, and was in accord with the ecclesiastical views Sheldon represented. These included, in any case, a belief in the necessary obedience of laymen to clergy which Walton was to cite as his main reason for complying. Other persuasions, he would suggest, were irrelevant.

Walton did know, though, that his congenial task was an item in a kind of propaganda war. Hooker's main work, *The Laws of Ecclesiastical Polity*, was disputed ground. Rather like the Bible, but in a lesser degree, its problem was that its authority for English Protestants was publicly conceded, and this meant that it was rifled for ammunition by every side in debates about the nature of conformity. Yet it had been written partly in response to such debates, and its printing history had been fragmented and interrupted by them. Right from the turn of the century parts of Hooker's manuscript had been unofficially censored, his arguments as they touched the divinely appointed nature of kings and bishops proving too provisional, too *discursive* to be made properly public. Very crudely, you could say the problem was that it was seen as a text which defined when in fact it argued. At the Restoration, a full uncut text was, through a series of blunders and cross-purposes, published with a prefatory *Life of Hooker* both too lukewarm and too moderate to please Sheldon, and a damage limitation exercise was now sought. This was where Walton came in. The edition he was to write for was also uncut, but Walton's remit included a command to throw doubt on the genuineness of the more dangerous passages. The *Life*, plus doubts, was to be printed singly – it came out in 1665 – before readers were allowed access to Hooker's text the next year. The struggle for appropriation the Church suffered was being repeated in microcosm over the *Laws*.

Walton fulfilled these obligations, apparently entirely believing everything he was told about the 'doubtful Books' (Books VI, VII and VIII) in the *Polity*. He had a tendency to trust his erudite betters. But the real service he performed in the *Life* was not to be found in any quasi-factual detail, but in the extraordinarily seductive picture of the exemplary goodness of a singular 'private man': Hooker himself. Walton wrote up a saint, of a particular and now-familiar kind. 'He was never known to be angry, or passionate, or extreme in any of his Desires . . . ' wrote Walton, 'never heard to utter an uncomly word'. His 'grave Behaviour' was a 'Divine Charm'. He avoided disputation whenever he could (though Walton had to concede that he was sometimes forced to it). His asceticism found a parallel in the life of St John the Baptist: he appeared an *obscure, harmless man . . . in poor Clothes . . . his body worn out, not with Age, but Study and Holy Mortifications*.

Walton's Hooker embodied a harmless reasonableness made powerful only by the strength of divine approval. Extreme neither for 'active Romanism' or 'restless Non-conformity', he represented 'The passive peaceable Protestant'. When not walking the newly built *via media*, he looked after his rural parish, his sermons 'neither long nor earnest'. He had weak sight and (by the time of the 1670 edition) a 'blessed . . . bashfulness'. He meditated on his deathbed on *the Number and Nature of Angels, and their blessed Obedience and Order*. He preferred the contained certainties of his masculine friendships to the shrewish demands of his wife. It is a pity Walton got his information about Mrs Hooker from relatives currently in litigation with her, but it allowed him to draw another telling pastoral landscape as Hooker, meekly enduring her monopoly of the family servant, tended sheep with one hand while trying to read the copy of Horace's *Odes* he held in the other. Walton had invented the prototype of a thousand rural vicars and drawn the 'Heat-Pimpled' face of Anglican spirituality. He had embodied holiness in a passionless masculinity that, while it owed something to a pre-Reformation model, combined a distrust of emotional extremes, a degree of personal asceticism, and a veneration for study in a mixture which became standard for Anglical clerical virtue. To some extent these were collegiate ideals, fostered first in a masculine community and then taken out and as far as possible preserved into the dangerous world of lay joys, griefs and practical needs.

George Eliot was to recognise what such an ideal excluded in her portrayal of the unsatisfactory marriage of Dorothea and Casaubon in *Middlemarch*. Dorothea, wrote Eliot 'retained very childlike ideas about marriage. She felt sure she would have accepted the judicious Hooker, if she had been born in time, to save him from that wretched mistake he made in matrimony . . . or any of the other great men whose odd habits it would have been glorious piety to endure'. Dorothea thought that in Casaubon she had detected a pastorally efficacious piety, because he was learned, ascetic and cool. In fact he is quite uninterested in her plans for model cottages for his tenants, and spends his time in misconceived and arid academic disputation he is unable to finish. Nor will he teach her Hebrew; and she learns that even her respect for his erudition requires her willing exclusion to be acceptable.

Walton's model, harmless in itself, favoured a drive towards celibacy and metaphysics which could court some kinds of extremes at the same time as it abjured others. The youthful Edward White Benson, later to become a wilfully ascetic Archbishop of Canterbury, could think of no 'more exact' way to express his admiration for Cardinal Newman's 'manner' in 1848 than to use 'the words which old Izaak Walton used of Hooker'.

By the time the *Life of Hooker* came out, Walton was living in the Close at Winchester as Bishop Morley's steward. He had travelled there from Worcester when Morley was translated to the Winchester See. His wife had died in 1662, at the age of fifty-two. She was buried at Worcester Cathedral, in the Lady Chapel, and Walton wrote her epitaph. Characteristically, it juxtaposes a very direct grief with a brief but explicit portrayal of the dead woman as exemplary. Walton was to spend the rest of his life at Winchester, and to write his last three prose works there: the *Life of Mr. George Herbert*, the *Life of Dr. Sanderson, late Bishop of Lincoln*, and the Popish plot polemic *Love and Truth*.

The *Life of Herbert* is the most ambitious, and arguably the most successful, of these final pieces. It was, Walton wrote a little later, a 'Free-Will-offering' of his, not a commissioned account, and it appeared alone in 1670 rather than as an adjunct to Herbert's own works. This seems important: not only because it shows how much biography had become an independent form, but because it might say something about how Walton saw Herbert himself. That he respected both Herbert's poetry and the prose of *The Country Parson* is not in doubt. But the nature of his extensive use of each does show that he regarded them primarily as sources from which to demonstrate the sanctity and vocation of their author. Herbert's *'most powerful eloquence'* for Walton was in his *'vertuous life'*. In writing it up, Walton was making it possible for Herbert's lived actions to become a kind of sermon, a posthumous exhortation to imitative virtue in the reader.

This implies that Walton was not interested in artistry as such, but only in lived piety. In fact, Walton was very ready to see the skills and beauties of art as corollaries to piety, because his religious sympathies so emphasised ceremony with its attendant musical and liturgical beauties. Though the *Life of Herbert* flattens the rhythms of its subject's spiritual songs, and the traverse of his internal journeys, into a prose paraphrase, we find both packed into a bold devotional metaphor, as Walton celebrates the *'Musick'* of a pious action performed on the road to Salisbury. In the same way, a felicitous and typical misreading of a source text allows Walton to convert the Temple which signified Herbert's physical body, and which edified the body of his poetry, into a real church building, beautified at Herbert's own expense with an unusual but fictional wainscotting.

Predictably, Walton is not much interested in Herbertian conflict or choler. Walton's Herbert, like his Hooker, distrusts passions, marrying a wife he has courted effectively by proxy, and reproving his family on his deathbed for weeping 'to an extremity'. He acknowledges that Herbert experienced spiritual struggles, but his own stress is on certainties, routines, serenities: a lived-out quietude. It is only in this century that Herbert and Donne have fully become poets again. Before that – although Herbert had a devotional value and both wrote a few hymns – the music of pious actions, arranged by Walton, had been their main utterance.

Bishop Sanderson has undergone a comparable transmutation. In this last biography of Walton's, Sanderson is a kind of generic royalist ecclesiastical figure who retains almost no traces of the grimly Calvinist outlook which saw unaided mankind as incompetent 'to subsist an hour if every man should be left to the wildness of his own nature, to do what mischief the devil and his own heart should put upon him'. The 'work' by Sanderson with which Walton's *Life* was bound in the first edition of 1678 was in fact a composite of different extracts. The Sanderson portrayed in the biography shares his qualities (and some of the events of his life) with the straightforwardly Laudian Dr Hammond, like Sanderson a chaplain of Charles I's in the 1640s. Both have bad memories and cannot preach *'without Book'* (seventeenth-century divines habitually preached from memory); both as young clergy-men are supposed to have intervened successfully between a grasping landlord and a suffering tenant. The eighty-five-year-old author manages his anecdotes gracefully, and they are what remain in the memory, especially the author's chance meeting with Sanderson in grim Civil War London, wearing 'sad-coloured clothes' and mourning the demise of the Prayer Book in prose which imitates its discredited liturgical elegance.

Both the *Life of Sanderson* and *Love and Truth*, Walton's last (and anonymous) printed work of 1680, are vehicles through which Walton could express his distrust and disapproval for the usurpation of theological ground (and thus of religious decisions) by untrained lay people. In *Sanderson* the target was extemporary prayer – '*"those raw unpremeditated expressions, to which many of the hearers could not say* Amen"'. In *Love and Truth* it was the theological arrogance of women who changed their religion with their dress, and shopkeepers who thought they could decide against conformity on the basis of their own reading and private conviction. It is peculiarly appropriate that the only time Walton should have engaged in religious debate, he should have spent it denying lay competence in religious questions. It is also like him to have cited his own *Life of Herbert* 'plainly and I hope truly writ' as an effective *argument* for trusting the clergy. It was not an argument but a narrative, always for Walton '*the most powerful eloquence to perswade*'.

Three years later he died. He left two children, another Anne and another Izaak. Anne married William Hawkins, whose *Life of Thomas Ken* continued the Waltonian tradition of spiritualised biography. Izaak went to university, and became a Canon of Salisbury.

Since Walton's death, feeling about his work has more or less divided into two. There is learned opinion, which in the last century particularly has become uneasy and irritated with his inaccuracies; and it is certainly true that you cannot learn how to fish from the *Angler* or pick up the causes of the English Revolution from the *Lives*. In a way, the problem with this approach is that Walton chose genres which seemed to require factual record but which also invited artistry, and thus creative invention. These genres no longer allow invention on quite the terms they once did, and since Walton's talents were bound up with making and depicting ideal worlds, it has become too easy to dismiss him (in the tart judgement of Leslie Stephen) as the writer of 'prose idyl'.

Then there are the people who read him as it were practically. Some, like Boswell, have seen him as essentially a devotional exercise, taking him at face value as an exemplary writer. Walton might have been a bit startled to find his *Lives* standing in for more conventional worship, as on the Sunday morning when Boswell read the *Life of Sanderson* in bed instead of 'being externally decent and going to church'. It did the trick for Boswell, though, who found 'the simplicity and pious spirit of Walton . . . transfused into my soul' in an operation not merely painless but absolutely effortless.

Others found in Walton a feeling which had as much to do with what they felt to be the 'natural goodnesses' of the very English natural world as it did with devotional pieties. Charles Kingsley, with a fine disregard for factual probability, wrote to his wife in 1844 after a day's fishing in Bemerton, George Herbert's parish, fantasising that he might have picked the 'very meadows' where not merely Herbert but 'Dr. Donne, and Izaak Walton, may have fished before me'. He then went on to have a self-consciously Waltonian experience:

> I killed . . . a brace of grayling . . . – a fish quite new to me, smelling just like cucumbers. The dazzling chalk-wolds sleeping in the sun, the clear river rushing and boiling down in one ever-sliding sheet of transparent silver, the birds bursting into song . . . everything stirred with the gleam of God's eye when 'he reneweth the face of the earth'!

It is impossible to unpick what bits of Kingsley's feeling here are about God and what bits are about an idea of 'Englishness'. In fact it is a very Anglican passage, packing and pouring its religious identity into landscape and vista as well as into the figures who are imagined to inhabit it. Kingsley was, as it happens, devout, but this can become an optional extra; the *Angler* in particular is read by many who affirm their English decencies in doing so without being necessarily very exercised by the presence of God.

In fact, the 'practical' readers of Walton do so in order to receive and be comforted by a vision of *goodness*. They are being nurtured by ideal history. 'There are no colours in the fairest sky / So fair as these' Wordsworth wrote of the world of the *Lives*, and in doing so acknowledged that such a world was not and is not, though it might exist in the virtues its imagined inhabitants might inspire in Walton's readers:

> O could we copy their mild virtues, then
> What joy to live, what blessedness to die!
> Methinks their very names shine still and bright;
> Apart – like glow-worms on a summer night;
> Or lonely tapers when from far they fling
> A guiding ray; or seen like stars on high,
> Satellites burning in a lucid ring
> Around meek Walton's heavenly memory.

Wordsworth was not interested in the factual truth of what he read in Walton, any more than Leslie Stephen had any patience with those components of Walton's 'prose idyl' which might seem to hold a different kind of truth from the factual for his readers. For a final assessment which unifies the detached and critical with the more involved, what I have called the 'practical' reader, the most just and fine seems to me to be Dr Johnson's. He called Walton a 'great panegyrist'. In such a judgement, we are at last allowed to see Walton's achievement whole.

A Note on the Selection

In making this selection I have tried to do justice to the range of different kinds of art Walton employed. I have, for instance, represented genres not automatically associated with Walton, such as celebratory verse and explicit polemic. As well as this I have tried to give, as far as possible, some idea of the shaping layers which went to make up finished work by including informal notes, such as his letter to the biographer Aubrey about Ben Jonson, and by rendering one famous passage (from the *Life of Donne*) with its revisions in parallel.

I have mostly preferred later revisions against earlier; on the whole Walton's second and third thoughts were improvements on his first. In practice this means the 1675 edition of the first four *Lives*, the 1678 (or first) edition of the *Life of Sanderson* and the 1676 (or fifth) edition of the *Angler* are quoted unless I have indicated otherwise, since each indicates Walton's last words on his texts. First editions of these appeared as follows: the *Compleat Angler* in 1653; the *Life of Donne* in 1640, as a preface to Donne's *LXXX Sermons*; the *Life of Wotton* in 1654, as a preface to Wotton's *Reliquiae Wottonianae*; the *Life of Hooker* in 1665, as a flyer for its appearance as a preface to Hooker's *Works* in 1666; and the *Life of Herbert* as a flyer for the *Collected Lives* in 1670. I don't feel, however, that Walton's revisions to his poetry necessarily improve it in quite the same way. In reprinting his Elegy for Donne I have used the first version of 1633, though revisions exist from 1635 and 1675; it has an imitatively Donne-like roughness which I like, full of parentheses, though other tastes might prefer the smoother Restoration lines of the last revision.

Walton's Notes for a Life of John Hales were unpublished during his lifetime, and date from the 1670s. They are reprinted from *The Compleat Walton*, edited by Geoffrey Keynes (London, 1929). The inscription on his marriage chest, the texts of the epitaph for David Hookham, and the commendatory verses for Jeremiah Rich are also printed from Keynes's edition. The extract from *Love and Truth* is from the anonymous pamphlet of 1680. The original of Walton's letter to Aubrey exists among Aubrey's MSS, endorsed by Aubrey: 'This account I received from Mr Isaac Walton (who wrote Dr Donne's Life, &c. Decemb. 3, 1680, he being then eighty-seven years of age. This is his own hand-writing "I.A."' The Elegy for Donne first appeared in *Poems, by J.D., with Elegies on the Authors Death* (London, 1633), and the lines on Donne's portrait are from the second edition of 1635, which Walton may have helped edit. The lines on Sibbes are written in Walton's hand in his copy of Sibbes' *The Returning Backslider* (1650), now in Salisbury Cathedral Library. The verses on William Cartwright's death first appeared in *Comedies, Tragi-Comedies, with other Poems, by Mr William Cartwright* . . . (London, 1661). The epitaph for Anne Ken, his second wife, is given as it is engraved on her monument at Worcester Cathedral. Walton writes a slightly different version of it in his prayer book.

I have chosen to retain Walton's orthography and italics throughout. In the case of those pieces printed in his lifetime, the spelling is not distractingly different, and upper case letters are used straightforwardly for emphasis. Though italics are an obsolete convention, they are here employed with some art. As well as being used for proper names and for quotation, they also helpfully indicate paraphrase, emphasis, and direct speech, and to remove them is to remove careful authorial pointers on how to read differently defined bits of text; for Walton always saw his own books through the press.

Four pieces stayed in MS until they were collected as Waltoniana some two hundred years later: the Notes for the Life of John Hales, the letter to Aubrey, the couplet on Richard Sibbes, and Walton's Will. I have retained the spelling (as eccentric as Walton's hand was difficult) here, too, as it usefully indicates the distinction between formally and informally presented work. I have silently regularised some punctuation, provided upper-case opening letters after full stops, and expanded contractions where the short form is not self-evident (e.g. M^{ris} does not become Mistress, but q^{ue} does become *quaere*).

.When quoting in the Introduction, I have not followed my rule about revisions. Since I chose to tell Walton's life chronologically, there seemed something rather dishonest about quoting any edition but the first as the books came out. So, for instance, the *Life of Donne* appears there in its very different form of 1640, though in the main text it is rendered as printed in 1675. Richard Franck, whose prolix book was first issued in 1694, appears here in the reprint of 1821.

Some other practical considerations have dictated the balance of texts reproduced, in particular the *Compleat Angler* as against the *Lives*. The *Angler* has never been out of print, and has been available since 1983 in a handsome and careful edition by the Walton scholar Jonquil Bevan. The *Lives* still await similar treatment and are not currently in print, while they contain some of Walton's finest prose. I have tried to redress the balance by giving them a generous representation here.

Further Reading

Lives of John Donne etc., Izaak Walton, ed. George Saintsbury (Oxford, 1927)

The Compleat Walton, ed. Geoffrey Keynes (London, 1929)

The Compleat Angler 1653-1676, ed. Jonquil Bevan (Oxford, 1983)

Judith Anderson, *Biographical Truth: The Representation of Historical Persons, in Tudor-Stuart Writing* (Yale, 1984)

R.C. Bald, 'Historical Doubts Respecting Walton's Life of Donne' in *Essays in English Literature from the Renaissance to the Victorian Age*, ed. Millar MacLure and F.W. Watt (Toronto, 1964) pp.69-84

Jonquil Bevan, 'Some Books from Walton's Library' in *The Library*, 6th Series, Vol. II, no. 3 (1980)

——, *Izaak Walton's* The Compleat Angler, *The Art of Recreation* (Brighton, 1988)

John Butt, 'Izaak Walton's Methods in Biography' in *Essays and Studies*, 19 (1933), pp.67-84

John Carey, 'Sixteenth and Seventeenth Century Prose' in *English Poetry and Prose 1540-1674*, ed. Christopher Ricks (London, 1970), pp. 339-431

Helen Gardner, 'Dean Donne's Monument in St. Paul's' in *Evidence in Literary Scholarship: Essays in Memory of James Marshall Osborne*, ed. René Wellek and Alvaro Ribeiro (Oxford, 1979), pp.29-44

Raoul Granqvist, 'Izaak Walton's *Lives* in the 19th and early 20th Centuries: A Study of a Cult Object' in *Studia Neophilologica*, 54 (2) (1982), pp.247-61

C.D. Lein, 'Art and Structure in Walton's *Life of Mr. George Herbert*' in *University of Toronto Quarterly*, 46 (1976-7), pp.162-76

David Novarr, *The Making of Walton's* Lives (Ithaca, New York, 1958)

——, 'The Anglican Quietude of Izaak Walton' in *Etudes Anglaises*, 28 (1975), pp.314-24

Donald Stauffer, *English Biography Before 1700* (Cambridge, Mass., 1930)

Richard Wendorf, *The Elements of Life: Biography and Portrait Painting in Stuart and Georgian England* (Oxford, 1990)

The Compleat Angler

From '*A Conference betwixt an* Angler, *a* Faulkner, *and a* Hunter, each commending his Recreation.'

PISCATOR.
VENATOR.
AUCEPS.

Pisc. You know Gentlemen, 'tis an easy thing to scoff at any Art or Recreation; a little *wit* mixt with ill nature, confidence and *malice* will do it; but though they often venture boldly, yet they are often caught even in their own trap [. . .]

And for you that have heard many grave serious men pity Anglers; let me tell you Sir, there be many men that are by others taken to be serious and grave men, which we contemn and pity. Men that are taken to be grave, because nature hath made them of a sowre complexion, money-getting-men, men that spend all their time first in getting, and next in anxious care to keep it; men that are condemned to be rich, and then always busie or discontented: for these poor-rich men, we Anglers pity them perfectly, and stand in no need to borrow their thoughts to think our selves so happy. No, no, Sir, we enjoy a contentedness above the reach of such dispositions, and as the learned and ingenuous[1] *Mountagne* sayes like himself freely, *When my Cat and I entertain each other with mutual apish tricks (as playing with a garter) who knows but that I make my Cat more sport than she makes me? shall I conclude her to be simple, that has her time to begin or refuse to play as freely as I my self have? nay, who knowes but that it is a defect of my not understanding her language (for doubtless Cats talk and reason with one another) that we agree no better: and who knowes but that she pitties me for being no wiser, than to play with her, and laughs and censures my follie for making sport for her when we two play together?*

Thus freely speaks *Mountaigne* concerning Cats, and I hope I may take as great a liberty to blame any man, and laugh at him

---

[1] *in Apol. for Ra. Sebend.* [– I.W.] (Montaigne, *Essayes*, tr. Florio (2nd edn, 1613), II.xii)

too let him be never so grave, that hath not heard what Anglers can say in justification of their Art and Recreation; which I may again tell you is so full of pleasure, that we need not borrow their thoughts to make our selves happy.

Venat. Sir, you have almost amazed me, for though I am no scoffer, yet I have (I pray let me speak it without offence) always looked upon Anglers as more patient and more simple men, then I fear I shall find you to be.

Pisc. Sir, I hope you will not judge my earnestness to be impatience: and for my *simplicity*, if by that you mean a harmlessness, or that simplicity which was usually found in the primitive Christians, who were (as most Anglers are) quiet men, and followers of peace; men that were so simply-wise, as not to sell their Consciences to buy riches, and with them vexation and a fear to die; If you mean such simple men as lived in those times when there were fewer Lawyers; when men might have had a Lordship safely conveyed to them in a piece of Parchment not bigger than your hand, (though several sheets will not do it safely in this wiser age) I say Sir, if you take us Anglers to be such simple men as I have spoke of, then my self and those of my profession will be glad to be so understood: But if by simplicity you meant to express a general defect in those that profess and practise the excellent Art of Angling, I hope in time to disabuse you, and make the contrary appear so evidently, that if you will but have patience to hear me, I shall remove all the Anticipations that discourse, or time, or prejudice have possess'd you with against that laudable and ancient art; for I know it is worthy the *knowledge* and *practise* of a wise man.

But (Gentlemen) though I be able to do this, I am not so unmannerly as to ingross all the discourse to my self; and therefore, you two having declared your selves, the one to be a lover of *Hawks*, the other of *Hounds*, I shall be most glad to hear what you can say in the commendation of that recreation which each of you love and practise; and having heard what you can say, I shall be glad to exercise your attention with what I can say concerning my own Recreation and Art of Angling, and by this means, we shall make the way to seem the shorter: and if you like my motion, I would have Mr. *Faulkner* to begin.

2

Auc. Your motion is consented to with all my heart, and to testifie it, I will begin as you have desired me.

And, first, for the Element I use to trade in, which is the Air, an Element of more worth than weight, an Element that doubtless exceeds both the Earth and Water; for though I sometimes deal in both, yet the Air is most properly mine, I and my hawks use that most, and it yields us most recreation; it stops not the high soaring of my noble and generous *Falcon*; in it she ascends to such an height, as the dull eyes of beasts and fish are not able to reach to; their bodies are too gross for such high elevations: in the Air my troops of Hawks soar up on high, and when they are lost in the sight of men, then they attend on and converse with the gods, therefore I think my *Eagle* is so justly titled *Joves servant in Ordinary*: and that very *Falcon*, that I am now going to see deserves no meaner a title, for she usually in her flight endangers her self, (like the son of *Daedalus*) to have her wings scorch'd by the Suns heat, she flyes so near it, but her mettle makes her careless of danger, for she then heeds nothing, but makes her nimble Pinions cut the fluid air, and so makes her high-way over the steepest mountains and deepest rivers, and in her glorious carere looks with contempt upon those high Steeples and magnificent Palaces which we adore and wonder at; from which height I can make her to descend by a word from my mouth (which she both knows and obeys) to accept of meat from my hand, to own me for her Master, to go home with me, and be willing the next day to afford me the like recreation. [. . .]

Nay more, the very birds of the air (those that be not Hawks) are both so many, and so useful and pleasant to mankind, that I must not let them pass without some observations: They both feed and refresh him; feed him with their choice bodies, and refresh him with their Heavenly voices. I will not undertake to mention the several kinds of Fowl by which this is done; and his curious palate pleased by day, and which with their very excrements afford him a soft lodging at night. These I will pass by, but not those little nimble Musicians of the air, that warble forth their curious Ditties, with which Nature hath furnished them to the shame of Art.

As first the *Lark*, when she means to rejoyce; to chear her self and those that hear her, she then quits the earth, and sings as she ascends higher into the air, and having ended her Heavenly imployment, grows then mute and sad to think she must descend to the dull earth, which she would not touch but for necessity.

How do the *Black-bird* and *Thrassel* with their melodious voices bid welcome to the chearful Spring, and in their fixed Months warble forth such ditties as no art or instrument can reach to?

Nay, the smaller birds also do the like in their particular seasons, as namely the *Leverock*, the *Tit-lark*, the little *Linnet*, and the honest *Robin*, that loves mankind both alive and dead.

But the *Nightingale* (another of my Airy Creatures) breaths such sweet loud musick out of her little instrumental throat, that it might make mankind to think Miracles are not ceased. He that at midnight (when the very labourer sleeps securely) should hear (as I have very often) the clear airs, the sweet descants, the natural rising and falling, the doubling and redoubling of her voice, might well be lifted above earth, and say; Lord, what Musick hast thou provided for the Saints in Heaven, when thou affordest bad men such musick on Earth! [. . .]

There is also a little contemptible winged Creature (an Inhabitant of my Aerial Element) namely, the laborious *Bee*, of whose *Prudence, Policy* and regular Government of their own Commonwealth I might say much, as also of their several kinds, and how useful their honey and wax is both for meat and Medicines to mankind; but I will leave them to their sweet labour, without the least disturbance, believing them to be all very busie at this very time amongst the herbs and flowers that we see nature puts forth this *May* morning.

And now to return to my Hawks from whom I have made too long a digression; you are to note, that they are usually distinguished into two kinds; namely, the long-winged and the short-winged Hawk: of the first kind, there be chiefly in use amongst us in this Nation,

> The *Gerfalcon* and *Jerkin*.
> The *Falcon* and *Tassel-gentel*.
> The *Laner* and *Laneret*.
> The *Bockerel* and *Bockeret*.
> The *Saker* and *Sacaret*.

The *Marlin* and *Jack Marlin*.

The *Hobby* and *Jack*.

There is the *Stelletto* of *Spain*.

The *Bloud* red *Rook* from *Turky*.

The *Waskite* from *Virginia*.

And there is of short-winged Hawks,

The *Eagle* and *Iron*.

The *Goshawk* and *Tarcel*.

The *Sparhawk* and *Musket*.

The French *Pye* of two sorts.

These are reckoned Hawks of note and worth, but we have also of an inferious rank,

The *Stanyel*, the *Ringtail*.

The *Raven*, the *Buzzard*.

The forked *Kite*, the bald *Buzzard*.

The *Hen-driver*, and others that I forbear to name.

Gentlemen, if I should enlarge my discourse to the observation of the *Eires*, the *Brancher*, the *Ramish Hawk*, the *Haggard*, and the two sorts of *Lentners*, and then treat of their several *Ayries*, their *Mewings*, rare order of casting, and the renovation of their *Feathers*; their reclaiming, dyeting, and then come into their rare stories of practice; I say, if I should enter into these, and many other observations that I could make, it would be much, very much pleasure to me: but lest I should break the rules of Civility with you, by taking up more than the proportion of time allotted to me, I will here break off, and entreat you Mr. *Venator*, to say what you are able in the commendation of Hunting, to which you are so much affected, and if time will serve, I will beg your favour for a further enlargement of some of those several heads of which I have spoken. But no more at present.

Venat. Well Sir, and I will now take my turn, and will first begin with a commendation of the earth, as you have done most excellently of the Air, the Earth being that Element upon which I drive my pleasant, wholsom, hungry trade. The Earth is a solid, setled Element; an Element most universally beneficial both to man and beast: to men who have their several Recreations upon it, as Horse-races, Hunting, sweet smells, pleasant walks. The Earth feeds man, and all those several beasts who both feed him, and afford him recreation: What pleasure doth man take in hunting the stately *Stag*, the generous *Buck*, the *Wild Boar*, the cunning *Otter*, the crafty *Fox*, and the fearful *Hare*? And if I may descend to a lower Game, what pleasure is it sometimes with Gins to betray the very vermine of the earth? as namely, the *Fichat*, the *Fulimart*, the *Ferret*, the *Pole-cat*, the *Mould-warp*, and the like creature that live upon the face, and within the bowels of the earth. How does the earth bring forth *herbs, flowers* and *fruits*, both for *physick* and the *pleasure* of mankind? and above all, to me at least, the fruitful *Vine*, of which, when I drink moderately, it clears my brain, chears my heart, and sharpens my wit. How could *Cleopatra* have feasted *Mark Antony* with eight Wild Boars roasted whole at one Supper, and other meat suitable, if the earth had not been a bountiful mother? But to pass by the mighty *Elephant*, which the earth breeds and nourisheth, and descend to the least of creatures, how doth the earth afford us a doctrinal example in the little *Pismire*, who in the Summer provides and lays up her Winter provision, and teaches man to do the like? The earth feeds and carries those horses that carry us. If I would be prodigal of my time and your patience, what might I not say in commendations of the earth? That puts limits to the proud and raging *Sea*, and by that means preserves both man and beast that it destroys them not, as we see it daily doth those that venture upon the Sea, and are there ship-wrackt, drowned, and left to feed Haddocks; when we that are so wise as to keep our selves on *earth*, *walk*, and *talk*, and *live*, and *eat*, and *drink*, and go a *hunting*: of which recreation I will say a little, and then leave Mr. *Piscator* to the commendation of Angling. [. . .]

I might enlarge my self in the commendation of *Hunting*, and of the noble Hound especially, as also of the docibleness of *dogs* in general; and I might make many observations of Land-creatures, that for composition, order, figure and constitution, approach nearest to the compleatness and understanding of man; especially of those creatures which *Moses* in the Law permitted to the Jews, (which have cloven Hoofs and chew the Cud) which I shall forbear to name because I will not be so uncivil to Mr. *Piscator*, as not to allow him a time for the commendations of *Angling*, which he calls an Art; but doubtless 'tis an easie one: and Mr. *Auceps*, I doubt we shall hear a watry discourse of it, but I hope 'twill not be a long one.

Auc. And I hope so too, though I fear it will.

Pisc. Gentlemen; let not prejudice prepossess you. I confess my discourse is like to prove suitable to my Recreation, *calm* and *quiet*; we seldome make the Welkin to roar, we seldom take the name of God into our mouths, but it is either to praise him or to pray to him; if others use it vainly in the midst of their recreations, so vainly as if they meant to conjure, I must tell you, it is neither our fault nor our custom; we, we protest against it. But, pray remember I accuse no body; for as I would not make a *watry* discourse, so would I not put too much *vinegar* into it; nor would I raise the reputation of my own Art by the diminution or ruine of anothers. And so much for the Prologue to what I mean to say.

And now for the *Water*, the Element that I trade in. The *water* is the eldest daughter of the Creation, the Element upon which the Spirit of God did first move, the Element which God commanded to bring forth living creatures abundantly; and without which those that inhabit the Land, even all creatures that have breath in their nostrils must suddenly return to putrefaction. *Moses*, the great Law-giver and chief Philosopher, skilled in all the learning of the Egyptians, who was called the friend of God, and knew the mind of the Almighty, names this Element the first in the Creation; this is the Element upon which the Spirit of God did first move, and is the chief Ingredient in the Creation: many Philosophers have made it to comprehend all the other Elements, and most allow it the chiefest in the mixtion of all living creatures. [. . .]

The *Water* is more productive than the *Earth*. Nay, the earth hath no fruitfulness without showers or dews; for all the *herbs*, and *flowers*, and *fruit* are produced and thrive by the water; and the very Minerals are fed by streams that run under ground, whose natural course carries them to the tops of many high mountains, as we see by several springs breaking forth on the tops of the highest hills; and this is also witnessed by the daily trial and testimony of several Miners.

Nay, the increase of those creatures that are bred and fed in the water, are not only more, and more miraculous, but more advantagious to man; not only for the lengthning of his life, but for the preventing of sickness; for 'tis observed by the most learned Physicians, that the casting off of Lent and other Fish-daies,[1] (which hath not only given the Lie to so many learned, pious, wise Founders of Colledges, for which we should be ashamed) hath doubtless been the chief cause of those many putrid, shaking, intermitting Agues, unto which this nation of ours is now more subject than those wiser Countries that feed on Herbs, Sallets, and plenty of Fish; of which it is observed in Story, that the greatest part of the world now do. And it may be fit to remember that *Moses* (*Lev.* 11. 9. *Deut* 14. 9.) appointed Fish to be the chief diet for the best Common-wealth that ever yet was.

And it is observable not only that there are *fish*, (as namely the *Whale*) three times as big as the mighty Elephant, that is so fierce in battel; but that the mightiest feasts have been of Fish. The *Romans* in the height of their glory have made Fish the mistress of all their entertainments; they have had Musick to usher in their *Sturgeon, Lampreys,* and *Mullet*, which they would purchase at rates rather to be wondred at than believed. He that shall view the Writings of *Macrobius* or *Varro*, may be confirmed and informedof this, and of the incredible value of their Fish and fish-ponds.

But, Gentlemen, I have almost lost my self, which I confess I may easily do in this Philosophical Discourse; I met with most of it very lately (and I hope happily) in a conference with a most learned Physician, Dr. *Wharton*, a dear Friend;[2] that loves both me and my Art of Angling. But however I will wade no deeper in these mysterious Arguments, but pass to such Observations as I can manage with more pleasure, and less fear of running into error. But I must not yet forsake the Waters, by whose help we have so many known advantages.

And first (to pass by the miraculous cures of our known *Baths*) how advantagious is the *Sea* for our daily Traffique; without

---

[1] For Lent, and other fast days in the Church year, people were expected to abstain from eating meat. The custom of eating fish on Fridays – a weekly fast day – still survives.

[2] Thomas Wharton (1614-73), physician and anatomist.

8

which we could not now subsist? How does it not only furnish us with food and Physick for the bodies, but with such Observations for the mind as ingenious persons would not want. [. . .]

Gentlemen, I might both enlarge and lose my self in such like Arguments; I might tell you that Almighty God is said to have spoken to a *Fish*, but never to a *Beast*; that he made a *Whale* a Ship to carry and set his prophet *Jonah* safe on the appointed shore.[1] Of these I might speak, but I must in manners break off, for I see *Theobalds* house. I cry you mercy for being so long, and thank you for your patience.

Auceps. Sir, my pardon is easily granted you: I except against nothing that you have said; nevertheless, I must part with you at this Park-wall, for which I am very sorry; but I assure you Mr. *Piscator*, I now part with you full of good thoughts, not only of your self, but your Recreation. And so Gentlemen, God keep you both.

¶ *Discourse on Angling*

Pisc. O Sir, doubt not but that *Angling* is an Art; is it not an Art to deceive a *Trout* with an artificial Flie? a *Trout*! that is more sharp sighted than any Hawk you have nam'd, and more watchful and timorous than your high mettled Marlin is bold? and yet, I doubt not to catch a brace or two to morrow, for a friends breakfast: doubt not therefore, Sir, but that *Angling* is an Art, and an Art worth your learning: the Question is rather, whether you be capable of learning it? for *Angling* is somewhat like *Poetry*, men are to be born so: I mean, with inclinations to it, though both may be heightened by discourse and practice, but he that hopes to be a good *Angler* must not only bring an inquiring, searching, observing wit; but he must bring a large measure of hope and patience, and a love and propensity to the Art it self; but having once got and practis'd it, then doubt not but *Angling* will prove to be so pleasant, that it will prove to be like Vertue, *a reward to it self.*

[1] Jonah 1:17 – 2:10

9

Venat. Sir, I am now become so full of expectation that I long much to have you proceed; and in the order that you propose.

Pisc. Then first, for the *antiquity* of *Angling*, of which I shall not say much, but onely this; Some say it is as ancient as *Deucalions* Flood: others that *Belus*, who was the first Inventor of Godly and vertuous Recreations, was the first Inventor of *Angling*: and some others say (for former times have had their disquisitions about the Antiquity of it) that *Seth*, one of the Sons of Adam,[1] taught it to his Sons, and that by them it was derived to posterity: others say, that he left it ingraven on those pillars which he erected, and trusted to preserve the knowledge of the *Mathematicks, Musick,* and the rest of that precious knowledge, and those useful Arts which by Gods appointment or allowance and his noble industry were thereby preserved from perishing in *Noahs* flood.[2]

These, Sir, have been the opinions of several men, that have possibly endeavored to make *Angling* more ancient than is needful, or may well be warranted; but for my part, I shall content my self in telling you that Angling is much more ancient than the Incarnation of our Saviour; for in the Prophet *Amos* mention is made of *fish-hooks*;[3] and in the book of *Job* (which was long before the days of *Amos*, for that book is said to be writ by *Moses*) mention is made also of fish-hooks, which must imply Anglers in those times.[4] [. . .]

And an ingenuous *Spaniard* says, *That rivers and the Inhabitants of the watry Element were made for wise men to contemplate, and fools to pass by without consideration.* And though I will not rank my self in the number of the first, yet give me leave to free my self from the last, by offering to you a short contemplation, first of *Rivers,* and then of *Fish*; concerning which I doubt not but to give you many observations that will appear very considerable: I am sure they have appeared so to me, and made many an hour pass away more pleasantly, as I have sate quietly on a flowry Bank by a calm River, and contemplated what I shall now relate to you.

And first concerning Rivers; there be so many wonders reported and written of them, and of the several Creatures that be bred and

[1] Genesis 5:3

[2] Genesis 5:28 – 9:29

[3] Amos 4:2

[4] Job 41:1-2

10

live in them; and, those by Authors of so good credit, that we need not to deny them an historical Faith.

As namely of a River in *Epirus*, that puts out any lighted Torch, and kindles any Torch that was not lighted. Some Waters being drank cause madness, some drunkenness, and some laughter to death. The River *Selarus* in a few hours turns a rod or wand to stone: and our *Cambden*[1] mentions the like in *England*, and the like in *Lochmere* in *Ireland*. There is also a River in *Arabia*, of which all the sheep that drink thereof have their wool turned into a Vermilion colour. And one of no less credit than *Aristotle*, tells us of a merry River, (the River *Elusina*) that dances at the noise of musick, for with musick it bubbles, dances and grows sandy, and so continues till the musick ceases, but then it presently returns to its wonted calmness and clearness. And *Cambden* tells us of a Well near to *Kerby* in *Westmoreland*, that ebbs and flows several times every day: and he tells us of a River in *Surry* (it is called *Mole*) that after it has run several miles, being opposed by hills, finds or makes it self a way under ground, and breaks out again so far off, that the Inhabitants thereabout boast, (as the *Spaniards* do of their River *Anus*) that they feed divers flocks of sheep upon a Bridge. And lastly, for I would not tire your patience, one of no less authority than *Josephus* that learned Jew, tells us of a River in *Judea*, that runs swiftly all the six days of the week, and stands still and rests all their *Sabbath*.

But I will lay aside my Discourse of Rivers and tell you some things of the Monsters, or Fish, call them what you will, that they breed and feed in them. *Pliny* the Philosopher says, (in the third Chapter of his ninth Book)[2] that in the *Indian Sea*, the fish call'd the *Balæna* or *Whirle-Pool* is so long and broad, as to take up more in length and bredth than two Acres of ground, and of other fish of two hundred cubits long; and that in the River *Ganges*, there be Eeles of thirty feet long. He says there, that these Monsters appear

[1] William Camden (1551-1623), historian and antiquarian. His *Britannia* (1586) was translated, under his direction, by Philemon Holland as *Britain, or a Choreographicall Description* in 1610; Walton uses the 1637 edition.

[2] Walton draws heavily on the *Historia Naturalis* (Natural History) of Pliny the Elder (AD 23-79). Pliny, though a naturalist, is no scientist.

11

in that Sea only, when the tempestuous winds oppose the Torrents of Waters falling from the Rocks into it, and so turning what lay at the bottom to be seen on the waters top. And he says, that the people of *Cadara* (an Island near this place) make the Timber for their houses of those Fish-bones. He there tells us, that there are sometimes a thousand of these great Eeles found wrapt, or interwoven together. He tells us there, that it appears that Dolphins love musick, and will come, when call'd for, by some men or boys, that know and use to feed them, and that they can swim as swift as an Arrow can be shot out of a Bow, and much of this is spoken concerning the *Dolphin*, and other Fish, as may be found also in learned Dr. *Casaubons* Discourse of Credulity, and Incredulity, printed by him about the year 1670.

I know, we Islanders are averse to the belief of these wonders: but, there be so many strange Creatures to be now seen (many collected by *John Tredescant*, and others added by my friend *Elias Ashmole* Esq; who now keeps them carefully and methodically at his house near to *Lambeth* near *London*) as may get some belief of some of the other wonders I mentioned. I will tell you some of the wonders that you may now see, and not till then believe, unless you think fit.

You may there see the *Hog-fish*, the *Dog-fish*, the *Dolphin*, the *Cony-Fish*, the *Parrot-fish*, the *Shark*, the *Poyson-fish, sword-fish*, and not only other incredible fish! but you may there see the *Salamander*, several sorts of *Barnacles*, of *Solan Geese*, the *bird* of *Paradise*, such sorts of *Snakes*, and such *birds-nests*, and of so various forms, and so wonderfully made, as may beget wonder and amusement in any beholder: and so many hundreds of other rarities in that Collection, as will make the other wonders I spake of, the less incredible; for, you may note, that the waters are natures storehouse, in which she locks up her wonders.

But, Sir, lest this Discourse may seem tedious, I shall now give it a sweet conclusion out of that holy Poet Mr. *George Herbert* his Divine Contemplation on Gods Providence.

> *Lord, who hath praise enough, nay, who hath any?*
> *None can express thy works, but he that knows them;*
> *And none can know thy works, they are so many,*
> *And so compleat, but only he that ows them.*

> We all acknowledg both thy power and love
> To be exact, transcendent and divine;
> Who dost so strangely and so sweetly move,
> Whilst all things have their end, yet none but thine.
>
> Wherefore, most sacred Spirit, I here present
> For me, and all my fellows, praise to thee;
> And just it is that I should pay the rent,
> Because the benefit accrues to me.

And as concerning Fish in that Psalm, (*Psal.* 104.) wherein for height of Poetry and Wonders the Prophet *David* seems even to exceed himself, how doth he there express himself in choice Metaphors, even to the amazement of a contemplative Reader, concerning the *Sea*, the *Rivers*, and the *Fish* therein contained? And the great Naturalist *Pliny* says, *That Natures great and wonderful power is more demonstrated in the Sea than on the Land.* And this may appear by the numerous and various Creatures inhabiting both in and about that Element; as to the Readers of *Gesner, Rondelitius, Pliny, Ausonius, Aristotle*, and others, may be demonstrated. But I will sweeten this Discourse also out of Contemplation in Divine *Dubartas*,[1] who says,

> God quickned in the sea and in the rivers,
> So many Fishes of so many features,
> That in the waters we may see all creatures,
> Even all that on the earth are to be found,
> As if the world were in deep waters drown'd.
> For seas (as well as skies) have Sun, Moon, Stars;
> (As well as air) Swallows, Rooks, and Stares;
> (As well as earth) Vines, Roses, Nettles, Melons,
> Mushrooms, Pinks, Gilliflowers, and many millions
> Of other plants, more rare, more strange than these,
> As very fishes living in the seas:
> As also Rams, Calves, Horses, Hares and Hogs,
> Wolves, Urchins, Lions, Elephants and Dogs;

[1] A reference to Joshua Sylvester's translation, *Du Bartas His Divine Weekes and Workes* (1608)

13

> *Yea men and Maids, and which I most admire,*
> *The mitred Bishop, and the cowled Fryer.*
> *Of which, Examples but a few years since,*
> *Were shewn the* Norway *and* Polonian *Prince.*

These seem to be wonders, but have had so many confirmations from men of learning and credit, that you need not doubt them; nor are the number, nor the various shapes of fishes, more strange or more fit for *contemplation*, than their different natures, inclinations and actions; concerning which I shall beg your patient ear a little longer.

The *Cuttle-fish* will cast a long line out of her throat, which (like an Angler doth his line) she sendeth forth and pulleth in again at her pleasure, according as she sees some little fish come near to her; and the *Cuttle-fish* (being then hid in the gravel) lets the smaller fish nibble and bite the end of it, at which time she by little and little draws the smaller fish so near to her, that she may leap upon her, and then catches and devours her: and for this reason some have called this fish the *Sea-Angler*.

And there is a fish called a *Hermit*, that at a certain age gets into a dead fishes shell, and like a Hermite dwells there alone, studying the wind and weather, and so turns her shell, that she makes it defend her from the injuries that they would bring upon her.

There is also a fish called by *Ælian* (in his 9. book of Living Creatures, Chap. 16.) the *Adonis*, or Darling of the Sea; so called, because it is a loving and innocent fish, a fish that hurts nothing that hath life, and is at peace with all the numerous Inhabitants of that vast watry Element: and truly I think most Anglers are so disposed to most of mankind. [. . .]

Sir, the Examples may, to you and others, seem strange; but they are testified some by *Aristotle*, some by *Pliny*, some by *Gesner*,[1] and by many others of credit, and are believed and known by divers, both of wisdom and experience, to be a Truth; and indeed are (as I said at the beginning) fit for the contemplation of a most serious and a most pious man. And doubtless this made the Prophet *David* say, *They that occupy themselves in deep*

[1] Conrad Gesner (1516-65), physician and naturalist. His influential *Historiae Animalium* (History of Animals) in five volumes, appeared between 1551 and 1587.

waters see the wonderful works of God:[1] indeed such wonders and pleasures too as the land affords not.

And that they be fit for the contemplation of the most prudent, and pious, and peaceable men, seems to be testifyed by the practise of so many devout and contemplative men, as the *Patriarchs* and *Prophets* of old; and of the *Apostles* of our Saviour in our latter times; of which twelve, we are sure he chose four that were simple Fisher-men, whom he inspired and sent to publish his blessed Will to the *Gentiles, and inspir'd them also with a power to speak all languages, and by their powerful Eloquence to beget faith in the unbelieving Jews: and themselves to suffer for that Saviour whom their fore fathers and they had Crucified, and, in their sufferings, to preach freedom from the incumbrances of the Law, and a new way to everlasting life:* this was the imployment of these happy Fishermen. Concerning which choice, some have made these Observations.

First that he never reproved these for their Imployment or Calling, as he did the *Scribes* and the *Mony-changers*.[2] And secondly, he found that the hearts of such men by nature were fitted for contemplation and quietnesse; men of mild, and sweet, and peaceable spirits, as indeed most Anglers are: these men our blessed Saviour, (who is observed to love to plant grace in good natures) though indeed nothing be too hard for him, yet these men he chose to call from their irreprovable imployment of Fishing, and gave them grace to be his Disciples, and to follow him and doe wonders, I say four of twelve. [. . .]

And if this hold in reason (as I see none to the contrary), then it may be probably concluded, that *Moses* (who, I told you before, writ the Book of *Job*) and the Prophet *Amos*, who was a Shepherd, were both Anglers; for you shall in all the Old Testament find Fish-hooks, I think but twice mentioned, namely, by meek *Moses* the friend of God, and by the humble Prophet *Amos*.

Concerning which last, namely the Prophet *Amos*, I shall make but this Observation, That he that shall read the *humble, lowly, plain style* of that *Prophet*, and compare it with the *high, glorious, eloquent style* of the Prophet *Isaiah* (though they be both equally

[1] Psalm 107: 23-4   [2] Matthew 21:12; Mark 11:15

15

true) may easily believe *Amos* to be, not only a Shepherd, but a good natur'd, plain *Fisher-man*.

Which I do the rather believe by comparing the affectionate, loving, lowly, humble Epistles of S. *Peter*, S. *James* and S. *John*, whom we know were all Fishers, with the glorious language and high Metaphors of S. *Paul*, who we may believe was not. [. . .]

I might here enlarge my self by telling you, what commendations our learned *Perkins* bestowes on Angling: and how dear a lover, and great a practiser of it our learned Doctor *Whitaker* was, as indeed many others of great learning have been. But I will content my self with two memorable men, that lived near to our own time, whom I also take to have been ornaments to the Art of Angling.

The first is Doctor *Nowel* sometimes Dean of the Cathedral Church of St. *Pauls* in *London*, where his Monument stands yet undefaced, a man that in the Reformation of Queen *Elizabeth* (not that of *Henry the VIII.*) was so noted for his meek spirit, deep learning, prudence and piety, that the then Parliament and Convocation both, chose, enjoyned and trusted him to be the man to make a Catechism for publick use, such a one as should stand as a rule for faith and manners to their posterity. And the good old man (though he was very learned, yet knowing that God leads us not to Heaven by many nor by hard questions) like an honest Angler, make that *good, plain, unperplext* Catechism which is printed with our good old Service Book. I say, this good man was as dear a lover, and constant practicer of Angling, as any Age can produce; and his custom was to spend besides his fixt hours of prayer, (those hours which by command of the Church were enjoyned the Clergy, and voluntarily dedicated to devotion by many Primi-tive Christians): I say, besides those hours, this good man was observed to spend a tenth part of his time in Angling; and also (for I have conversed with those which have conversed with him) to bestow a tenth part of his Revenue, and usually all his fish, amongst the poor that inhabited near to those Rivers in which it was caught: saying often, *That charity gave life to Religion*: and at his return to his House would praise God he had spent that day free from worldly trouble; both harmlessly, and in a recreation that became a Church-man. [. . .]

16

My next and last example shall be that under-valuer of mony, the late Provost of *Eton* Colledge, Sir *Henry Wotton*, (a man with whom I have often fish'd and convers'd) a man whose forreign Imployments in the service of this *Nation*, and whose *experience, learning, wit* and *chearfulness* made his company to be esteemed one of the delights of mankind; this man, whose very approbation of Angling were sufficient to convince any modest censurer of it, this man was also a most dear lover, and a frequent practiser of the art of angling; of which he would say, *'Twas an imployment for his idle time, which was then not idly spent*: for angling was after tedious Study, *a rest to his mind, a chearer of his spirits, a diverter of sadness, a calmer of unquiet thoughts, a moderator of passions, a procurer of contentedness*: and *that it begat habits of* peace *and* patience *in those that profess'd and practis'd it*. Indeed, my friend, you will find angling to be like the vertue of Humility, which has a calmness of spirit, and a world of other blessings attending upon it.

Sir, This was the saying of that learned man, and I do easily believe that *peace*, and *patience*, and a calm *content* did cohabit in the chearful heart of Sir *Henry Wotton*, because I know that when he was beyond seventy years of age, he made this description of a part of the present pleasure that possess'd him, as he sate quietly in a Summers evening on a bank a Fishing; it is a description of the Spring, which, because it glided as soft and sweetly from his pen, as that river does at this time by which it was then made, I shall repeat it unto you.

This day dame Nature seem'd in love:
The lusty sap began to move;
Fresh juice did stir th'embracing Vines,
And birds had drawn their Valentines,
The jealous Trout, *that low did lye,*
Rose at a well dissembled flie;
There stood my friend with patient skill,
Attending of his trembling quill.
Already were the eaves possest
With the swift Pilgrims dawbed nest:
The Groves already did rejoyce,

17

In Philomels *triumphing voice:*
The showers were short, the weather mild,
The morning fresh, the evening smil'd.
Jone *takes her neat rub'd pail, and now*
She trips to milk the sand-red Cow;
Where, for some sturdy foot-ball Swain,
Jone strokes a sillibub *or twain.*
The fields and gardens were beset
With Tulips, Crocus, Violet,
And now, though late, the modest Rose
Did more than half a blush disclose.
Thus all looks gay, and full of chear
To welcome the new livery'd year.   [. . .]

Venat. Sir, you have Angled me on with much pleasure to the *Thatcht-house*: and I now find your words true *That good company makes the way seem short*, for trust me, Sir, I thought we had wanted three miles of this *House* till you shewed it to me: but now we are at it, we'l turn into it, and refresh our selves with a cup of drink and a little rest.

Pisc. Most gladly (Sir) and we'l drink a civil cup to all the *Otter Hunters* that are to meet you to morrow.

Ven. That we will Sir, and to all the lovers of Angling too, of which number, I am now willing to be one my self, for by the help of your good discourse and company, I have put on new thoughts both of the Art of Angling, and of all that professe it: and if you will but meet me to morrow at the time and place appointed, and bestow one day with me and my friends in hunting the *Otter*, I will dedicate the next two dayes to wait upon you, and we two will for that time do nothing but angle, and talk of fish and fishing.

Pisc. 'Tis a match, Sir, I'l not fail you, God willing, to be at Amwel-hill to morrow morning before Sun-rising.

¶ On Caterpillars

Pliny holds an opinion, that many have their birth or being from a dew that in the Spring falls upon the leaves of trees; and that some kinds of them are from a dew left upon herbs or flowers; and others from a dew left upon Coleworts or Cabbages: All which kinds of dews being thickned and condensed, are by the Suns generative heat most of them hatch'd, and in three days made living creatures; and these of several shapes and colours; some being hard and tough, some smooth and soft; some are horned in their head, some in their tail, some have none: some have hair, some none: some have sixteen feet, some less, and some have none, but (as our *Topsel* hath with great diligence observed)[1] those which have none, move upon the earth or upon broad leaves, their motion being not unlike to the waves of the Sea. Some of them he also observes to be bred of the Eggs of other Caterpillars, and that those in their time turn to be *Butter-flies*: and again, that their Eggs turn the following year to be *Caterpillars*. And some affirm, that every plant has his particular flie or Caterpillar, which it breeds and feeds. I have seen, and may therefore affirm it, a green Caterpillar, or worm, as big as a small Peascod, which had fourteen legs, eight on the belly, four under the neck, and two near the tail. It was found on a hedge of Privet, and was taken thence, and put into a large Box, and a little branch or two of Privet put to it, on which I saw it feed as sharply as a dog gnaws a bone: it lived thus five or six daies, and thrived, and changed the colour two or three times, but by some neglect in the keeper of it, it then dyed and did not turn to a flie: but if it had lived, it had doubtless turned to one of those flies that some call flies of prey, which those that walk by the Rivers may in Summer, see fasten on smaller flies, and I think make them their food. And 'tis observable, that as there be these *flies of prey* which be very large, so there be others very little, created, I think, only to feed them, and bred out of I know not what; whose life, they say,

---

[1] In his history of Serpents. [– I.W.] Edward Topsell (d.1638) wrote *The History of Foure-Footed Beastes . . .* (1607) and *The History of Serpents . . .* (1608), which draw heavily on Gesner.

Nature intended not to exceed an hour, and yet that life is thus made shorter by other flies, or accident. [. . .]

Nay, the very colours of *Caterpillars* are, as one has observed, very elegant and beautiful: I shall (for a taste of the rest) describe one of them, which I will sometime next month shew you feeding on a Willow-tree, and you shall find him punctually to answer this very description: *His lips and mouth somewhat yellow, his eyes black as Jet, his forehead purple, his feet and hinder parts green, his tail two forked and black, the whole body stained with a kind of red spots which run along the neck and shoulder-blade, not unlike the form of Saint* Andrew's *Cross, or the letter X, made thus cross-wise, and a white line drawn down his back to his tail; all which add much beauty to his whole body.* And it is to me observable, that at a fixed age this *Caterpillar* gives over to eat, and towards Winter comes to be covered over with a strange shell or crust called an *Aurelia*, and so lives a kind of dead life, without eating all the Winter; and (as others of several kinds turn to be several kinds of flies and vermin the Spring following) so this *Caterpillar* then turns to be a painted *Butter-fly*.[1]

¶ *On making artificial flies*

First, you must arm your hook with the line on the inside of it, then take your Scissors, and cut so much of a brown Mallards feather as in your own reason will make the wings of it, you having withal regard to the bigness or littleness of your hook, then lay the outmost part of your feather next to your hook, then the point of your feather next the shank of your hook; and having so done, whip it three or four times about the hook with the same Silk, with which your hook was armed, and having made the Silk fast, take the hackle of a *Cock* or *Capons* neck, or a *Plovers* top, which is usually better: take off the one side of the feather, and then take the hackle, Silk, or Crewel, Gold or Silver thred, make

[1] View Sir Fra. Bacon exper. 728 & 90. in his Natural History. [– I.W.] Wotton refers to Bacon's *Sylva Sylvarum, or a Naturall History* (see 1650 edn, pp.153, 24).

these fast at the bent of the hook, that is to say, below your arming; then you must take the hackle, the Silver or Gold thred, and work it up to the wings, shifting or still removing your fingers as you turn the Silk about the hook: and still looking at every stop or turn, that your Gold, or what materials soever you make your Flie of, do lie right and neatly; and if you find they do so, then when you have made the head, make all fast, and then work your hackle up to the head, and make that fast: and then with a needle or pin divide the wing into two, and then with the arming Silk whip it about cross-waies betwixt the wings; and then with your thumb you must turn the point of the feather towards the bent of the hook, and then work three or four times about the shank of the hook, and then view the proportion, and if all be neat and to your liking fasten.

I confess, no direction can be given to make a man of a dull capacity able to make a Flie well: and yet I know, this with a little practice will help an ingenuous Angler in a good degree: but to see a Flie made by an Artist in that kind, is the best teaching to make it, and then an ingenuous Angler may walk by the River and mark what flies fall on the water that day, and catch one of them, if he see the *Trouts* leap at a flie of that kind: and then having alwaies hooks ready hung with him, and having a bag also always with him, with Bears hair, or the hair of a brown or sad-coloured Heifer, hackles of a Cock or Capon, several coloured Silk and Crewel to make the body of the flie, the feathers of a Drakes head, black or brown Sheeps wool, or Hogs wool, or hair, thred of Gold and of Silver: Silk of several colours (especially sad coloured to make the flies head): and there be also other coloured feathers both of little birds and of peckled foul. I say, having those with him in a bag, and trying to make a flie, though he miss at first, yet shall he at last hit it better, even to such a perfection, as none can well teach him, and if he hit to make his Flie right, and have the luck to hit also where there is a store of *Trouts*, a dark day, and a right wind, he will catch such store of them, as will encourage him to grow more and more in love with the Art of *Fly-making*. [. . .]

And now, Scholar, my direction for flie-fishing is ended with this showre, for it has done raining; and now look about you, and see how pleasantly that Meadow looks; nay, and the Earth smells as sweetly too. Come, let me tell you what holy Mr. *Herbert* says of such days and flowers as these, and then we will thank God that we enjoy them, and walk to the River and sit down quietly, and try to catch the other brace of *Trouts*.

> *Sweet day, so cool, so calm, so bright,*
> *The bridal of the earth and skie,*
> *Sweet dews shall weep thy fall to night,*
> > *for thou must die.*

> *Sweet Rose, whose hew angry and brave*
> *Bids the rash gazer wipe his eye,*
> *Thy root is ever in its grave,*
> > *and thou must die.*

> *Sweet Spring, full of sweet days and roses,*
> *A box where sweets compacted lye;*
> *My Musick shews you have your closes,*
> > *and all must dye.*

> *Only a sweet and vertuous soul,*
> *Like seasoned Timber never gives,*
> *But when the whole world turns to coal,*
> > *then chiefly lives.*

Venat. I thank you, good Master, for your good direction for Flie-fishing, and for the sweet enjoyment of the pleasant day, which is so far spent without offence to God or man: and I thank you for the sweet close of your discourse with Mr. *Herberts* Verses, who I have heard loved Angling: and I do the rather believe it, because he had a spirit suitable to Anglers, and to those primitive Christians, that you love, and have so much commended.

Pisc. Well my loving Scholar, and I am pleased, to know that you are so well pleased with my direction and discourse.

And since you like these Verses of Mr. *Herberts* so well, let me tell you what a reverend and learned Divine that professes to imitate him (and has indeed done so most excellently) hath writ of our *Book of Common Prayer*, which I know you will like the better, because he is a friend of mine, and I am sure no enemy to Angling.

What? pray'r by th'book? and common? Yes, why not?
The Spirit of grace,
And supplication,
Is not left free alone
For time and place,
But manner too: to read or speak by rote,
Is all alike to him, that prayes
In's heart, what with his mouth he says.

They that in private by themselves alone
Do pray, may take
What liberty they please,
In chusing of the ways
Wherein to make
Their souls must intimated affections known
To him that sees in secret, when
Th'are most conceal'd from other men.

But he, that unto others leads the way
In publick prayer,
Should do it so
As all that hear may know
They need not fear
To tune their hearts unto his tongue, and say,
Amen; *nor doubt they were betray'd*
To blaspheme, *when they meant to have* pray'd.

Devotion will add Life unto the Letter,
And why should not
That which Authority
Prescribes, esteemed be
Advantage got?
If th'prayer be good, the commoner the better,
Prayer in the Churches words as well
As sense, *of all prayers bears the bell.*

Ch. Harvie.

And now, Scholar, I think it will be time to repair to our Angle-rods, which we left in the water, to fish for themselves, and you shall chuse which shall be yours; and it is an even lay, one of them catches.

¶ *Observations of the* Luce *or* Pike, *with directions how to fish for him.*

Pisc. The mighty *Luce* or *Pike* is taken to be the Tyrant (as the *Salmon* is the King) of the fresh waters. 'Tis not to be doubted, but that they are bred, some by generation, and some not: as namely, of a Weed called *Pickerel-weed*, unless learned *Gesner* be much mistaken, for he says, this weed and other glutinous matter, with the help of the Suns heat in some particular Months, and some Ponds apted for it by nature, do become *Pikes*. But doubtless divers *Pikes* are bred after this manner, or are brought into some Ponds some such other wayes as is past mans finding out, of which we have daily testimonies.

Sir *Francis Bacon* in his History of Life and Death, observes the *Pike* to be the longest lived of any fresh-water-fish, and yet he computes it to be not above ten years; and yet *Gesner* mentions a *Pike* taken in *Swedeland* in the Year 1449. with a Ring about his neck, declaring he was put into that Pond by *Frederick* the second, more than two hundred years before he was last taken, as by the Inscription in that Ring (being Greek) was interpreted by the then Bishop of *Worms*. But of this no more, but that it is observed, that the old or very great Pikes have in them more of state than goodness; the smaller or middle sized Pikes being by the most and choicest Palates observed to be the best meat; and contrary, the Eel is observed to be the better for age and bigness.

All Pikes that live long prove chargeable to their Keepers, because their life is maintained by the death of so many other Fish, even those of their own kind, which has made him by some Writers to be called the *Tyrant* of the Rivers, or the *Freshwater-wolf*, by reason of his bold, greedy devouring disposition; which is so keen, as *Gesner* relates, a man going to a Pond (where it seems a

24

Pike had devoured all the fish) to water his Mule, had a *Pike* bit his Mule by the lips; to which the *Pike* hung so fast, that the Mule drew him out of the water, and by that accident the owner of the Mule angled out the *Pike*. And the same *Gesner* observes, that a maid in *Poland* had a *Pike* bit her by the foot as she was washing clothes in a Pond. And I have heard the like of a woman in *Killing-worth* Pond, not far from *Coventry*. But I have been assured by my friend Mr. *Seagrave*, (of whome I spake to you formerly), that keeps tame *Otters*, that he hath known a *Pike* in extream hunger fight with one of his Otters for a Carp that the Otter had caught and was then bringing out of the water. I have told you who relates these things, and tell you they are persons of credit, and shall conclude this observation, by telling you what a wise man has observed, *It is a hard thing to perswade the belly, because it has no ears.*

But if these relations be disbelieved, it is too evident to be doubted, that a *Pike* will devour a Fish of his own kind, that shall be bigger than his belly or throat will receive, and swallow a part of him, and let the other part remain in his mouth till the swallowed part be digested, and then swallow that other part that was in his mouth, and so put it over by degrees; which is not unlike the Ox and some other beasts, taking their meat not out of their mouth immediately into their belly, but first into some place betwixt, and then chaw it, or digest it by degrees after, which is called *Chewing the Cud*. And doubtless *Pikes* will bite when they are not hungry, but as some think even for very anger, when a tempting bait comes near to them. [. . .]

The *Pike* is also observed to be a solitary, melancholy and a bold Fish: Melancholy, because he always swims or rests himself alone, and never swims in sholes or with company, as *Roach* and *Dace*, and most other Fish do: And bold, because he fears not a shadow, or to see or be seen of any body, as the *Trout* and *Chub*, and all other Fish do.

And it is observed by *Gesner*, that the Jaw-bones, and Hearts, and Galls of *Pikes* are very medicinable for several diseases, or to stop blood, to abate Fevers, to cure Agues, to oppose or expel the infection of the Plague, and to be many ways medicinable and useful for the good of Mankind; but he observes, that the biting of a *Pike* is venemous and hard to be cured.

And it is observed, that the *Pike* is a fish that breeds but once a year, and that other fish (as namely *Loaches*) do breed oftner: as we are certain tame Pigeons do almost every month, and yet the *Hawk* (a Bird of Prey, as the *Pike* is of Fish) breeds but once in twelve months: and you are to note, that his time of breeding or spawning is usually about the end of *February*, (or somewhat later, in *March*, as the weather proves colder or warmer) and to note, that his manner of breeding is thus, a He and a She *Pike* will usually go together out of a River into some ditch or creek, and that there the Spawner casts her eggs, and the Melter hovers over her all that time that she is casting her spawn, but touches her not.

I might say more of this, but it might be thought curiosity or worse, and shall therefore forbear it, and take up so much of your attention, as to tell you, that the best of *Pikes* are noted to be in *Rivers*, next those in great *Ponds*, or *Meres*, and the worst in small Ponds. [. . .]

[Y]ou may fish for a *Pike*, either with a *ledger* or a *walking-bait*; and you are to note, that I call that a Ledger bait, which is fixed, or made to rest in one certain place when you shall be absent from it: and I call that a walking bait, which you take with you, and have ever in motion. Concerning which two, I shall give you this direction; That your ledger bait is best to be a living bait, though a dead one may catch, whether it be a fish or a frog; and that you may make them live the longer, you may or indeed you must take this course.

First, for your live bait of fish, a *Roach* or *Dace* is (I think) best and most tempting, and a *Pearch* is the longest lived on a hook, and having cut off his fin on his back, which may be done without hurting him, you must take your knife (which cannot be too sharp) and betwixt the head and the fin on the back, cut or make an incision, or such a scar, as you may put the arming wire of your hook into it, with as little bruising or hurting the fish as art and diligence will enable you to do; and so carrying your arming wire along his back, unto, or near the tail of your Fish, betwixt the skin and the body of it, draw out that wire or arming of your hook at another scar near to his tail: then ty him about it with thred, but no harder than of necessity to prevent hurting the fish;

26

and the better to avoid hurting the fish, some have a kind of probe to open the way, for the more easie entrance and passage of your wire or arming: but as for these, time, and a little experience will teach you better than I can by words; therefore I will for the present say no more of this, but come next to give you some directions, how to bait your hook with a frog. [. . .]

Put your hook into his mouth, which you may easily do from the middle of *April* till *August*, and then the frogs mouth grows up, and he continues so for at least six moneths without eating, but is sustained, none but he whose name is Wonderful, knows how; I say, put your hook, I mean the arming wire through his mouth, and out at his gills, and then with a fine needle and silk sow the upper part of his leg with only one stitch to the arming wire of your hook, or tie the frogs leg above the upper joynt to the armed wire; and in so doing, use him as though you loved him, that is, harm him as little as you may possibly, that he may live the longer. [. . .]

Or if you bait your hooks thus with live Fish or Frogs, and in a windy day, fasten them thus to a bough or bundle of straw, and by the help of that wind can get them to move cross a *Pond* or *mere*, you are like to stand still on the shore and see sport presently if there be any store of *Pikes*; or these live baits may make sport, being tied about the body or wings of a *Goose* or *Duck*, and she chased over a *Pond*: and the like may be done with turning three or four live baits thus fastened to bladders, or boughs, or bottles of hay or flags, to swim down a River, whilst you walk quietly along on the shore, and are still in expectation of sport. The rest must be taught you by practice, for time will not allow me to say more of this kind of fishing with live baits.

And for your dead bait for a Pike, for that you may be taught by one daies going a fishing with me, or any other body that fishes for him, for the baiting your hook with a dead *Gudgeon* or a *Roach*, and moving it up and down the water, is too easie a thing to take up any time to direct you to do it; and yet, because I cut you short in that, I will commute for it, by telling you that was told me for a secret: it is this:

Dissolve Gum *of* Ivy *in Oyl of* Spike, *and therewith anoynt your dead bait for a* Pike; *and then cast it into a likely place, and when it has*

27

lain a short time at the bottom, *draw it towards the top of the water and so up the stream; and it is more than likely that you have a* Pike *follow with more than common eagerness.*

And some affirm, that any bait anointed with the marrow of the Thigh-bone of an *Hern* is a great temptation to any Fish.

These have not been tryed by me, but told me by a friend of note, that pretended to do me a courtesie, but if this direction to catch a *Pike* thus, do you no good, yet I am certain this direction how to roast him when he is caught, is choicely good, for I have tryed it; and it is somewhat the better for not being common; but with my direction you must take this Caution, that your *Pike* must not be a small one, that is, it must be more than half a Yard, and should be bigger.

First open your Pike *at the gills, and if need be, cut also a little slit towards the belly; out of these take his guts, and keep his liver, which you are to shred very small with* Time, Sweet-marjoram, *and a little* Winter-savoury; *to these put some pickled* Oysters, *and some* Anchovies, *two or three, both these last whole (for the* Anchovies *will melt, and the* Oysters *should not); to these you must adde also a pound of sweet butter, which you are to mix with the herbs that are shred, and let them all be well salted (if the* Pike *be more than a yard long, then you may put into these herbs more than a pound, or if he be less, then less Butter will suffice): these being thus mixt with a blade or two of* Mace, *must be put into the* Pikes *belly, and then his belly so sowed up, as to keep all the Butter in his belly if it be possible, if not, then as much of it as you possibly can, but take not off the scales; then you are to thrust the spit through his mouth out at his tail, and then take four, or five, or six split sticks, or very thin lathes, and a convenient quantity of Tape or Filleting, these lathes are to be tyed round about the* Pikes *body from his head to his tail, and the Tape tyed somewhat thick to prevent his breaking or falling off from the spit; let him be roasted very leasurely, and often basted with* Claret *wine, and* Anchovyes, *and Butter mixt together, and also with what moisure falls from him into the pan: when you have rosted his sufficiently you are to hold under him (when you unwind or cut the Tape that ties him) such a dish as you purpose to eat him out of; and let him fall into it with the sawce that is rosted in his belly, and by this means the* Pike *will be kept unbroken and compleat: then, to the sawce which was within, and also that sawce in the pan, you*

28

are to add a fit quantity of the best Butter, and to squeeze the juyce of three or four Oranges: lastly, you may either put into the Pike *with the* Oysters, *two cloves of Garlick, and take it whole out, when the* Pike *is cut off the spit, or to give the sawce a* hogo, *let the dish (into which you let the* Pike *fall) be rubbed with it: the using or not using of this Garlick is left to your discretion.* M.B.

This dish of meat is too good for any but Anglers or very honest men; and I trust, you will prove both, and therefore I have trusted you with this secret.

¶ *Observations of the* Eel, *and other fish that want scales, and how to fish for them.*

Pisc. It is agreed by most men, that the *Eel* is a most daintie fish; the Romans have esteemed her the *Helena* of their feasts, and some *The Queen of palat pleasure.* But most men differ about their breeding: some say they breed by generation as other fish do, and others, that they breed (as some worms do) of mud, as Rats and Mice, and many other living creatures are bred in *Egypt*, by the Suns heat when it shines upon the overflowing of the River *Nilus*: or out of the putrefaction of the earth, and divers other wayes. Those that deny them to breed by generation as other fish do; ask: if any man ever saw an *Eel* to have a Spawn or Melt? and they are answered, that they may be as certain of their breeding as if they had seen Spawn: for they say, that they are certain that *Eels* have all parts fit for generation, like other fish, but so small as not to be easily discerned, by reason of their fatness; but that discerned they may be, and that the He and the She *Eel* may be distinguished by their fins. And *Rondelitius*[1] saies, he has seen *Eels* cling together like *Dew-worms*.

And others say, that Eels growing old breed other *Eels* out of the corruption of their own age, which Sir *Francis Bacon* sayes, exceeds not ten years. And others say, that as *Pearls* are made of

[1] Guillaume Rondelet (1507-66), naturalist and physician, author of *Libri de Piscibus Marinis* (Books on Marine Fish), 1554-5.

glutinous dew-drops, which are condensed by the Suns heat in those Countries, so *Eels* are bred of a particular dew falling in the months of *May* or *June* on the banks of some particular Ponds or Rivers (apted by nature for that end) which in a few dayes are by the Suns heat turned into *Eels* that are thus bred, *The Off-spring of Jove*. I have seen in the beginning of *July*, in a River not far from *Canterbury*, some parts of it covered over with young *Eels*, about the thickness of a straw; and these *Eels* did lie on the top of that water, as thick as motes are said to be in the Sun: and I have heard the like of other Rivers, as namely in *Severn*, (where they are called *Yelvers*) and in a *pond* or *mere* near unto *Stafford-shire*, where about a set time in Summer, such small *Eels* abound so much, that many of the poorer sort of people, that inhabit near to it take such *Eels* out of this Mere, with sieves or sheets, and make a kind of Eel-cake of them, and eat it like as Bread. And *Gesner* quotes venerable *Bede* to say, that in *England* there is an Island called *Ely*, by reason of the innumerable number of *Eels* that breed in it. But that *Eels* may be bred as some worms, and some kind of *Bees* and *Wasps* are, either of *dew*, or out of the corruption of the earth, seems to be made probable by the *Barnacles* and young *Goslings* bred by the Suns heat, and the rotten planks of an old Ship, and hatched of trees; both which are related for truths by *Dubartas* and *Lobel*, and also by our learned *Cambden*, and laborious *Gerard*[1] in his *Herbal*.

It is said by *Rondelitius*, that those *Eels* that are bred in Rivers that relate to, or be nearer to the Sea, never return to the fresh waters (as the *Salmon* does always desire to do) when they have once tasted the salt water; and I do the more easily believe this, because I am certain that powdered Beef is a most excellent bait to catch an *Eel*: and though Sir *Francis Bacon* will allow the *Eels* life to be but ten years; yet he in his History of Life and Death, mentions a *Lamprey* belonging to the *Roman* Emperour to be made tame, and so kept for almost threescore years: and that such useful and pleasant observations were made of this *Lamprey*, that *Crassus* the Orator (who kept her) lamented her Death. And we

[1] John Gerard (1545-1612), herbalist, whose famous *Herball* appeared in 1597.

read (in Doctor *Hackwel*)[1] that *Hortensius* was seen to weep at the death of a *Lamprey* that he had kept long, and loved exceedingly.

It is granted by all, or most men, that *Eels*, for about six months (that is to say, the six cold months of the year) stir not up and down, neither in the Rivers, nor in the Pools in which they usually are, but get into the soft earth or mud, and there many of them together bed themselves, and live without feeding upon any thing (as I have told you some *Swallows* have been observed to do in hollow trees for those six cold months): and this the *Eel* and *Swallow* do, as not being able to endure winter weather: For *Gesner* quotes *Albertus* to say, that in the year 1125. (that years winter being more cold than usually) *Eels* did by natures instinct get out of the water into a stack of hay in a Meadow upon drie ground, and there bedded themselves, but yet at last a frost kill'd them. And our *Cambden* relates, that in *Lancashire* Fishes were dig'd out of the earth with Spades, where no water was near to the place. I shall say little more of the Eel, but that, as it is observed he is impatient of cold; so it hath been observed, that in warm weather an *Eel* has been known to live five days out of the water.

And lastly, let me tell you that some curious searchers into the natures of Fish, observe that there be several sorts or kinds of *Eels*, as the *silver Eel*, and green or *greenish Eel* (with which the River of *Thames* abounds, and those are called *Grigs*); and a *blackish Eel*, whose head is more flat and bigger than ordinary *Eels*; and also an *Eel* whose Fins are reddish, and but seldom taken in this Nation, (and yet taken sometimes): These several kinds of *Eels* are (say some) diversely bred; as namely, out of the corruption of the earth, and some by dew, and other ways, (as I have said to you): and yet it is affirmed by some for a certain, that the *silver Eel* is bred by generation, and not by Spawning as other Fish do, but that her brood come alive from her, being then little live Eels no bigger nor longer than a pin; and I have had too many testimonies of this to doubt the truth of it my self, and if I thought it needful I might prove it, but I think it is needless.

And this Eel of which I have said so much to you, may be caught with divers kinds of Baits: as namely with powdered Beef, with a

[1] George Hakewill (1578-1649), in *Apologie of the Power and Providence of God* (1627).

31

Lob or *Garden-worm*, with a *Minnow*, or gut of a *Hen, Chicken*, or the guts of any Fish, or with almost any thing, for he is a greedy Fish; but the Eel may be caught especially with a little, a very little *Lamprey* which some call a *Pride*, and may in the hot months be found many of them in the River *Thames*, and in many mud-heaps in other Rivers, yea, almost as usually as one finds worms in a dunghill.

Next note, that the Eel seldom stirs in the day, but then hides himself, and therefore he is usually caught by night with one of these baits of which I have spoken, and may be then caught by laying hooks, which you are to fasten to the bank or twigs of a tree; or by throwing a string cross the stream with many hooks at it, and those baited with the aforesaid Baits, and a clod, or plummet, or stone, thrown into the River with this line, that so you may in the morning find it near to some fixt place, and then take it up with a Drag-hook or otherwise: but these things are indeed too common to be spoken of, and an hours fishing with any Angler will teach you better, both for these and many other common things in the practical part of *Angling*, than a weeks discourse. I shall therefore conclude this direction for taking the *Eel*, by telling you, that in a warm day in Summer I have taken many a good Eel by *snigling* and have been much pleased with that sport.

And because you that are but a young Angler know not what snigling is, I will now teach it to you. You remember I told you that Eels do not usually stir in the day time, for then they hide themselves under some covert, or under boards or planks about Flood-gates, or Weires, or Mills, or in holes in the River banks; so that you observing your time in a warm day, when the water is lowest, may take a strong small hook tied to a strong line, or to a string about a yard long, and then into one of these holes, or between any boards about a Mill, or under any great stone or plank, or any place where you think an Eel may hide or shelter her self, you may with the help of a short stick put in your bait, but leasurely, and as far as you may conveniently: and it is scarce to be doubted, but that if there be an Eel within the sight of it, the Eel will bite instantly, and as certainly gorge it: and you need not doubt to have him if you pull him not out of the hole too quickly, but pull him out by degrees, for he lying folded double in his hole, will with the help of his tail break all, unless you give him time to be wearied with pulling, and so get him out by degrees; not pulling too hard.

And to commute for your patient hearing this long Direction I shall next tell you how to make this *EEL* a most excellent dish of meat:

First, wash him in water and salt, then pull off his skin below his vent or navel, and not much further: having done that, take out his guts as clean as you can, but wash him not: then give him three or four scotches with a knife, and then put into his belly and those scotches, sweet herbs, an Anchovy, and a little Nutmeg grated or cut very small, and your herbs and Anchovis must also be cut very small, and mixt with good butter and salt; having done this, then pull his skin over him all but his head, which you are to cut off, to the end you may tie his skin about that part where his head grew, and it must be so tyed as to keep all his moisture within his skin: and having done this, tie him with Tape or Pack-thred to a spit, and rost him leasurely, and baste him with water and salt till his skin breaks, and then with Butter: and having rosted him enough, let what was put into his belly, and what he drips be his sawce. S.F.*

When I go to dress an Eel thus, I wish he were as long and big, as that which was caught in *Peterborough* River in the year 1667, which was a yard and three quarters long. If you will not believe me? then go and see at one of the *Coffee-houses* in *King-street* in *Westminster*. [. . .]

And Scholar, there is also a Flounder, a Sea-fish, which will wander very far into fresh Rivers, and there lose himself, and dwell and thrive to a hands breadth, and almost twice so long, a fish without scales, and most excellent meat, and a fish that affords much sport to the Angler, with any small worm, but especially a little blewish worm, gotten out of Marsh ground or Meadows, which should be well scowred; but this though it be most excellent meat, yet it wants scales, and is as I told you therefore an abomination to the Jews.

But Scholar, there is a fish that they in *Lancashire* boast very much of, called a *Char*, taken there, (and I think there only) in a

Mere called *Winander Mere*; a Mere, says *Cambden*, that is the largest in this Nation, being ten miles in length, and some say as smooth in the bottom as if it were paved with polisht marble: this fish never exceeds fifteen or sixteen inches in length; and 'tis spotted like a *Trout*, and has scarce a bone but on the back: but this, though I do not know whether it make the Angler sport, yet I would have you take notice of it, because it is a rarity, and of so high esteem with persons of great note.

Nor would I have you ignorant of a rare fish called a *Guiniad*, of which I shall tell you what *Cambden*, and others speak. The River *Dee* (which runs by *Chester*) springs in *Merionethshire*, and as it runs toward *Chester* it runs through *Pemble-Mere*, which is a large water. And it is observed, that though the River *Dee* abounds with *Salmon*, and *Pemble-Mere* with the *Guiniad*, yet there is never any *Salmon* caught in the *Mere*, nor a *Guiniad* in the River.

¶ *Arrival*

Pisc. I will tell you Scholar, I have heard a grave Divine say, that God has two dwellings; one in Heaven; and, the other in a meek and thankful heart. *Which Almighty God grant to me, and to my honest Scholar: and so, you are welcom to* Tottenham High-Cross.

*Venat.*Well Master, I thank you for all your good directions, but, for none more than this last of thankfulness, which I hope I shall never forget. And pray let's now rest our selves in this sweet shady Arbour, which nature her self has woven with her own fine fingers; 'tis such a contexture of *Woodbines*, *Sweetbrier*, *Jessamine*, and *Mirtle*; and so interwoven, as will secure us both from the Suns violent heat; and from the approaching shower, and being sate down I will requite a part of your courtesies with a bottle of *Sack*, *Milk*, *Oranges*, and *Sugar*; which all put together, make a drink like *Nectar*, indeed too good for any body but us *Anglers*: and so Master, here is a full glass to you of that liquor, and when you have pledged me, I will repeat the Verses which I promised you; it is a Copy printed amongst some of Sir *Henry Wottons*: and doubtless made either by him, or by a lover of Angling: Come Master, now drink a glass to me, and then I will pledge you, and fall to my repetition; it is a description of such *Country-Recreations* as I have enjoyed since I had the happiness to fall into your company.

Quivering fears, *heart-tearing* cares,
Anxious sighs, *untimely* tears,
  Flye, flye to Courts,
  Flye to fond wordlings sports
Where strain'd Sardonick smiles are glosing still,
And grief *is forc'd to* laugh *against her will.*
  Where mirth's but mummery,
  And sorrows only real be.

*Fly from our Country-*pastimes, *fly,*
Sad troops of humane misery,
  Come serene looks,
  Clear as the chrystal Brooks,
Or the pure azur'd heaven that smiles to see
The rich attendance on our poverty;
  Peace and a secure mind,
  Which all men seek, we only find.

Abused Mortals, *did you know*
Where joy, hearts-ease *and* comforts *grow?*
  Youl'd scorn proud Towers,
  And seek them in these Bowers,
Where winds *sometimes our woods perhaps may shake,*
But blustring care *could never tempest make,*
  Nor murmurs ere come nigh us,
  Saving, of fountains that glide by us.

Here's no fantastick Mask nor Dance,
But of our Kids that frisk and prance;
  Nor wars *are seen,*
  Unless upon the green
Two harmless Lambs *are butting one the other,*
Which done, both bleating run each to his Mother.
  And wounds are never found,
  Sve what the plough-share gives the ground.

Here are no entrapping baits
To hasten too, too hasty fates,
 Unless it be
 The fond credulity ∘
Of silly fish, which (wordling like) still look
Upon the bait, but never on the hook:
 Nor envy, 'nless among
 The birds for price of their sweet song.

Go, let the diving Negro *seek*
For Gems hid in some forlorn creek:
 We all pearls scorn,
 Save what the dewy morn
Congeals upon each little spire of grass,
Which careless, shepherds beat down as they pass:
 And gold ne're here appears,
 Save what the yellow Ceres *bears.*

Blest silent groves, oh may you be
For ever mirths best nursery!
 My pure contents
 For ever pitch their tents
Upon these downs, *these* meads, *these* rocks, *these* mountains,
And Peace still slumber by these purling fountains:
 Which we may every year
 Meet when we come a fishing here.

[. . .] I thank you for your many instructions, which (God willing) I will not forget: and as St. *Austin* in his Confessions (*book* 4.
chap. 3.) commemorates the kindness of his friend *Verecundus*, for
lending him and his companion a *Country-house*, because there
they rested and enjoyed themselves free from the troubles of the
world; so, having had the like advantage, both by your conversation, and the Art you have taught me, I ought ever to do the like:
for indeed, your company and discourse have been so useful and
pleasant, that I may truly say, *I have only lived since I enjoyed them,
and turned Angler, and not before.* Nevertheless, here I must part
with you, here in this now sad place where I was so happy as first

36

to meet you: But I shall long for the ninth of *May*, for then I hope again to enjoy your beloved company at the appointed time and place. And now I wish for some *somniferous potion*, that might force me to sleep away the intermitted time, which will pass away with me as tediously, as it does with men in sorrow; nevertheless I will make it as short as I can by my *hopes* and *wishes*. And my good Master, I will not forget the doctrine which you told me *Socrates* taught his Scholars, *That they should not think to be honoured so much for being* Philosophers, *as to honour* Philosophy *by their vertuous lives*. You advised me to the like concerning *Angling*, and I will endeavour to do so, and to live like those many *worthy men*, of which you made mention in the former part of your discourse. This is my firm resolution; and as a pious man advised his friend, *That to beget* Mortification *he should frequent* Churches; *and view* Mountains, *and* Charnel-houses, *and then and there consider, how many dead bones time had pil'd up at the gates of death*. So when I would beget *content*, and increase confidence in the *Power*, and *Wisdom*, and *Providence* of Almighty God, I will walk the *Meadows* by some gliding stream, and there contemplate the *Lillies* that take no care, and those very many other various little living *creatures*, that are not only created but fed (man knows not how) by the goodness of the God of *Nature*, and therefore trust in him. This is my purpose: and so, *Let every thing that hath breath praise the Lord*. And let the blessing of St. *Peters* Master be with mine.

Pisc. And upon all that are lovers of *Vertue*; and dare trust in his *providence*, and be *quiet*, and go a *Angling*.

Study to be quiet, 1 Thes. 4. 11.

FINIS.

THE
LIFE
OF
Dr. *JOHN DONNE*,
Late Dean of St. *Paul's* Church,
LONDON.

¶ *The Introduction*

If that great Master of Language and Art, Sir Henry Wotton, *the late Provost of* Eaton Colledge, *had liv'd to see the Publication of these Sermons, he had presented the World with the* Authors Life *exactly written; And, 'twas pity he did not; for it was a work worthy his undertaking, and he fit to undertake it: betwixt whom, and the Author, there was so mutual a knowledge, and such a friendship contracted in their Youth, as nothing but death could force a separation. And, though their bodies were divided, their affections were not: for that learned Knight's love followed his Friends fame beyond death and the forgetful grave; which he testified by intreating me, whom he acquainted with his design, to inquire of some particulars that concern'd it, not doubting but my knowledge of the Author, and love to his memory, might make my diligence useful: I did most gladly undertake the employment, and continued it with great content 'till I had made my Collection ready to be augmented and compleated by his matchless Pen: but then, Death prevented his intentions.*

When I heard that sad news, and heard also that these Sermons *were to be printed, and want the* Authors Life, *which I thought to be very remarkable: Indignation or grief (indeed I know not which) transported me so far, that I reviewed my forsaken-Collections, and resolv'd the World should see the best plain Picture of the* Authors Life *that my artless Pensil, guided by the hand of truth, could present to it.*

And, If I shall now be demanded as once Pompey's *poor bondsman was,[1] (The grateful wretch had been left alone on the Sea-shore, with the*

---

[1] Plutark [– I.W.]. A reference to Plutarch's Life of Pompey, in his *Lives . . . of the Nobles Grecians and Romans*, translated into English by Thomas North (1579).

forsaken dead body of his once glorious lord and master: and, was then gathering the scatter'd pieces of an old broken boat to make a funeral pile to burn it' (which was the custom of the Romans) who art thou that alone hast the honour to bury the body of *Pompey* the Great? *so,* who am I that do thus officiously set the Authors memory on fire? *I hope the question will prove to have in it, more of wonder then disdain; But wonder indeed the Reader may, that I who profess my self artless should presume with my faint light to shew forth his Life whose very name makes it illustrious! but be this to the disadvantage of the person represented: Certain I am, it is to the advantage of the beholder, who shall here see the Authors Picture in a natural dress, which ought to beget faith in what is spoken: for he that wants skill to deceive, may safely be trusted.*

And if the Authors glorious spirit, which now is in Heaven; can have the leasure to look down and see me, the poorest, the meanest of all his friends, in the midst of this officious duty, confident I am, that he will not disdain this well-meant sacrifice to his memory: for, whilst his Conversation made me and many others happy below, I know his Humility and Gentleness was then eminent; and, I have heard Divines say, those Vertues that were but sparks upon Earth, become great and glorious flames in Heaven.

Before I proceed further, I am to intreat the Reader to take notice, that when *Doctor Donn*'s Sermons were first printed, this was then my excuse for daring to write his life; and, I dare not now appear without it.

¶ *His birth, education and marriage*

Master *John Donne* was born in *London*, in the year 1573. of good and vertuous Parents: and, though his own Learning and other multiplyed merits may justly appear sufficient to dignifie both Himself and his Posterity: yet, the Reader may be pleased to know, that his Father was masculinely and lineally descended from a very antient Family in *Wales*, where many of his name now live, that deserve and have great reputation in that Countrey.

By his Mother he was descended of the Family of the famous and learned Sir *Thomas Moor*, sometime Lord *Chancellour* of *England*: as also, from that worthy and laborious *Judge Rastall*, who left Posterity the vast Statutes of the Law of this Nation most exactly abridged.

He had his first breeding in his Fathers house, where a private Tutor had the care of him, until the tenth year of his age; and, in his eleventh year, was sent to the University of *Oxford*; having at that time a good command both of the French and Latine Tongue. This and some other of his remarkable Abilities, made one then give this censure of him; *That this age had brought forth another* Picus Mirandula; of whom Story says, *That he was rather born, than made wise by study.*

There he remained for some years in *Hart-Hall*, having for the advancement of his studies Tutors of several Sciences to attend and instruct him, till time made him capable, and his learning expressed in publick exercises declared him worthy to receive his first degree in the Schools, which he forbore by advice from his friends, who being for their Religion of the Romish perswasion, were *conscionably* averse to some parts of the Oath that is alwaies tendered at those time; and not to be refused by those that expect the titulary honour of their studies.

About the fourteenth year of his age, he was transplanted from *Oxford* to *Cambridge*; where, that he might receive nourishment from both Soils, he staied till his seventeenth year; all which time he was a most laborious Student, often changing his studies, but endeavouring to take no degree, for the reasons formerly mentioned.

About the seventeenth year of his age, he was removed to *London*, and then admitted into *Lincolns-Inne*, with an intent to study the *Law*; where he gave great testimonies of his Wit, his Learning, and of his Improvement in that profession: which never served him for other use than an Ornament and Self-satisfaction.

His Father died before his admission into this Society; and being a Merchant, left him his portion in money (it was 3000 l.). His Mother and those to whose care he was committed, were watchful to improve his knowledge, and to that end appointed him Tutors both in the *Mathematicks*, and in all the other *Liberal*

Sciences, to attend him. But with these Arts they were advised to instil into him particular Principles of the *Romish Church*; of which those Tutors profest (though secretly) themselves to be members.

They had almost obliged him to their faith; having for their advantage, besides many opportunities, the example of his dead and pious Parents, which was a most powerful perswasion, and did work much upon him, as he professeth in his Preface to his *Pseudo-Martyr*; a Book of which the Reader shall have some account in what follows.

He was now entered into the eighteenth year of his age; and at that time had betrothed himself to no Religion that might give him any other denomination than *a Christian*. And Reason and Piety had both perswaded him, that there could be no such sin as *Schism*, if an adherence to some visible Church were not necessary.

About the nineteenth year of his age, he, being then unresolv'd what Religion to adhere to, and, considering how much it concern'd his soul to choose the most Orthodox, did therefore (though his youth and health, promised him a long life) to rectifie all scruples that might concern that, presently lay aside all study of the Law: and, of all other Sciences that might give him a denomination; and begun seriously to survey, and consider the Body of Divinity, as it was then controverted betwixt the *Reformed* and the *Roman Church*. And as *Gods blessed Spirit did then awaken him to the search, and in that industry did never forsake him,* (they be his own words[1]) *so he calls the same holy Spirit to witness this Protestation; that, in that disquisition and search, he proceeded with humility and diffidence in himself; and, by that which he took to be the safest way; namely, frequent Prayers, and an indifferent affection to both parties*; and, indeed, truth had too much light about her to be hid from so sharp an Inquirer; and, he had too much ingenuity, not to acknowledge he had found her.

Being to undertake this search, he believed the *Cardinal Bellarmine* to be the best defender of the *Roman cause*, and therefore betook himself to the examination of his Reasons. The Cause was

[1] In his Preface to *Pseudo-Martyr*. [– I.W.]

41

weighty: and wilful delays had been inexcusable both towards God and his own Conscience; he therefore proceeded in this search with all moderate haste, and about the twentieth year of his age, did shew the then *Dean* of *Gloucester* (whose name my memory hath now lost) all the Cardinals works marked with many weighty observations under his own hand; which works were bequeathed by him at his death as a Legacy to a most dear Friend.

About a year following he resolved to travel; and the Earl of *Essex* going first to the *Cales*, and after the *Island voyages*, the first *Anno* 1596. the second 1597. he took the advantage of those opportunities, waited upon his Lordship, and was an eye-witness of those happy and unhappy employments. [. . .]

Not long after his return into *England*, that exemplary Pattern of Gravity and Wisdom, the Lord *Elsemore*, then Keeper of the Great Seal, and *Lord Chancellour of England*, taking notice of his Learning, Languages, and other Abilities, and much affecting his Person and Behaviour, took him to be his chief Secretary; supposing and intending it to be an Introduction to some more weighty Employment in the State; for which, his Lordship did often protest, he thought him very fit. [. . .]

He continued that employment for the space of five years, being daily useful, and not mercenary to his Friends. During which time he (I dare not say unhappily) fell into such a liking, as (with her approbation) increased into a love with a young Gentlewoman that lived in that Family, who was Niece to the Lady *Elsemore*, and Daughter to Sir *George Moor*, then Chancellor of the Garter and Lieutenant of the Tower.

Sir *George* had some intimation of it, and knowing prevention to be a great part of wisdom, did therefore remove her with much haste from that to his own house at *Lothesley*, in the County of *Surry*; but too late, by reason of some faithful promises which were so interchangeably passed, as never to be violated by either party.

These promises were only known to themselves, and the friends of both parties used much diligence, and many arguments to kill or cool their affections to each other: but in vain; for love is a flattering mischief, that hath denied aged and wise men a foresight of those evils that too often prove to be the children of that blind

42

father, a passion! that carries us to commit *Errors* with as much ease as whirlwinds remove feathers, and begets in us an unwearied industry to the attainment of what we desire. And such an Industry did, notwithstanding much watchfulness against it, bring them secretly together (I forbear to tell the manner how) and at last to a marriage too, without the allowance of those friends, whose approbation always was, and ever will be necessary, to make even a vertuous love become lawful.

And that the knowledge of their marriage might not fall, like an unexpected tempest, on those that were unwilling to have it so: and, that preapprehensions might make it the less enormous, when it was known: it was purposely whispered into the ears of many that it was so, yet by none that could affirm it. But, to put a period to the jealousies of Sir *George* (Doubt often begetting more restless thoughts then the certain knowledge of what we fear) the news was in favour to Mr. *Donne*, and with his allowance, made known to Sir *George*, by his honourable friend and neighbour *Henry* Earl of *Northumberland*: but it was to Sir *George* so immeasurably unwelcome, and, so transported him; that as though his passion of anger and inconsideration, might exceed theirs of love and errour, he presently engaged his Sister the Lady *Elsemore*, to join with him to procure her Lord to discharge Mr. *Donne* of the place he held under his Lordship. – This request was followed with violence; and though Sir *George* were remembred, that Errors might be overpunished, and desired therefore to forbear till second considerations might clear some scruples: yet, he became restless until his suit was granted, and the punishment executed. And though the *Lord Chancellor* did not at Mr. *Donnes* dismission, give him such a Commendation as the great Emperour *Charles* the fifth, did of his Secretary *Eraso*, when he presented him to his Son and Successor *Philip* the Second, saying, *That in his* Eraso, *he gave to him a greater gift then all his Estate, and all the Kingdoms which he then resigned to him*: yet the Lord *Chancellor* said, *He parted with a Friend; and such a Secretary as was fitter to serve a King then a Subject.*

Immediately after his dismission from his service, he sent a sad Letter to his Wife, to acquaint her with it: and, after the subscription of his name, writ,

John Donne, Anne Donne, Vn-done,
and God knows it proved too true.

For this bitter Physick of Mr. *Donnes* dismission was not strong enough to purge out all Sir *George's* choler; for, he was not satisfied till Mr. *Donne* and his sometime Compupil in *Cambridge* that married him; namely, *Samuel Brook* (who was after Doctor in Divinity, and Master of Trinity Colledge) and his brother Mr. *Christopher Brook*, sometime Mr. *Donnes* Chamber-fellow in *Lincolns-Inn*, who gave Mr. *Donne* his Wife, and witnessed the marriage, were all committed, to three several prisons.

Mr. *Donne* was first enlarged, who neither gave rest to his body or brain, nor to any friend in whom he might hope to have an interest, until he had procured an enlargement for his two imprisoned friends.

He was now at liberty; but his days were still cloudy: and being past these troubles, others did still multiply upon him; for his wife was (to her extream sorrow) detained from him; and though with *Jacob* he endured not an hard service for her,[1] yet he lost a good one, and, was forced to make good his title, and to get possession of her by a long and restless suit in Law; which proved troublesome and sadly-chargeable to him, whose youth, and travel, and needless bounty, had brought his estate into a narrow compass.

It is observed, and most truly, that silence and submission are charming qualities, and work most upon passionate men; and it proved so with Sir *George*; for these, and a general report of Mr. *Donnes* merits, together with his winning behaviour (which when it would intice, had a strange kind of elegant irresistible art) these, and time had so dispassionated Sir *George*, that as the world had approved his Daughters choice, so he also could not but see a more then ordinary merit in his new son: and this at last melted him into so much remorse (for Love and Anger are so like Agues, as to have hot and cold fits; and love in Parents, though it may be quenched, yet is easily rekindled, and expires not, till death denies mankind a natural heat) that he laboured his Sons restauration to his place; using to that end, both his own and his Sisters

[1] Genesis 29: 10-30

power to her Lord; but with no success; for his Answer was, *That though he was unfeignedly sorry for what he had done, yet it was inconsistent with his place and credit, to discharge and readmit servants at the request of passionate petitioners.*

Sir *Georges* endeavour for Mr. *Donnes* readmission, was by all means to be kept secret (for men do more naturally reluct for errors, then submit to put on those blemishes that attend their visible acknowledgment.) But however it was not long before Sir *George* appeared to be so far reconciled, as to wish their happiness; and not to deny them his paternal blessing, but yet, refused to contribute any means that might conduce to their livelyhood.

Mr. *Donnes* estate was the greatest part spent in many and chargeable Travels, Books and dear-bought Experience: he out of all employment that might yield a support for himself and wife, who had been curiously and plentifully educated; both their natures generous, and accustomed to confer, and not to receive Courtesies: These and other considerations, but chiefly that his wife was to bear a part in his sufferings, surrounded him with many sad thoughts, and some apparent apprehensions of want.

But his sorrows were lessened and his wants prevented by the seasonable courtesie of their noble kinsman Sir *Francis Wolly* of *Pirford* in *Surry*, who intreated them to a cohabitation with him; where they remained with much freedom to themselves, and equal content to him for some years; and, as their charge encreased (she had yearly a child) so did his love and bounty. [. . .]

¶ *Mitcham*

Sir *Francis* being dead, and that happy family dissolved, Mr. *Donne* took for himself a house in *Micham* (near to *Croydon* in *Surry*) a place noted for good air and choice company: there his wife and children remained: and for himself he took lodgings in *London*, near to White-Hall, whither his friends and occasions drew him very often, and where he was as often visited by many of the Nobility and others of this Nation, who used him in their Counsels of greatest consideration: and with some rewards for his better subsistence.

Nor did our own Nobility only value and favour him, but his acquaintance and friendship was sought for by most Ambassadours of forraign Nations, and by many other strangers, whose learning or business occasioned their stay in this Nation.

He was much importuned by many friends to make his constant residence in *London*, but he still denied it, having setled his dear wife and children at *Micham*, and near some friends that were bountiful to them and him: for they, God knows, needed it: and that you may the better now judge of the then present Condition of his mind and fortune, I shall present you with an extract collected out of some few of his many Letters.

────── *And the reason why I did not sent an answer to your last weeks letter, was, because it then found me under too great a sadness; and at present 'tis thus with me: There is not one person, but my self, well of my family: I have already lost half a Child, and with that mischance of hers, my wife is fallen into such a discomposure, as would afflict her too extreamly, but that the sickness of all her other children stupifies her: of one of which, in good faith, I have not much hope: and these meet with a fortune so ill provided for Physick, and such relief, that if God should ease us with burials, I know not how to perform even that: but I flatter myself with this hope, that I am dying too: for I cannot waste faster then by such griefs. As for, ──────*

From my hospital at

Aug. 10. *Micham,*

JOHN DONNE.

Thus he did bemoan himself: And thus in other letters.

────── *For, we hardly discover a sin, when it is but an omission of some good, and no accusing act; with this or the former, I have often suspected myself to be overtaken; which is,* with an over earnest desire of the next life: *and though I know it is not meerly a weariness of this, because I had the same desire when I went with the tide, and injoyed fairer hopes then I now do: yet, I doubt worldly troubles have increased it: 'tis now Spring, and all the pleasures of it displease me; every other tree blossoms, and I wither: I grow older and not better; my strength diminisheth and my load grows heavier; and yet, I would fain be or do something; but, that I cannot tell what, is no wonder in this time of my* sadness; for, to chuse is to do; but, to be no part of any body, is as to be nothing; and so I am, and shall so judge my self, unless I could be so incorporated into a part of the world, as by business to contribute some sustentation[1] to the whole. This I made account, I began early when I understood the study of our Laws: but was diverted by leaving that and imbracing the worst voluptuousness, an hydroptique[2] immoderate desire of humane learning and languages: *Beautiful ornaments indeed to men of great fortunes; but mine was grown so low as to need an occupation: which I thought I entred well into, when I subjected my self to such a service as I thought might exercise my poor abilities: and there I stumbled, and fell too: and now I am become so little, or such a nothing, that I am not a subject good enough for one of my own letters; – Sir, I fear my present discontent does not proceed from a good root, that I am so well content to be nothing, that is, dead. But, Sir, though my fortune hath made me such, as that I am rather a Sickness or a Disease of the world, than any part of it, and therefore neither love it nor life; yet I would gladly live to become some such thing as you should not repent loving me: Sir, your own Soul cannot be more zealous for your good then I am, and, God, who loves that zeal in me, will not suffer you to doubt it: you would pity me now, if you saw me write, for my pain hath drawn my head so much awry, and holds it so, that my eye cannot follow my pen. I therefore receive you into my Prayers with mine own weary soul, and Commend my self to yours. I doubt not but next week will bring you good news, for I have either mending or dying on my side: but If I do continue longer thus, I shall have Comfort in this, That my blessed Saviour in exercising his Justice upon my two worldly parts,* my Fortune *and* my Body, *reserves all his Mercy for that which most needs it,* my Soul! *which is, I doubt, too like a Porter, that is very often near the gate, and yet goes not out. Sir, I profess to you truly, that my lothness to give over writing now, seems to my self a sign that I shall write no more* ——

Your poor friend, *and*
Gods poor patient
JOHN DONNE.

Sept. 7.

<hr />

[1] maintenance

[2] dropsical; in this context, diseasedly over-thirsty

By this you have seen, a part of the picture of his narrow fortune, and the perplexities of his generous mind; and thus it continued with him for about two years; all which time his family remained constantly at *Micham*; and to which place he often retir'd himself, and destined some days to a constant study of some points of Controversie betwixt the *English* and *Roman Church*; and especially those of *Supremacy* and *Allegiance*: and, to that place and such studies he could willingly have wedded himself during his life: but the earnest perswasion of friends became at last to be so powerful, as to cause the removal of himself and family to *London*, where Sir *Robert Drewry*, a Gentleman of a very noble estate, and a more liberal mind, assigned him and his wife an useful apartment in his own large house in *Drewry lane*, and not only rent-free, but was also a cherisher of his studies, and such a friend as sympathized with him and his in all their joy and sorrows.

At this time of Mr. *Donne's*, and his wives living in Sir *Roberts* house, the Lord *Hay* was by King *James* sent upon a glorious Embassie to the then *French* King *Henry* the fourth, and, Sir *Robert* put on a suddain resolution to accompany him to the *French* Court, and, to be present at his audience there. And, Sir *Robert* put on as suddain a resolution, to solicit Mr. *Donne* to be his Companion in that Journey: And this desire was suddainly made known to his wife, who was then with Child, and otherways under so dangerous a habit of body, as to her health, that she profest an unwillingness to allow him any absence from her; saying, *her divining soul boded her some ill in his absence*; and therefore, desired him not to leave her. This made Mr. *Donne* lay aside all thoughts of the Journey, and really to resolve against it. But Sir *Robert* became restless in his perswasions for it; and, Mr. *Donne* was so generous, as to think he had sold his liberty when he received so many Charitable kindnesses from him: and, told his wife so; who did therefore with an unwilling-willingness give a faint Consent to the Journey, which was proposed to be but for two months: for about that time they determin'd their return. – Within a few days after this resolve, the *Embassador*, Sir *Robert*, and Mr. *Donne* left *London*; and were the twelfth day all got safe to *Paris*. – two days after their arrival there, Mr. *Donne* was left alone, in that room in which Sir *Robert*, and he, and some other friends had din'd together. To this place Sir *Robert* return'd within half an hour; and, as he left, so he found Mr. *Donne* alone; but, in such an Extasie, and so alter'd as to his looks, as amaz'd Sir *Robert* to behold him: insomuch that he earnestly desired Mr. *Donne* to declare what had befaln him in the short time of his absence? to which, Mr. *Donne* was not able to make a present answer: but, after a long and perplext pause, did at last say, *I have seen a dreadful Vision since I saw you: I have seen my dear wife pass twice by me through this room, with her hair hanging about her shoulders, and a dead child in her arms: this, I have seen since I saw you.* To which, Sir *Robert* reply'd; *Sure, Sir, you have slept since I saw you; and, this is the result of some melancholy dream, which I desire you to forget, for you are now awake.* To which Mr. *Donnes* reply was: *I cannot be surer that I now live, then that I have not slept since I saw you: and am, as sure, that at her second appearing, she stopt, and look'd be in the face, and vanisht.* —— Rest and sleep, had not alter'd Mr. *Donne's* opinion the next day: for, he then affirm'd this Vision with a more deliberate, and, so confirm'd a confidence, that he inclin'd Sir *Robert* to a faint belief that the Vision was true. —— It is truly said, *that desire, and doubt, have no rest*: and it prov'd so with Sir *Robert*, for he immediately sent a servant to *Drewry* house with a charge to hasten back, and bring him word, whether Mrs. *Donne* were alive? and if alive, in what condition she was, as to her health? – The twelfth day the Messenger returned with this account – That he found and left Mrs. *Donne* very sad, and sick in her bed: and, that after a long and dangerous labor she had been deliver'd of a dead child. And, upon examination, the abortion prov'd to be the same day, and about the very hour that Mr. *Donne* affirm'd he saw her pass by him in his Chamber.

This is a relation that will beget some wonder: and, it well may; for most of our world are at present possest with an opinion that *Visions* and *Miracles* are ceas'd. And, though 'tis most certain, that two Lutes, being both strung and tun'd to an equal pitch, and then, one plaid upon, the other, that is not totcht, being laid upon a Table at a fit distance, will (like an Eccho to a trumpet) warble a faint audible harmony, in answer to the same tune: yet many will not believe there is any such thing, as a *sympathy* of *souls*; and I am well pleas'd, that every Reader do injoy his own opinion: but if the unbelieving will not allow the believing Reader of this story, a liberty to believe that it may be true; then, I wish him to consider, many Wise men have believed, that, the ghost of *Julius Cæsar* did appear to *Brutus*, and that both St. *Austin*,[1] and *Monica* his mother, had Visions in order to his Conversion. [. . .]

¶ *The second St Austine*

In the first and most blessed times of Christianity, when the Clergy were look'd upon with reverence, and deserved it, when they overcame their opposers by high examples of Vertue, by a blessed Patience and long Suffering: those only were then judged worthy the Ministry, whose quiet and meek spirits did make them look upon that sacred calling with an humble adoration and fear to undertake it; which indeed requires such great degrees of *humility*, and *labour*, and *care*, that none but such were then thought worthy of that celestial dignity. And such only were then sought out, and solicited to undertake it. This I have mentioned because forwardness and inconsideration, could not in Mr. *Donne*, as in many others, be an argument of insufficiency or unfitness; for he had considered long, and had many strifes within himself concerning the strictness of life and competency of learning required in such as enter into sacred Orders; and doubtless, considering his own demerits, did humbly ask God with St. *Paul, Lord, who is sufficient for these things*? and, with meek *Moses, Lord, who am I*?[2] And sure, if he had consulted with flesh and blood, he had not for these reasons put his hand to that holy plough. But God who is able to prevail, wrestled with him, as the *Angel* did with *Jacob, and marked him;*[3] mark'd him for his own; mark'd him with a blessing; a blessing of obedience to the motions of his blessed Spirit. And then, as he had formerly asked God with *Moses, Who am I?* So now being inspired with an apprehension of Gods particular mercy to him, in the Kings and other solicitations of him, he came

---

[1] Augustine   [2] 2 Corinthians 2:16; Exodus 3:11   [3] Genesis 32:24-32

to ask *King Davids* thankful question, *Lord, who am I, that thou art so mindful of me?*[1] So mindful of me, as to lead me for more then forty years through this wilderness of the many temptations, and various turnings of a dangerous life: so merciful to me, as to move the learned'st of Kings, to descend to move me to serve at the Altar! so merciful to me, as at last, to move my heart to imbrace this holy motion: thy motions I will and do imbrace: And, I now say with the blessed Virgin, *Be it with thy servant as seemeth best in thy sight:*[2] and so, *blessed Jesus*, I do take the cup of Salvation, and will call upon thy Name, and will preach thy Gospel.

Such strifes as these St. *Austine* had, when St. *Ambrose* indeavoured his conversion to Christianity; with which he confesseth, he acquainted his friend *Alipius*. Our learned Author (a man fit to write after no mean Copy) did the like. And declaring his intentions to his dear friend Dr. *King* then *Bishop* of *London*, a man famous in his generation, and no stranger to Mr. *Donne*'s abilities, (for he had been Chaplain to the Lord Chancellor, at the time of Mr. *Donne*'s being his Lordships Secretary) That Reverend man did receive the news with much gladness; and, after some expressions of joy, and a perswasion to be constant in his pious purpose, he proceeded with all convenient speed to ordain him first *Deacon*, and then *Priest* not long after.

Now the *English Church* had gain'd a second St. *Austine*, for, I think, none was so like him before his Conversion: none so like St. *Ambrose* after it: and if his youth had the infirmities of the one, his age had the excellencies of the other; the learning and holiness of both.

And now all his studies which had been occasionally diffused, were all concentred in Divinity. Now he had a new calling, new thoughts, and a new imployment for his wit and eloquence: Now all his earthly affections were changed into divine love; and all the faculties of his own soul, were ingaged in the Conversion of others: In preaching the glad tidings of Remission to repenting Sinners, and peace to each troubled soul. To these he applied himself with all care and diligence: and now, such a change was wrought in him, that he could say with *David, Oh how amiable are*

---

[1] Psalm 8:4   [2] paraphrase of Luke 38

thy tabernacles, O Lord God of Hosts![1] Now he declared openly, *that when he required a temporal, God gave him a spiritual blessing.* And that, *he was now gladder to be a door-keeper in the house of God, then he could be to injoy the noblest of all temporal imployments.*[2]

Presently after he entred into his holy profession, the King sent for him, and made him his Chaplain in Ordinary; and promised to take a particular care for his preferment.

And though his long familiarity with Scholars, and persons of greatest quality, was such as might have given some men boldness enough to have preached to any eminent Auditory; yet his modesty in this imployment was such, that he could not be perswaded to it, but went usually accompanied with some one friend, to preach privately in some village, not far from *London*: his first Sermon being preached at *Paddington*. This he did, till His Majesty sent and appointed him a day to preach to him at *White-hall*, and, though much were expected from him, both by His Majesty and others, yet he was so happy (which few are) as to satisfie and exceed their expectations: preaching the Word so, as shewed his own heart was possest with those very thoughts and joys that he laboured to distill into others: A Preacher in earnest; weeping sometimes for his Auditory, sometimes with them: alwayes preaching to himself, like an Angel from a cloud, but in none; carrying some, as St. *Paul* was, to Heaven in holy raptures,[3] and inticing others by a sacred Art and Courtship to amend their lives; here picturing a vice so as to make it ugly to those that practised it; and a vertue so, as to make it be beloved even by those that lov'd it not; and all this with a most particular grace and an unexpressible addition of comeliness.

There may be some that may incline to think (such indeed as have not heard him) that my affection to my Friend, hath transported me to an immoderate Commendation of his Preaching. If this meets with any such, Let me intreat, though I will omit many, yet that they will receive a double witness for what I say; it being attested by a Gentleman of worth (Mr. *Chidley*, a frequent hearer of his Sermons) in part of a funeral Elogie writ by him on Dr. *Donne*; and is a known truth, though it be in Verse.

[1] Psalm 84:1   [2] Psalm 84:10   [3] 2 Corinthians 12:2-4

—— Each Altar had his fire ——
He kept his love, but not his object: wit,
He did not banish, but transplanted it;
Taught it both time and place, and brought it home
To Piety, *which it doth best become.*
For say, had ever pleasure such a dress?
Have you seen crimes so shap't, or loveliness
Such as his lips did clothe Religion in?
Had not reproof a beauty, passing sin?
Corrupted nature sorrowed that she stood
So near the danger of becoming good.
And, when he preach't she wish't her ears exempt
From Piety, *that had such pow'r to tempt.*
How did his sacred flattery beguile
Men to amend? ——

More of this, and more witnesses might be brought, but I forbear and return.

That Summer, in the very same month in which he entred into sacred Orders, and was made the *Kings Chaplain*, His Majesty then going his Progress, was intreated to receive an entertainment in the University of *Cambridge*. And Mr. *Donne* attending his Majesty at that time, his Majesty was please to recommend him to the University, to be made *Doctor* in *Divinity; Doctor Harsnet* (after Archbishop of *York*) was then *Vice-Chancellor*, who knowing him to be the Author of that learned Book the *Pseudo-Martyr*, required no other proof of his Abilities, but proposed it to the *University*, who presently assented, and exprest a gladness, that they had such an occasion to intitle him to be theirs.

His Abilities and Industry in his Profession were so eminent, and he so known, and so beloved by Persons of Quality, that within the first year of his entring into sacred Orders, he had fourteen Advowsons of several Benefices presented to him: But they were in the Countrey, and he could not leave his beloved *London*, to which place he had a natural inclination, having received both his Birth and Education in it, and there contracted a friendship with many, whose conversation multiplied the joys of his life: But, an imployment that might affix him to that place would be welcome; for he needed it.

Immediately after his return from *Cambridge*, his wife died; leaving him a man of a narrow unsetled estate, and (having buried five) the careful father of seven children then living, to whom he gave a voluntary assurance, never to bring them under the subjection of a step-mother; which promise he kept most faithfully, burying with his tears, all his earthly joys in his most dear and deserving wives grave; and betook himself to a most retired and solitary life.

In this retiredness, which was often from the sight of his dearest friends, he became *crucified to the world*, and all those vanities, those imaginary pleasures that are daily acted on that restless stage; and they were as perfectly crucified to him. Nor is it hard to think (being passions may be both changed, and heightned by accidents) but that that abundant affection which once was betwixt him and her, who had long been the delight of his eyes, and the Companion of his youth; her, with whom he had divided so many pleasant sorrows, and contented fears, as Common-people are not capable of; not hard to think but that she, being now removed by death, a commeasurable grief took as full a possession of him as joy had done; and so indeed it did: for now his very soul was elemented of nothing but sadness; now, grief took so full a possession of his heart, as to leave no place for joy: If it did? It was a joy to be alone, where like a *Pelican in the wilderness*,[1] he might bemoan himself without witness or restraint, and pour forth his passions like *Job* in the days of his affliction, *Oh that I might have the desire of my heart! Oh that God would grant the thing that I long for!* For then, *as the grave is become her house*, so I would hasten to make it mine also; *that we two might there make our beds together in the dark.*[2] [. . .]

¶ *Dean of Pauls*

But God who is the God of all wisdom and goodness, turn'd it to the best; for this employment (to say nothing of the event of it) did not only divert him from those too serious studies, and sad

---

[1] Psalm 102:6   [2] Job 17:13

thoughts; but seemed to give him a new life by a true occasion of joy, to be an eye-witness of the health of his most dear and most honoured Mistress the Queen of *Bohemia*, in a forraign Nation; and to be a witness of that gladness which she expressed to see him: Who, having formerly known him a Courtier, was much joyed to see him in a Canonical habit, and more glad to be an ear-witness of his excellent and powerful Preaching.

About fourteen months after his departure out of England, he returned to his friends of Lincolns-Inne with his sorrows moderated, and his health improved; and there betook himself to his constant course of Preaching.

About a year after his return out of *Germany*, Dr. *Cary* was made Bishop of *Exeter*, and by his removal the Deanry of St. *Pauls* being vacant, the King sent to Dr. *Donne*, and appointed him to attend him at Dinner the next day. When his Majesty was sate down, before he had eat any meat, he said after his pleasant manner, Dr. *Donne*, *I have invited you to Dinner; and, though you sit not down with me, yet I will carve to you of a dish that I know you love well; for knowing you love* London, *I do therefore make you Dean of Pauls; and when I have dined, then do you take your beloved dish home to your study; say grace there to your self, and much good may it do you.*

Immediately after he came to his Deanry, he employed workman to repair and beautifie the Chapel; suffering, as holy *David* once vowed, *his eyes and temples to take no rest, till he had first beautified the house of God.*[1] [. . .]

¶ *Sickness & Death*

In *August* 1630. being with his eldest Daughter Mrs. *Harvy* at Abury hatch in *Essex*, he there fell into a Fever, which with the help of his constant infirmity (vapours from the spleen) hastened him into so visible a Consumption, that his beholders might say, as St. *Paul* of himself, *He dyes daily*; and he might say with *Job, My*

[1] Psalm 132

welfare passeth away as a cloud, the days of my affliction have taken
hold of me, and weary nights are appointed for me.[1]

> *Reader, This sickness continued long, not only weakning but*
> *wearying him so much, that my desire is, he may now take some rest:*
> *and that before I speak of his death, thou wilt not think it an imper-*
> *tinent digression to look back with me, upon some observations of his*
> *life, which, whilst a gentle slumber gives rest to his spirits, he may,*
> *I hope, not unfitly exercise thy consideration.*

His marriage was the remarkable error of his life; an error
which though he had a wit able and very apt to maintain Para-
doxes, yet he was very far from justifying it: and though his wives
Competent years, and other reasons might be justly urged to
moderate severe Censures; yet he would occasionally condemn
himself for it: and doubtless it had been attended with an heavy
Repentance, if God had not blest them with so mutual and cor-
dial affections, as in the midst of their sufferings made their bread
of sorrow taste more pleasantly then the banquets of dull and
low-spirited people.

The Recreations of his youth were *Poetry*, in which he was so
happy, as if nature and all her varieties had been made only to
exercise his sharp wit, and high fancy; and in those pieces which
were facetiously Composed and carelesly scattered (most of them
being written before the twentieth year of his age) it may appear
by his choice Metaphors, that both *Nature* and all the *Arts* joyned
to assist him with their utmost skill.

It is a truth, that in his penitential years, viewing some of those
pieces that had been loosely (God knows too loosely) scattered in
his youth, he wish't they had been abortive, or so short liv'd that
his own eyes had witnessed their funerals: But though he was no
friend to them, he was not so fallen out with heavenly Poetry as
to forsake that: no not in his declining age; witnessed then by many
Divine Sonnets, and other high, holy, and harmonious Com-
posures. Yea, even on his former sick-bed he wrote this heavenly
Hymn, expressing the great joy that then possest his soul in the
Assurance of Gods favour to him when he Composed it.

[1] 1 Corinthians 15:31; Job 30:15

An Hymn to God the Father.

Wilt thou forgive that sin where I begun,
   Which was my sin, though it were done before;
Wilt though forgive that sin through which I run,
   And do run still though still I do deplore?
   When thou hast done, thou hast not done,
                For I have more.

Wilt thou forgive that sin, which I have won
   Others to sin, and made my sin their door?
Wilt thou forgive that sin which I did shun
   A year or two, but wallowed in a score?
   When thou hast done, thou hast not done,
                For I have more.

I have a sin of fear, that when I've spun
   My last thread, I shall perish on the shore:
But swear by thy self, that at my death thy Son
   Shall shine as he shines now, and heretofore;
   And having done that, thou hast done,
                I fear no more.

I have the rather mentioned this *Hymn,* for that he caus'd it to be set to a most grave and solemn Tune, and to be often sung to the *Organ* by the *Choristers* of St. *Pauls* Church, in his own hearing; especially at the Evening Service, and at his return from his Customary Devotions in that place, did occasionally say to a friend, *The words of this* Hymn *have restored to me the same thoughts of joy that possest my Soul in my sickness when I composed it. And, O the power of Church-musick! that Harmony added to this Hymn has raised the Affections of my heart, and quickned my graces of zeal and gratitude;* and I observe, *that I always return from paying this publick duty of* Prayer *and* Praise *to God, with an unexpressible tranquillity of mind,* and a willingness *to leave the world.*

After this manner did the Disciples of our Saviour, and the best of Christians in those Ages of the Church nearest to his time, offer their praises to Almighty God. And the reader of St. *Augustines* life may there find, that towards his dissolution he wept abundantly, that the enemies of Christianity had broke in upon them, and prophaned and ruined their *Sanctuaries*; and because their *Publick Hymns* and Lauds were lost out of their Churches. And after this manner have many devout Souls lifted up their hands and offered acceptable Sacrifices unto Almighty God where Dr. *Donne* offered his, and now lyes buried.

But now, oh Lord, how is that place $\left.\right\}$ 1656
become desolate.

Before I proceed further, I think fit to inform the Reader, that not long before his death he caused to be drawn a figure of the Body of Christ extended upon an Anchor, like those which Painters draw when they would present us with the picture of Christ crucified on the Cross: his varying no otherwise then to affix him not to a Cross but to an anchor (the Emblem of hope) this he caused to be drawn in little, and then many of those figures thus drawn to be ingraven very small in *Helitropian* Stones, and set in gold, and of these he sent to many of his dearest friends to be used as *Seals*, or *Rings*, and kept as memorials of him, and of his affection to them. [. . .]

And in this enumeration of his friends, though many must be omitted, yet that man of primitive piety, Mr. *George Herbert* may not; I mean that *George Herbert*, who was the Author of the *Temple*, or *Sacred Poems and Ejaculations*. A Book, in which by declaring his own spiritual Conflicts, he hath Comforted and raised many a dejected and discomposed Soul, and charmed them into sweet and quiet thoughts: A Book, by the frequent reading whereof, and the assistance of that Spirit that seemed to inspire the Author, the Reader may attain habits of *Peace* and *Piety*, and all the gifts of the *Holy Ghost* and *Heaven*: and may by still reading, still keep those sacred fires burning upon the Altar of so pure a heart, as shall free it from the anxieties of this world, and keep it fixt upon things that are above; betwixt this *George Herbert* and Dr. *Donne* there was a long and dear friendship, made up by such a Sympathy of inclinations, that they coveted and joyed to be in each others Company; and this happy friendship, was still maintained by many sacred indearments; of which, that which followeth may be some Testimony.

58

To Mr. *George Herbert*; sent him with one of my Seals of the *Anchor* and *Christ*. (A sheaf of Snakes used heretofore to be my Seal, which is the Crest of our poor Family.)

Qui prius assuetus serpentum falce tabellas
  Signare, hæc nostræ Symbola parva domus
Adscitus domui domini.——

Adopted in Gods family, and so
  My old Coat lost into new Arms I go.
The Cross *my seal in Baptism spread below,*
  Does by that form into an Anchor grow.
Crosses grow Anchors, bear as thou should'st do
  Thy Cross, and that Cross grows an Anchor too.
But he that makes our Crosses Anchors thus,
  Is Christ; *who there is crucified for us.*
Yet with this I may my first Serpents hold:
  (God gives new blessings, and yet leaves the old)
The Serpent may as wise my pattern be;
  My poison, as he feeds on dust, that's me.
And, as he rounds the earth to murder, sure
  He is my death; but on the Cross my cure.
Crucifie nature then; and then implore
  All grace from him, crucify'd there before.
When all is Cross, *and that* Cross *Anchor grown,*
  This seals a Catechism, not a seal alone.
Vnder that little seal great gifts I send,
  Both works and prayers, pawns & fruits of a friend;
Oh may that Saint that rides on our great Seal,
  To you that bear his name large bounty deal.

                                                    John Donne.

In Sacram Anchoram Piscatoris
GEORGE HERBERT.

Quod Crux nequibat fixa clavique additi,
Tenere Christum scilicet ne ascenderet
Tuive Christum ———

Although the Cross could not Christ here detain,
When nail'd unto't, but he ascends again:
Nor yet thy eloquence here keep him still,
But only whilst thou speak'st; this Anchor will:
Nor canst thou be content, unless thou to
This certain Anchor add a seal, and so
The water *and the* earth, *both unto thee*
Do owe the Symbole of their certainty.
Let the world reel, we and all ours stand sure,
This Holy Cable's from all storms secure.

George Herbert.

I return to tell the Reader, that besides these verses to his dear Mr. *Herbert*, and that *Hymn* that I mentioned to be sung in the *Quire* of St. *Pauls Church*; he did also shorten and beguile many sad hours by composing other sacred Ditties; and he writ an Hymn on his death-bed, which bears this title.

An Hymn to God, my God, in my
sickness, *March* 23. 1630.

Since I am coming to that holy room,
Where, with thy Quire of Saints for evermore
I shall be made thy musique, as I come
I tune my Instrument here at the dore,
And what I must do then, think here before.

Since my Physitians by their loves are grown
Cosmographers! and I their map, who lye
Flat on this bed ———

So, in his purple wrapt receive me, Lord!
By these, his thorns, *give me his other* Crown:
And, as to other souls I preach'd thy Word,
Be this my Text: my Sermon to mine own.
That, he may raise; therefore, the Lord throws down.

If these fall under the censure of a soul, whose too much mixture with earth makes it unfit to judge of these high raptures and illuminations; let him know that many holy and devout men have thought the Soul of *Prudentius* to be most refined, when not many days before his death *he charged it to present his God each morning and evening with a new and spiritual song*; justified, by the example of King *David* and the good King *Hezekias*, who upon the renovation of his years paid his thankful vows to Almighty God in a *royal Hymn*, which he concludes in these words, *The Lord was ready to save, therefore I will sing my songs to the stringed instruments all the days of my life in the temple of my God.*[1] [. . .]

We left the Author sick in *Essex*, where he was forced to spend much of that Winter, by reason of his disability to remove from that place: And having never for almost twenty years omitted his personal attendance on His Majesty in that month in which he was to attend and preach to him; nor having ever been left out of the Roll and number of Lent-Preachers, and there being then (in *January* 1630.) a report brought to *London*, or raised there, that Dr. *Donne* was dead: That report gave him occasion to write this following Letter to a dear friend.

    Sir,

    This advantage you and my other friends have by my frequent Fevers, that I am much the oftner at the gates of Heaven; and this advantage by the solitude and close imprisonment that they reduce me to after, that I am so much the oftner at my prayers, in which I shall never leave out your happiness; and I doubt not among his other blessings, God will add some one to you for my prayers. A man would almost be content to dye (if there were no other benefit in death) to hear of so much sorrow, and so much good testimony from good men as I (God be blessed for it) did upon the report of my death; yet I perceive it went not through all; for one writ to me that some (and he said of my friends) conceived I was not so ill as I pretended, but withdrew my self to live at ease, discharged of preaching. It is an unfriendly, and God knows an ill-grounded interpretation; for I have always been sorrier when I could not preach, than any could be they could not hear me. It hath been

[1] Isaiah 38:21

my desire, and God may be pleased to grant it, that I might dye in the Pulpit; if not that, yet that I might take my death in the Pulpit, that is, dye the sooner by occasion of those labours. Sir, I hope to see you presently after *Candlemas*,[1] about which time will fall my *Lent-Sermon at Court*, except my *Lord Chamberlain* believe me to be dead, and so leave me out of the Roll; but as long as I live, and am not speechless, I would not willingly decline that service. I have better leisure to write, than you to read; yet I would not willingly oppress you with too much Letter. God so bless you and your Son as I wish, to

> *Your poor friend and Servant*
> *in Christ Jesus,*
> J. Donne.

Before that month ended, he was appointed to preach upon his old constant day, the first *Friday* in *Lent*; he had notice of it, and had in his sickness so prepared for that imployment, that as he had long thirsted for it: so he resolved his weakness should not hinder his journey; he came therefore to *London*, some few days before his appointed day of preaching. At his coming thither, many of his friends (who with sorrow saw his sickness had left him but so much flesh as did only cover his bones) doubted his strength to perform that task; and did therefore disswade him from undertaking it, assuring him however, it was like to shorten his life; but he passionately denied their requests; saying, *he would not doubt that that God who in so many weaknesses had assisted him with an unexpected strength, would now withdraw it in his last employment; professing an holy ambition to perform that sacred work.* And, when to the amazement of some beholders he appeared in the Pulpit, many of them thought he presented himself not to preach mortification by a living voice: but, mortality by a decayed body and a dying face. And doubtless, many did secretly ask that question in *Ezekiel*; *Do these bones live?*[2] *or, can that soul organize that*

---

[1] Feast of the Purification of the Virgin Mary, or the presentation of Christ in the Temple, celebrated by a great display of candles on 2 February.

[2] Ezekiel 37:3 [– I.W.]

tongue, to speak so long time as the sand in that glass will move towards
its centre, and measure out an hour of this dying mans unspent life?
Doubtless it cannot; and yet, after some faint pauses in his zealous
prayer, his strong desires enabled his weak body to discharge his
memory of his preconceived meditations, which were of dying:
the Text being, *To God the Lord belong the issues from death.*[1] Many
that then saw his tears, and heard his faint and hollow voice, professing they thought the Text prophetically chosen, and that Dr.
Donne *had preach't his own Funeral Sermon.*

Being full of joy that God had enabled him to perform this
desired duty, he hastened to his house; out of which he never
moved, till like St. *Stephen, he was carried by devout men to his
Grave.*[2]

The next day after his Sermon, his strength being much wasted,
and his spirits so spent, as indisposed him to business, or to talk:
A friend that had often been a witness of his free and facetious
discourse, asked him, *Why are you sad?* To whom he replied with
a countenance so full of chearful gravity, as gave testimony of an
inward tranquillity of mind, and of a soul willing to take a farewell of this world; And said,

'I am not sad, but most of the night past I have entertained
my self with many thoughts of several friends that have left
me here, *and are gone to that place from which they shall not
return;*[3] And, that within a few days *I shall also go hence, and be
no more seen.*[4] And my preparation for this change is become
my nightly meditation upon my bed, which my infirmities
have now made restless to me. But, at this present time, I was
in a serious contemplation of the providence and goodness of
God to me: to me *who am less than the least of his mercies;*[5] and
looking back upon my life past, I now plainly see it was his
hand that prevented me from all temporal employment; and
that it was his Will I should never settle nor thrive till I entred
into the Ministry; in which, I have now liv'd almost twenty

[1] Psalm 68:20
[2] Acts 8:2
[3] Job 10:21, 16:22
[4] Psalm 39:13
[5] Genesis 32:10

years (I hope to his glory) and by which I most humbly thank him, I have been enabled to requite most of those friends which shewed me kindness when my fortune was very low, as God knows it was: and (as it hath occasioned the expression of my gratitude) I thank God most of them have stood in need of my requital. I have liv'd to be useful and comfortable to my good Father-in-law Sir *George Moore*, whose patience God hath been pleased to exercise with many temporal Crosses; I have maintained my own Mother, whom it hath pleased God after a plentiful fortune in her younger days, to bring to a great decay in her very old age. I have quieted the Consciences of many that have groaned under the burthen of a wounded spirit, whose prayers I hope are available for me: I cannot plead innocency of life, especially of my youth: But I am to be judged by a merciful God, *who is not willing to see what I have done amiss.* And, though of my self I have nothing to present to him but sins and misery; yet, I know he looks not upon me now as I am of my self, but as I am in my Saviour, and hath given me even at this present time some testimonies of his Holy Spirit, that I am of the number of his Elect: *I am therefore full of unexpressible joy, and shall dye in peace.'*

I must here look so far back, as to tell the Reader, that at his first return out of *Essex* to preach his last Sermon, his old Friend and Physitian, Dr. *Fox*, a man of great worth, came to him to consult his health; and that after a sight of him, and some queries concerning his distempers, he told him, *That by Cordials, and drinking milk twenty days together, there was a probability of his restauration to health*; but he passionately denied to drink it. Nevertheless, Dr. *Fox*, who loved him most intirely, wearied him with sollicitations, till he yielded to take it for ten days; at the end of which time, he told Dr. *Fox, he had drunk it more to satisfie him, than to recover his health; and, that he would not drink it ten days longer upon the best moral assurance of having twenty years added to his life: for he loved it not; and was so far from fearing death, which to others is the King of terrors: that he long'd for the day of his dissolution.*

It is observed, that a desire of glory or commendation is rooted in the very nature of man; and that those of the severest and most mortified lives, though they may become so humble as to banish self-flattery, and such weeds as naturally grow there: yet they have not been able to kill this desire of glory, but that, like our radical heat, it will both live and dye with us; and many think it should do so; and we want not sacred examples to justifie the desire of having our memory out-live our lives: which I mention, because Dr. *Donne*, by the perswasion of Dr. *Fox*, easily yielded at this very time to have a Monument made for him; but Dr. *Fox* undertook not to perswade him how, or what Monument it should be; that was left to Dr. *Donne* himself.

A Monument being resolved upon, Dr. *Donne* sent for a Carver to make for him in wood the figure of an *Vrn*, giving him directions for the compass and height of it; and to bring with it a board of the just height of his body. 'These being got: then without delay a choice Painter was got to be in a readiness to draw his Picture, which was taken as followeth. —— Several Charcole-fires being first made in his large Study, he brought with him into that place his winding-sheet in his hand, and, having put off all his cloaths, had this sheet put on him, and so tyed with knots at his head and feet, and his hands so placed, as dead bodies are usu-ally fitted to be shrowded and put into their Coffin, or grave. Upon this *Vrn* he thus stood with his eyes shut, and with so much of the sheet turned aside as might shew his lean, pale, and death-like face, which was purposely turned toward the East, from whence he expected the second coming of his and our Saviour Jesus.' In this posture he was drawn at his just height; and when the Picture was fully finished, he caused it to be set by his bed-side, where it continued, and became his hourly object till his death: and, was then given to his dearest friend and Executor Doctor *Henry King*, then chief Residentiary of St. *Pauls*, who caused him to be thus carved in one entire piece of white Marble, as it now stands in that Church; and by Doctor *Donns*'s own appointment, these words were to be affixed to it as his Epitaph:

JOHANNES DONNE
Sac. Theol. Profess.
Post varia Studia quibus ab annis tenerrimis fi-
deliter, nec infeliciter incubuit;
Instinctu & impulsu Sp. Sancti, Monitu
& Hortatu
REGIS JACOBI, *Ordines Sacros am-*
plexus Anno sui Jesu, 1614. & *suæ ætatis* 42.
Decanatu hujus Ecclesiæ indutus 27. *Novem-*
bris 1621.
Exutus morte ultimo Die Martii 1631.
Hic licet in Occiduo Cinere Aspicit Eum
Cujus nomen est Oriens.

And now, having brought him through the many labyrinths and perplexities of a various life: even to the gates of death and the grave; my desire is, he may rest till I have told my Reader, that I have seen many Pictures of him, in several habits, and at several ages, and in several postures: And I now mention this, because I have seen one Picture of him, drawn by a curious hand at his age of eighteen; with his sword and what other adornments might then suit with the present fashions of youth, and the giddy gayeties of that age: and his Motto then was,

> *How much shall I be chang'd,*
> *Before I am chang'd.*

And if that young, and his now dying Picture, were at this time set together, every beholder might say, Lord! *How much is Dr.* Donne *already chang'd, before he is chang'd?* And the view of them might give my Reader occasion, to ask himself with some amazement, Lord! *How much may I also, that am now in health be chang'd, before I am chang'd? before this vile, this changeable body shall put off mortality?* and therefore to prepare for it. —— But this is not writ so much for my Readers *Memento,* as to tell him, that Dr. *Donne* would often in his private discourses, and often publickly in his Sermons, mention the many changes both of his body and mind: especially of his mind from a vertiginous giddiness; and would as often say, *His great and most blessed change was from a temporal, to a spiritual imployment*: in which he was so happy, that he accounted the former part of his life to be lost. And, the beginning of it to be, from his first entring into *sacred Orders*; and serving his most merciful God at his Altar.

Upon *Monday* after the drawing this Picture, he took his last leave of his beloved Study; and, being sensible of his hourly decay, retired himself to his bed-chamber: and that week sent at several times for many of his most considerable friends, with whom he took a solemn and deliberate farewell; commending to their considerations some sentences useful for the regulation of their lives, and then dismist them, as good *Jacob* did his sons, with a spiritual benediction.[1] The *Sunday* following he appointed his servants, that if there were any business yet undone that concerned him or themselves, it should be prepared against *Saturday* next; for after that day he would not mix his thoughts with any thing that concerned this world; nor ever did: But, as *Job*, so he *waited for the appointed day of his dissolution.*[2]

And now he was so happy as to have nothing to do but to dye; to do which, he stood in need of no longer time, for he had studied it long; and to so happy a perfection, that in a former sickness he called God to witness[3] *he was that minute ready to deliver his soul into his hands, if that minute God would determine his dissolution.* In that sickness he beg'd of God the constancy to be preserved in that estate for ever; and his patient expectation to have his immortal soul disrob'd from her garment of mortality, makes me confident he now had a modest assurance that his Prayers were then heard, and his Petition granted. He lay fifteen days earnestly expecting his hourly change; and, in the last hour of his last day, as his body melted away and vapoured into spirit, his soul having, I verily believe, some Revelation of the Beatifical Vision, he said, *I were miserable if I might not dye*; and after those words, closed many periods of his faint breath, by saying often, *Thy Kingdom come, Thy Will be done.* His speech, which had long been his ready and faithful servant, left him not till the last minute of his life, and

---

[1] Genesis 49:28   [2] Job 30:23

[3] In his Book of Devotions written then. [– I.W.]

then forsook him not to serve another Master (for who speaks like him) but dyed before him, for that it was then become useless to him that now conversed with God on earth, as Angels are said to do in heaven, *only by thoughts and looks.* Being speechless, and seeing heaven by that illumination by which he saw it; he did, as St. *Stephen, look stedfastly into it, till he saw the Son of man, standing at the right hand of God his Father;*[1] and being satisfied with this blessed sight, as his soul ascended, and his last breath departed from him, he closed his own eyes; and then disposed his hands and body into such a posture as required not the least alteration by those that came to shroud him.

Thus *variable,* thus *vertuous* was the Life; thus *excellent,* thus *exemplary* was the Death of this memorable man.

He was buried in that place of St. *Pauls* Church which he had appointed for that use some years before his death; and by which he passed daily to pay his publick devotions to Almighty God (who was then served twice a day by a publick form of Prayer and Praises in that place) but he was not buried privately, though he desired it; for, beside an unnumbred number of others, many persons of Nobility, and of eminency for Learning, who did love and honour him in his life, did shew it at his death, by a voluntary and sad attendance of his body to the grave, where nothing was so remarkable as a publick sorrow.

To which place of his Burial some mournful Friend repaired, and as *Alexander the Great* did to the grave of the famous *Achilles,* so they strewed his with an abundance of curious and costly Flowers, which course they (who were never yet known) continued morning and evening for many days; not ceasing, till the stones that were taken up in that Church to give his body admission into the cold earth (now his bed of rest) were again by the Masons art so levelled and firm'd, as they had been formerly; and his place of Burial undistinguishable to common view.

The next day after his Burial, some unknown friend, some one, of the many lovers and admirers of his vertue and learning; writ this *Epitaph* with a cole on the wall, over his grave.

---

[1] Acts 7:55-6

Reader! I am to let thee know,
Donne's *Body only, lyes below:*
For, could the grave his Soul comprize,
Earth would be richer then the skies.

Nor was this all the Honor done to his reverend Ashes; for as there be some persons that will not receive a reward for that for which God accounts himself a Debtor: persons, that dare trust God with their Charity, and without a witness; so there was by some grateful unknown Friend, that thought Dr. *Donne's* memory ought to be perpetuated, an hundred Marks sent to his two faithful Friends[1] and Executors, towards the making of his Monument. It was not for many years known by whom; but, after the death of Dr. *Fox*, it was known that 'twas he that sent it; and he lived to see as lively a representation of his dead Friend, as Marble can express; a Statue indeed so like Dr. *Donne*, that (as his Friend Sir *Henry Wotton* hath expressed himself) *it seems to breath faintly; and, Posterity shall look upon it as a kind of artificial Miracle.*

He was of Stature moderately tall, of a strait and equally-proportioned body, to which all his words and actions gave an unexpressible addition of Comeliness.

The melancholy and pleasant humor, were in him so contempered, that each gave advantage to the other, and made his Company one of the delights of Mankind.

His fancy *was unimitably high, equalled only by his great wit; both being made useful by a commanding judgment.*

His aspect *was chearful, and such, as gave a silent testimony of a clear knowing soul, and of a Conscience at peace with it self.*

His melting eye, *shewed that he had a soft heart, full of noble compassion; of too brave a soul to offer injuries, and too much a Christian not to pardon them in others.*

He did much contemplate (especially after he entred into his Sacred Calling) the mercies *of Almighty God, the* immortality of the Soul, *and the* joyes of Heaven; *and would often say, in a kind of sacred*

---

[1] Dr. *King* and Dr. *Monfort*. [– I.W.] Henry King (1592-1669), poet and Bishop of Chichester.

extasie —— Blessed be God that he is God only, and divinely like himself.

He was by nature highly passionate, but more apt to reluct at the excesses of it. A great lover of the offices of humanity, and of so merciful a spirit, that he never beheld the miseries of Mankind without pity and relief.

He was earnest and unwearied in the search of knowledge; with which, his vigorous soul is now satisfied, and employed in a continual praise of that God that first breathed it into his active body; that body, which once was a Temple of the Holy Ghost, *and is now become a small quantity of* Christian dust:

But I shall see it reanimated.

J.W.

Feb. 15. 1639.

1573

66

THE
LIFE
OF
Sir *HENRY WOTTON.*

¶ *His Birth and Birthplace*

Sir *Henry Wotton* (whose Life I now intend to write) was born in
the Year of our Redemption 1568. in *Bocton-Hall* (commonly
called *Bocton*, or *Bougton*-place, or Palace) in the Parish of *Bocton
Malherb*, in the fruitful Country of *Kent: Bocton-hall* being an
ancient and *goodly Structure*, beautifying, and being beautified by
the Parish Church of *Bocton Malherb* adjoyning unto it; and both
seated within a fair Park of the *Wottons*, on the Brow of such a
Hill, as gives the advantage of a large Prospect, and of equal *pleasure* to all Beholders. [. . .]

   This being premised, I proceed to tell the Reader, that the Father
of Sir *Henry Wotton* was twice married, first to *Elizabeth*, the
Daughter of Sir *John Rudstone* Knight; after whose death, though
his inclination was averse to all Contentions; yet necessitated he
was to several Suits in Law: in the prosecution whereof (which
took up much of his time, and were the occasion of many Discontents) he was by divers of his friends earnestly perswaded to a *re-
marriage*; to whom as he often answered, That if ever he did put
on a resolution to marry, *he was seriously resolved to avoid three sorts
of persons:*

namely, those ⎱ that had *Children*
⎰ that had *Law-suits*
⎰ that were of his *Kindred*.

   And yet, following his own Law-suits, he met in *Westminster-
hall* with Mrs. *Elionora Morton*, Widow to *Robert Morton* of *Kent*
Esquire; who was also engaged in several Suits in Law: and, he
observing her Comportment at the time of hearing one of her
Causes before the Judges, could not but at the same time both
compassionate her Condition, and affect her Person (for, *the tears*

71

of Lovers, or *Beauty drest in sadness*, are observ'd to have in them a Charming Eloquence; and to become very often too strong to be resisted) which I mention, because it prov'd so with this *Thomas Wotton*, for although there were in her a concurrence of all those accidents, against which he had so seriously resoved, yet his affection to her grew then so strong, that he resolved to solicite her for a Wife; and did, and obtained her. [. . .]

¶ *The dream of Nicholas Wotton*

And here, though this good man be dead, yet I wish a Circumstance or two that concern him, may not be buried without a Relation; which I shall undertake to do, for that I suppose, they may so much concern the Reader to know, that I may promise my self a pardon for a short digression.

In the year of our Redemption, 1553. *Nicholas Wotton* Dean of *Canterbury* (whom I formerly mentioned) being then Ambassador in *France*, dream'd, that his Nephew, this *Thomas Wotton*, was inclined to be a party in such a project, as, if he were not suddenly prevented, would turn both to the loss of his life, and ruine of his *Family*.

Doubtless, the good Dean did well know, that common Dreams are but a senseless paraphrase on our waking thoughts; or, of the business of the day past; or, are the result of our over-engaged affections, when we betake our selves to rest; and knew that the observation of them, may turn to silly Superstitions; as they too often do: But, though he might know all this, and might also believe that Prophesies are ceased; yet, doubtless he could not but consider, that all Dreams are not to be neglected or cast away without all consideration: and did therefore rather lay this Dream aside, then intend totally to lose it; and dreaming the same again the Night following, when it became a double Dream, like that of the *Pharaoh* (of which double dreams, the learned have made many observations)[1] and considering that it had no dependance

[1] Genesis 41:32

on his waking thoughts, much less on the desires of his heart, then he did more seriously consider it; and remembred that Almighty God was pleased in a Dream to reveal and to assure *Monica* the Mother of St. *Austin, that he, her Son for whom she wept so bitterly, and prayed so much, should at last become a Christian*:[1] This I believe, the good Dean considered; and considering also that Almighty God (though the causes of Dreams be often unknown) hath even in these latter times also, by a certain *illumination* of the Soul in sleep, discovered many things that humane wisdon could not foresee: Upon these considerations, he resolved to use so prudent a remedy by way of prevention, as might introduce no great inconvenience either to himself or to his Nephew. And to that end, he wrote to the *Queen* ('twas *Queen Mary*) and besought her, *That she would cause his Nephew* Thomas Wotton, *to be sent for out of* Kent: *and that the Lords of her Council might interrogate him in some such feigned Questions, as might give a colour for his Commitment into a favourable* Prison; *declaring, that he would acquaint her Majesty with the true reason of his request, when he should next become so happy as to see, and speak to her Majesty.*

'Twas done as the *Dean* desired: and in Prison I must leave Mr. *Wotton*, till I have told the Reader what followed.

At this time a Marriage was concluded betwixt our *Queen Mary*, and *Philip King* of *Spain*: And though this was concluded with the advice, if not by the perswasion of her Privy Council, as having many probabilities of advantage to this Nation: yet divers persons of a contrary perswasion, did not only declare against it, but also raised Forces to oppose it; believing (as they said) it would be a means to bring *England* to be under a subjection to *Spain*, and make those of this Nation slaves to *Strangers*.

And of this number Sir *Thomas Wyat* of *Boxley-Abbey* in *Kent* (betwixt whose Family, and the Family of the *Wottons*, there had been an ancient and entire friendship) was the principal Actor; who having perswaded many of the Nobility and Gentry (especially of *Kent*) to side with him, and he being defeated, and taken Prisoner, was legally arraigned and condemned, and lost his life: So did the Duke of *Suffolk*, and divers others, especially many of

---

[1] St. Austin's [Augustine's] *Confession*. [– I.W.]

the Gentry of *Kent*, who were there in several places executed as *Wyat*'s assistants.

And of this number, in all probability, had Mr. *Wotton* been if he had not been confin'd: for, though he could not be ignorant that *another mans Treason makes it mine by concealing it*; yet he durst confess to his Uncle, when he returned into *England*, and then came to visit him in Prison, *that he had more then an intimation of* Wyat's *intentions*; and thought he had not continued actually *innocent*, if his Uncle had not so happily dream'd him into a *Prison*; out of which place, when he was delivered by the same hand that caused his Commitment, they both considered the Dream more seriously; and then, both joined in praising God for it; *That God, who tyes himself to no Rules, either in preventing of evil, or in shewing of mercy to those, whom of good pleasure he hath chosen to love.* [. . .]

And it may yet be more considerable, that this *Nicholas* and *Thomas Wotton* should both (being men of holy lives, of even tempers, and much given to fasting and prayer) foresee and foretell the very days of their own death: *Nicholas* did so, being then Seventy years of age, and in perfect health. *Thomas* did the like in the sixty fifth year of his age; who being then in *London* (where he dyed) and foreseeing his death there, gave direction in what manner his Body should be carried to *Bocton*; and, though he thought his Uncle *Nicholas* worthy of that noble Monument which he built for him in the *Cathedral Church* of *Canterbury*; yet this humble man gave direction concerning himself, to be buried privately, and especially without any pomp at his Funeral. This is some account of this Family, which seemed to be beloved of God. [. . .]

¶ *'A pleasant definition of an Ambassador'*

At his first going Ambassadour into *Italy*, as he passed through *Germany*, he stayed some days at *Augusta*; where having been in his former Travels well known by many of the best note for Learning and Ingeniousness (those that are esteemed the *Virtuosi* of that Nation) with whom he passing an evening in merriments, was requested by *Christopher Flecamore* to write some Sentence in his *Albo*; (a Book of white Paper, which for that purpose many of the *German* Gentry usually carry about them) and Sir *Henry Wotton* consenting to the motion, took an occasion from some accidental discourse of the present Company, to write a pleasant definition of an Ambassadour, in these very words:

> *Legatus est vir bonus peregrè missius ad mentiendum*
> *Reipublicæ causâ.*

Which Sir *Henry Wotton* could have been content should have been thus Englished:

> *An Embassadour is an honest man, sent to* lie *abroad*
> *for the good of his Country.*

But the word for *lye* (being the hinge upon which the Conceit was to turn) was not so exprest in Latine, as would admit (in the hands of an Enemy especially) so fair a construction as Sir *Henry* thought in *English*. Yet as it was, it slept quietly among other Sentences in this *Albo*, almost *eight years*, till by accident it fell into the hands of *Jasper Scioppius*, a Romanist, a man of a restless spirit, and a malicious Pen: who with Books against King *James*, prints this as a Principle of that Religion professed by the King, and his Ambassador Sir *Henry Wotton*, then at *Venice*: and in *Venice* it was presently after written in several Glass-windows, and spitefully declared to be Sir *Henry Wottons*. [. . .]

¶ *Wotton is granted the Provostship of Eton*

It pleased the God of providence, that in this juncture of time, the Provostship of His Majesties Colledge of *Eaton* became void by the death of Mr. *Thomas Murray*, for which there were (as the place deserv'd) many earnest and powerful Suitors to the *King*. And Sir *Henry* who had for many years (like *Sisyphus*) rolled the restless stone of a State-imployment; knowing experimentally, that the great blessing of sweet content was not to be found in multitudes of men or business: and, that a *Colledge* was the fittest place to nourish *holy thoughts*, and to afford rest both to his body and mind, which his age (being now almost threescore years) seemed to require, did therefore use his own, and the interest of all his friends to procure that place. By which means, and quitting the King of his promised reversionary Offices, and a piece of honest policy (which I have not time to relate) he got a Grant of it from His Majesty. [. . .]

Being thus setled according to the desires of his *heart*, his first *study* was the Statutes of the *Colledge*: by which, he conceiv'd himself bound to enter into *Holy Orders*, which he did; being made *Deacon* with all convenient speed; shortly after which time, as he came in his *Surplice* from the *Church-service*, an old Friend, a person of Quality, met him so attired, and joyed him of his new habit; to whom Sir *Henry Wotton* replied, *I thank God and the* King, *by whose goodness I now am in this condition; a condition, which that Emperor* Charles *the Fifth seem'd to approve: who, after so many remarkable Victories, when his glory was great in the eyes of all men, freely gave up his* Crown, *and the many cares that attended it, to* Philip *his Son, making a holy retreat to a Cloysteral life, where he might by devout meditations consult with God* (which the rich or busie men seldom do) *and have leisure both to examine the errors of his life past, and prepare for that great day, wherein all flesh must make an account of their actions: And after a kind of tempestuous life, I now have the like advantage from him,* that makes the out-goings of the morning to praise him; *even from my God, whom I daily magnifie for this particular mercy, of an exemption from business, a quiet mind, and a liberal maintenance, even in this part of my life, when my age and infirmities seem to sound me a retreat from the pleasures of this world, and invite me to contemplation, in which I have ever taken the greatest felicity.*

And now to speak a little of the imployment of his *time* in the Colledge. After his customary publick Devotions, his use was to retire into his *Study*, and there to spend some hours in reading the Bible, and Authors in Divinity, closing up his meditations with private prayer; this was, for the most part, his imployment in the Forenoon: But when he was once sate to Dinner, then nothing but chearful thoughts possess'd his mind; and those still increased by constant company at his Table, of such persons as brought thither additions both of Learning and Pleasure; but some part of most days was usually spent in *Philosophical Conclusions*. Nor did he forget his innate pleasure of *Angling*, which he would usually call, *his idle time, not idly spent*; saying often, he would rather live five *May months*, then *forty Decembers*.

He was a great lover of his Neighbours, and a bountiful entertainer of them very often at his Table, where his meat was choice, and his discourse better.

He was a constant Cherisher of all those youths in that School, in whom he found either a constant diligence, or a *Genius* that prompted them to Learning; for whose encouragement, he was (beside many other things of necessity and beauty) at the charge of setting up in it two rows of *Pillars*, on which he caused to be choicely drawn, the pictures of divers of the most famous *Greek* and *Latin Historians, Poets*, and *Orators*; perswading them not to neglect *Rhetorick*, because *Almighty God has left Mankind affections to be wrought upon*: And he would often say, *That none despised Eloquence, but such dull souls as were not capable of it*. He would also often make choice of some Observations out of those *Historians* and *Poets*: and would never leave the School, without dropping some choice *Greek* or *Latin Apothegm* or sentence, that might be worthy of a room in the memory of a growing Scholar.

He was pleased constantly to breed up one or more hopeful Youths, which he picked out of the *School*, and took into his own Domestick care, and to attend him at his Meals; out of whose *Discourse* and *Behaviour*, he gathered observations for the better compleating of his intended work of *Education*: of which, by his still striving to make the whole better, he lived to leave but part to Posterity.

He was a great enemy to *wrangling Disputes* of *Religion*, concerning which, I shall say a little, both to testifie that, and to shew the readiness of his Wit.

Having at his being in *Rome* made acquaintance with a pleasant *Priest*, who invited him one Evening to hear their Vesper *Musick* at *Church*, the Priest seeing Sir *Henry* stand obscurely in a corner, sends to him by a Boy of the Quire this Question, writ in a small piece of Paper, *Where was your Religion to be found before* Luther? To which Question Sir *Henry* presently under-writ, *My*

Religion was to be found then, *where yours is not to be found* now, *in the written Word of God.*

The next Vesper, Sir *Henry* went purposely to the same Church, and sent one of the Quire-boyes with this Question, to his honest, pleasant friend, the Priest; *Do you believe all those many thousands of poor Christians were damn'd, that were Excommunicated, because the* Pope, *and the Duke of* Venice, *could not agree about their temporal power?* even those poor Christians that knew not why they quarrel'd. Speak your Conscience. To which he under-writ in *French, Monsieur, excusay moy.*

To one that asked him, *Whether a Papist may be saved?* he replied, *You may be saved without knowing that.* Look to your self.

To another, whose earnestness exceeded his knowledge, and was still railing against the *Papists*, he gave this advice, *Pray Sir forbear, till you have studied the Points better; for the wise* Italians *have this Proverb; He that understands amiss, concludes worse:* And take heed of thinking, *The farther you go from the Church of* Rome, *the nearer you are to God.* [. . .]

¶ *A diplomat's advice to diplomats*

And here it offers it self (I think not unfitly) to tell the Reader, that a friend of Sir *Henry Wottons*, being designed for the imployment of an *Ambassador*, came to *Eaton*, and requested from him some experimental Rules for his prudent and safe carriage in his Negotiations; to whom he smilingly gave this for an infallible *Aphorism; That, to be in safety himself, and serviceable to his* Country, *he should always, & upon all occasions speak the* truth (*it seems a* State-Paradox) *for*, says Sir Henry Wotton, *you shall never be believed; and by this means, your truth will secure your self, if you shall ever be called to any account; and 'twill also put your Adversaries (who will still hunt counter) to a loss in all their disquisitions and undertakings.*

¶ *Sickness and death*

The next thing wherewith I shall acquaint the Reader, is, That he went usually once a year, if not oftner, to the beloved *Bocton-hall*, where he would say, *he found a cure for all cares, by the chearful company*, which he called the living furniture of that place: and *a restoration of his strength, by the Connaturalness of that, which he called his* genial *air*.

He yearly went also to *Oxford*. But the Summer before his death he changed that for a journey to *Winchester*-Colledge; to which School he was first removed from *Bocton*. And as he returned from *Winchester*, towards *Eaton*-Colledge, said to a friend, his Companion in that Journey; *How useful was that advice of a Holy Monk, who perswaded his friend to* perform his Customary devotions in a constant place, because in that place, we usually meet with those very thoughts which possessed us at our last being there; *And I find it thus far experimentally true; that, at my now being in that School, and seeing that very place where I sate when I was a Boy, occasioned me to remember those very thoughts indeed, that promised my growing years numerous pleasures, without mixtures of cares; and those to be enjoyed, when time (which I therefore thought slow pac'd) had changed my* youth *into* manhood: *But age and experience have taught me, that those were but empty hopes: For I have always found it true, as my* Saviour *did foretell*, Sufficient for the day is the evil thereof. *Nevertheless, I saw there a succession of Boys using the same recreations, and questionless possessed with the same thoughts that then possessed me. Thus, one generation succeeds another, both in their* lives, recreations, hopes, fears, and death.

After his return from *Winchester* to *Eaton* (which was about five Moneths before his death) he became much more retir'd, and contemplative; in which time he was often visited by Mr. *John Hales*, (learned Mr. *John Hales*) then a Fellow of that Colledge, to whom upon an occasion he spake to this purpose —— *I have in my passage to my grave met with most of those Joys of which a discoursive soul is capable: and, being entertain'd with more inferior pleasures then the sons of men are usually made partakers of: nevertheless, in this voyage I have not always floated on the calm Sea of Content; but have oft met with cross winds and storms, and with many troubles of mind*

79

and temptations to evil. And yet, though I have been and am a man com-
pass'd about with humane frailties, Almighty God hath by his grace pre-
vented me from making shipwrack *of* faith and a good Conscience;
the thought of which is now the joy of my heart, and I must humbly
praise him for it; And I humbly acknowledge that it was not my self but
he that hath kept me to this great age, and let him take the glory of his
great mercy. —— *And my dear Friend, I now see that I draw near my*
harbour of death: that harbor, that will secure me from all the future
storms and waves of this restless world; and I praise God I am willing
to leave it, and expect a better; that world, wherein dwelleth Righteousness, and I long for it. —— These, and the like expressions
were then utter'd by him at the beginning of a Feavourish distemper, at which time he was also troubled with an *Asthma*, or
short spitting; but after less then twenty fits, by the help of familiar Physick and a spare Diet, this Feaver abated; yet so, as to leave
him much weaker then it found him: and his *Asthma* seem'd also
to be overcome in a good degree by his forbearing *Tobacco*, which,
as many thoughtful men do, he also had taken somewhat immod-
erately. —— This was his then present condition, and, thus he
continued till about the end of *October* 1639, which was about a
moneth before his death, at which time, he again fell into a *Feaver*,
which, though he seem'd to recover, yet these still left him so
weak, that they and those other common infirmities that accompany age, and were wont to visit him like civil friends, and after
some short time to leave him; came now, both oftner and with
more violence, and at last took up their constant habitation with
him, still weakning his Body and abating his chearfulness: of
both which he grew more sensible, and did the oftner retire into
his Study, and there made many Papers that had pass'd his Pen
both in the days of his youth, and in the busie part of his life, useless, by a fire made there to that purpose. —— These and several
unusual expressions to his Servants and Friends, seem'd to foretell that the day of his death drew near: for which, he seem'd to
those many friends that observ'd him, to be well prepar'd, & to
be both patient, and free from all fear; as several of his Letters
writ on this his last sick-bed may testifie: and thus he continued
till about the beginning of *December* following, at which time he
was seiz'd more violently with a *Quotidian Feaver*, in the tenth fit

of which Feaver, his better part, that part of Sir *Henry Wotton* which could not dye, put off mortality with as much content and chearfulness as humane frailty is capable of; being then in great tranquillity of mind, and in perfect peace with God and man.

And thus the Circle of Sir *Henry Wotton's* Life – (that Circle which began at *Bocton*, and in the *Circumference* thereof, did first touch at *Winchester-School*, then at *Oxford*, and after upon so many remarkable parts and passages in *Christendom*) That *Circle* of his *Life*, was by *Death* thus closed up and compleated, in the seventy and second year of his *Age*, at *Eaton Colledge*, where, according to his Will, he now lies buried, with his Motto on a plain Gravestone over him; dying worthy of his Name and *Family*, worthy of the love and favour of so many *Princes*, and Persons of eminent *Wisdom* and *Learning*, worthy of the trust committed unto him, for the Service of his *Prince* and *Countrey*.

And all Readers are requested to believe, that he was worthy of a more worthy Pen, to have preserved his Memory, *and commended his* Merits *to the imitation of Posterity*.

Iz. Wa.

THE
LIFE
OF
Mr. *RICHARD HOOKER*

¶ *His birth and education*

It is not to be doubted but that *Richard Hooker* was born at *Heavy-tree*, near or within the Precincts, or in the City of *Exeter*; a City which may justly boast, that it was the Birth-place of him, and Sir *Tho. Bodley*; as indeed the County may in which it stands, that it hath furnished this Nation with Bishop *Jewel*, Sir *Francis Drake*, Sir *Walter Raleigh*, and many others, memorable for their Valour and Learning. He was born about the Year of our Redemption 1553, and of Parents that were not so remarkable for their Extraction or Riches, as for their Virtue and Industry, and Gods blessing upon both; by which they were enabled to educate their Children in some degree of Learning, of which our *Richard Hooker* may appear to be one fair testimony; and that Nature is not so partial, as always to give the great blessings of Wisdom and Learning, and with them the greater blessings of Virtue and Government, to those only that are of a more high and honourable Birth.

His Complexion (if we may guess by him at the age of Forty) was Sanguine, with a mixture of Choler; and yet his Motion was slow even in his Youth, and so was his Speech, never expressing an Earnestness in either of them, but an humble Gravity suitable to the Aged. And 'tis observed (so far as Inquiry is able to look back at this distance of Time) that at his being a School-boy he was an early Questionist, quietly inquisitive *Why this was, and that was not, to be remembred? Why this was granted, and that denied?* This being mixt with a remarkable Modesty, and a sweet serene quietness of Nature, and with them a quick apprehension of many perplext parts of Learning imposed then upon him as a Scholar, made his Master and others to believe him to have an inward Divine Light, and therefore to consider him to a little wonder. For in that, Children were less pregnant, less confident, and more malleable, than in this wiser, but not better, Age. [. . .]

¶ His patron, the Bishop of Salisbury

About the second or third Year of her Reign,[1] this *John Jewel* was made Bishop of *Salisbury*; and there being always observed in him a willingness to do good, and to oblige his Friends, and now a power added to this willingness: this *John Hooker* gave him a Visit in *Salisbury, and besought him for Charity's sake to look favourably upon a poor Nephew of his, whom Nature had fitted for a Scholar, but the Estate of his Parents was so narrow, that they were unable to give him the advantage of Learning; and that the Bishop would therefore become his Patron, and prevent him from being a Tradesman; for he was a Boy of remarkable hopes.* And though the Bishop knew, men do not usually look with an indifferent eye upon their own Children and Relations, yet he assented so far to *John Hooker*, that he appointed the Boy and his Schoolmaster should attend him about *Easter* next following at that place: which was done accordingly; and then, after some Questions and observations of the Boys learning and gravity, and behaviour, the Bishop gave his Schoolmaster a reward, and took order for an annual Pension for the Boys Parents: promising also, to take him into his care for a future preferment, which he performed; for about the Fifteenth Year of his age, which was *Anno* 1567, he was by the Bishop appointed to remove to *Oxford*, and there to attend Dr. *Cole*, then President of *Corpus-Christi* Colledge. Which he did; and Dr. *Cole* had (according to a promise made to the Bishop) provided for him both a Tutor (which was said to be the learned Dr. *John Reynolds*) and a Clerks place in that Colledge: which place, though it were not a full maintenance, yet with the contribution of his Uncle, and the continued Pension of his Patron the good Bishop, gave him a comfortable subsistence. And in this condition he continued unto the Eighteenth Year of his age, still increasing in Learning and Prudence, and so much in Humility and Piety, that he seemed to be filled with the Holy Ghost, and even like St. *John Baptist*, to be sanctified from his Mothers womb, who did often bless the day in which she bare him.[2]

About this time of his age he fell into a dangerous Sickness,

---

[1] Elizabeth I   [2] Luke I:5-25

which lasted two Months; all which time his Mother, having notice of it, did in her hourly prayers as earnestly beg his life of God, as *Monica* the Mother of St. *Augustine* did that he might become a true Christian; and their prayers were both so heard as to be granted. Which Mr. *Hooker* would often mention with much joy, *and as often pray that he might never live to occasion any sorrow to so good a Mother; of whom, he would often say, he loved her so dearly, that he would endeavor to be good even as much for hers, as for his own sake.*

As soon as he was perfectly recovered from this Sickness, he took a journey from *Oxford* to *Exeter*, to satisfie and see his good Mother, being accompanied with a Countreyman and Companion of his own Colledge, and both on foot; which was then either more in fashion, or want of money, or their humility made it so: But on foot they went, and took *Salisbury* in their way, purposely to see the good Bishop, who made Mr. *Hooker* and his Companion dine with him at his own Table; which Mr. *Hooker* boasted of with much joy and gratitude when he saw his Mother and Friends: And at the Bishops parting with him, the Bishop gave him good Counsel, and his Benediction, but forgot to give him money; which when the Bishop had considered, he sent a Servant in all haste to call *Richard* back to him, and at *Richards* return, the Bishop said to him, *Richard, I sent for you back to lend you a Horse, which hath carried me many a Mile, and I thank God with much ease;* and presently delivered into his hand a Walking-staff, with which he professed he had travelled through many parts of *Germany;* and he said, *Richard, I do not give, but lend you my Horse; be sure you be honest, and bring my Horse back to me at your return this way to* Oxford. *And I do now give you Ten Groats to bear your charges to* Exeter; *and here is Ten Groats more, which I charge you to deliver to your Mother, and tell her, I send her a Bishops Benediction with it, and beg the continuance of her prayers for me. And if you bring my Horse back to me, I will give you Ten Groats more to carry you on foot to the Colledge, and so God bless you, good* Richard.

And this, you may believe, was performed by both Parties. But, alas! the next News that followed Mr. *Hooker* to *Oxford*, was, that his learned and charitable Patron had changed this for a *better life.* Which happy change may be believed, for that as he lived, so he dyed, in devout meditation and prayer; and in both so zealously, that it became a religious question, *Whether his last Ejaculations, or his Soul, did first enter into Heaven?* [. . .]

¶ At Oxford

[A]mongst other Testimonies this still remains of him: That in four years, he was but twice absent from the Chappel prayers; and that his Behaviour there was such as shewed an awful reverence of that God which he then worshipped and prayed to; giving all outward testimonies that his Affections were set on heavenly things. This was his Behaviour towards God; and for that to Man; it is observable that he was never known to be angry, or passionate, or extream in any of his Desires; never heard to repine or dispute with Providence, but by a quiet gentle submission and resignation of his Will to the Wisdom of his Creator, bore the burthen of the day with Patience; never heard to utter an uncomly word: and by this, and a grave Behaviour, which is a Divine Charm, he begot an early Reverence unto his Person, even from those that at other times, and in other companies, took a liberty to cast off that strictness of Behaviour and Discourse that is required in a Collegiate Life. And when he took any liberty to be pleasant, his Wit was never blemisht with Scoffing, or the utterance of any Conceit that border'd upon, or might beget a thought of Looseness in his hearers. Thus mild, thus innocent and exemplary was his Behaviour in his Colledge; and, thus this good man continued till his death, still increasing in Learning, in Patience, and Piety.

¶ 'Those corroding cares that attend a married priest'

I return to Mr. *Hooker* in his *Colledge*, where he continued his studies with all quietness, for the space of three years; about which time, he enter'd into Sacred Orders, being then made Deacon and Priest; and, not long after, was appointed to preach at St. *Pauls Cross*.

In order to which Sermon, to *London* he came, and immediately to the *Shunamites house;*[1] (which is a House so called, for that, besides the Stipend paid the Preacher, there is provision made also for his Lodging and Diet for two days before, and one day after his Sermon;) this house was then kept by *John Churchman*, sometimes a Draper of good Note in *Watling-street*, upon whom poverty had at last come like an armed man, and brought him into a necessitous condition; which, though it be a punishment, is not always an argument of Gods disfavour, for he was a vertuous man: I shall not yet give the like testimony of his Wife, but leave the Reader to judge by what follows. But to this house Mr. *Hooker* came so wet, so weary, and weather-beaten, that he was never known to express more passion, than against a Friend that dissuaded him from footing it to *London*, and for finding him no easier an Horse; supposing the Horse trotted, when he did not: And at this time also, such a faintness and fear possest him, that he would not be perswaded two days rest and quietness, or any other means could be used to make him able to preach his Sunday Sermon; but a warm Bed, and Rest, and Drink, proper for a Cold, given him by Mrs. *Churchman*, and her diligent attendance added unto it, enabled him to perform the office of the day, which was in or about the Year 1581.

And in this first publick appearance to the World, he was not so happy as to be free from Exceptions against a point of Doctrine delivered in his Sermon; which was, *That in God there were two Wills, an Antecedent, and a Consequent Will; his first Will, that all Mankind should be saved; but his second Will was, that those only should be saved, that did live answerable to that degree of Grace which he had offered, or afforded them.* This seemed to cross a late Opinion of Mr. *Calvins*, and then taken for granted by many that had not a capacity to examine it, as it had been by him before, and hath been since by Master *Henry Mason*, Dr. *Jackson*, Dr. *Hammond*, and others of great Learning, who believ'd that a contrary Opinion intrenches upon the Honour and Justice of our merciful God. How he justified this, I will not undertake to declare, but it was not excepted against (as Mr. *Hooker* declares in his rational Answer

[1] See 2 Kings 4:8-17

to Mr. *Travers*) by *John Elmer*, then Bishop of *London*; at this time one of his Auditors, and at last one of his Advocates too, when Mr. *Hooker* was accused for it.

But the justifying of this Doctrine did not prove of so bad consequence, as the kindness of Mrs. *Churchmans* curing him of his late Distemper and Cold; for that was so gratefully apprehended by M. *Hooker*, that he thought himself bound in conscience to believe all that she said; so that the good man came to be perswaded by her, *that he was a man of a tender constitution*, and *that it was best for him to have a Wife, that might prove a Nurse to him*; such an one as *might both prolong his life, and make it more comfortable; and such a one she could and would provide for him, if he thought fit to marry*. And he not considering, that *the children of this world are wiser in their generation, than the children of light*; but, like a true *Nathanael*,[1] fearing no guile, because he meant none, did give her such a power as *Eleazar* was trusted with, (you may read it in the book of *Genesis*) when he was sent to choose a Wife for *Isaac*;[2] for even so he trusted her to choose for him, promising upon a fair summons to return to *London*, and accept her choice; and he did so in that or about the year following. Now the Wife provided for him, was her Daughter *Joan*, who brought him neither Beauty nor Portion; and for her Conditions, they were too like that Wife's which is by *Solomon* compar'd to a *dripping house*; so that the good man had no reason to *rejoice in the Wife of his Youth*; but too just cause to say with the holy Prophet, *Wo is me that I am constrained to have my habitation in the tents of Kedar*.[3]

This choice of Mr. *Hookers* (if it were his choice) may be wondred at; but let us consider that the Prophet *Ezekiel* says, *There is a wheel within a wheel*, a secret Sacred wheel of Providence (most visible in Marriages) guided by his hand, that *allows not the race to the swift*, nor *bread to the wise*,[4] nor good wives to good men: and he that can bring good out of evil, (for Mortals are blind to this Reason) only knows why this blessing was denied to patient *Job*,

---

[1] Luke 16:8; John 1:45 ff and 21:2   [2] Genesis 24

[3] Proverbs 19:13, 5:18; Psalm 120:5

[4] Ezekiel 1:16, 10:10; Ecclesiastes 9:11. It is not clear why Walton thought Job and Moses had shrewish wives.

to meek *Moses*, and to our as meek and patient Mr. *Hooker*. But so it was; and let the Reader cease to wonder, for *Affliction is a Divine diet*, which though it be not pleasing to Mankind, yet Almighty God hath often, very often imposed it as good, though bitter Physick to those children whose Souls are dearest to him.

And by this marriage the good man was drawn from the tranquillity of his Colledge, from that Garden of Piety, of Pleasure, of Peace, and a sweet Conversation, into the thorny Wilderness of a busie World; into those corroding cares that attend a married Priest, and a Countrey Parsonage: which was *Draiton Beauchamp* in *Buckinghamshire*, not far from *Alesbury*, and in the Diocess of *Lincoln*; to which he was presented by *John Cheny* Esquire, then Patron of it, the 9*th* of *December* 1584. where he behaved himself so as to give no occasion of evil, but (as St. *Paul* adviseth a Minister of God) *in much patience, in afflictions, in anguishes, in necessities; in poverty, and no doubt in long-suffering:*[1] yet troubling no man with his discontents and wants.

And in this condition he continued about a year, in which time his two Pupils, *Edwin Sandys* and *George Cranmer*, took a journey to see their Tutor, where they found him with a Book in his hand (it was the *Odes* of *Horace*) he being then like humble and innocent *Abel*, tending his small allotment of sheep in a common field, which he told his Pupils he was forced to do then, for that his servant was gone home to Dine, and assist his Wife to do some necessary household business. But when his servant returned and released him, then his two Pupils attended him unto his house, where their best entertainment was his quiet company, which was presently denied them: for, *Richard was call'd to rock the Cradle*; and the rest of their welcom was so like this, that they staid but till the next morning, which was time enough to discover and pity their Tutors condition; and they having in that time rejoiced in the remembrance, and then paraphrased on many of the innocent recreations of their younger days, and other like diversions, and thereby given him as much present comfort as they were able, they were forced to leave him to the company of his wife *Joan*, and seek themselves a quieter Lodging for next

[1] 2 Corinthians 6:4-5

night: But at their parting from him, Mr. *Cranmer* said, *Good Tutor, I am sorry your lot is fall'n in no better ground as to your Parsonage; and more sorry that your Wife proves not a more comfortable Companion after you have wearied your self in your restless studies.* To whom the good man replied, *My dear* George, *If Saints have usually a double share in the miseries of this life, I that am none, ought not to repine at what my wise Creator hath appointed for me, but labour, (as indeed I do daily) to submit mine to his Will, and possess my soul in patience, and peace.* [. . .]

¶ The 'Errors and Animosities' of Nonconformism considered

These Errors and Animosities were so remarkable, that they begot wonder in an ingenious *Italian*, who being about this time come newly into this nation, and considering them, writ scoffingly to a friend in his own Country, to this purpose, *That the Common people of* England *were wiser than the wisest of his Nation; for here the very* Women *and* Shopkeepers, *were able to judge of Predestination, and to determine what Laws were fit to be made concerning Church-government; and then, what were fit to be obeyed or abolisht: That they were more able (or at least thought so) to raise and determine perplext Cases of Conscience, than the wisest of the most learned Colledges in* Italy; *That men of the slightest Learning, and the most ignorant of the Common people, were mad for a new, or,* Super- *or* Re-reformation *of Religion; and that in this* they appeared like that man, who would never cease to whet and whet his knife, till there was no steel left to make it useful. And he concluded his Letter with this observation, *That those very men that were most busie in Oppositions, and Disputations, and Controversies, and finding out the faults of their Governors, had usually the least of* Humility *and* Mortification, *or of the* power *of* Godliness. [. . .]

¶ *Mr Hooker defends the Church with Reason and sweet Language*

[H]e designed to write a deliberate sober Treatise of the Churches power to make Canons for the use of Ceremonies, and by Law to impose an obedience to them, as upon her Children; and this he proposed to do in *eight Books of the Laws of Ecclesiastical Polity*; intending therein to shew such Arguments as should force an assent from all men, if Reason, delivered in sweet Language, and void of any provocation, were able to do it; And that he might prevent all prejudice, he wrote before it a large Preface or Epistle to the *Dissenting Brethren*, wherein there were such Bowels of Love, and such a Commixture of that *Love* with *Reason*, as was never exceeded but in Holy Writ, and particularly by that of St. *Paul* to his dear Brother and Labourer *Philemon*: than which, none was ever more like this Epistle of Mr. *Hookers*; so that his dear friend and Companion in his Studies Doctor *Spenser*, might after his death justly say, *What admirable height of Learning and depth of Judgment dwelt in the lowly mind of this truly humble man, great in all wise mens eyes except his own; with what gravity and Majesty of speech his Tongue and Pen uttered Heavenly Mysteries; whose eyes in the Humility of his Heart were always cast down to the ground; how all things that proceeded from him were breathed as from the Spirit of Love, as if he, like the Bird of the Holy Ghost, the Dove, had wanted Gall; let those that knew him not in his Person, judge by these living Images of his soul, his Writings.*

The foundation of these Books was laid in the Temple; but he found it no fit place to finish what he had there designed; and he therefore earnestly solicited the Archbishop for a remove from that place, to whom he spake to this purpose. My Lord, *When I lost the freedom of my Cell, which was my Colledge, yet I found some degree of it in my quiet Country Parsonage: but I am weary of the noise and oppositions of this place; and indeed, God and Nature did not intend me for Contentions, but for Study and quietness:* My Lord, *My particular contests with Mr.* Travers *here have proved the more unpleasant to me, because I believe him to be a good man; and, that belief hath occasioned me to examine mine own Conscience concerning his Opinions: and, to satisfie that, I have consulted the Scripture, and other Laws both*

Humane and Divine, whether the Conscience of him and others of his judgment ought to be so far complyed with as to alter our frame of Church Government, our manner of Gods Worship, our Praising and Praying to him, and, our established Ceremonies as often as his and others tender Consciences shall require us; and, in this examination, I have not only satisfied my self, but have begun a treatise, in which I intend a Justification of the Laws of our Ecclesiastical Polity: *in which design God and his holy Angels shall at the last great day bear me that witness which my Conscience now does; that my meaning is not to provoke any, but rather to satisfie all tender Consciences, and I shall never be able to do this, but where I may Study, and pray for Gods blessing upon my indeavours, and keep my self in Peace and Privacy, and behold Gods blessing spring out of my Mother Earth, and eat my own bread without oppositions; and therefore, if your Grace can Judge me worthy of such a favour, let me beg it, that I may perfect what I have begun.*

About this time the Parsonage or Rectory of *Boscum*, in the Diocess of *Sarum*, and six miles from that City, became void. The Bishop of *Sarum* is Patron of it; but in the vacancy of that See (which was three years betwixt the Translation of Bishop *Peirce* to the See of *York*, and Bishop *Caldwells* admission into it) the disposal of that and all Benefices belonging to that See, during this said vacancy, came to be disposed of by The Archbishop of *Canterbury*, and he presented *Richard Hooker* to it, in the year 1591. And *Richard Hooker* was also in the said year Instituted, *July* 17. to be a minor Prebend of *Salisbury*, the Corps of it being *Nether-Havin*, about ten miles from that City: which Prebend was of no great value, but intended chiefly to make him capable of a better preferment in that Church. In this *Boscum* he continued till he had finished four of his eight proposed Books of the Laws of Ecclesiastical Polity, and these were entered into the register Book in Stationers Hall, the 9*th* of *March* 1592. but not published till the year 1594. and then were with the before-mentioned large and affectionate Preface, which he directs *to them that seek (as they term it) the Reformation of the Laws and Orders Ecclesiastical in the Church of England*; of which Books I shall yet say nothing more, but that he continued his laborious diligence (of all which more properly hereafter) but at *Boscum* he finisht and publisht but only the first four; being then in the 39*th* year of his Age.

He left *Boscum* in the year 1595. by a surrender of it into the hands of Bishop *Caldwell*, and he presented *Benjamin Russel*, who was Instituted into it the 23 of *June* in the same year.

The Parsonage of *Bishops Borne* in *Kent*, three miles from *Canterbury*, is in that Archbishops gift; but, in the latter end of the year 1594. Doctor *William Redman* the Rector of it was made *Bishop* of *Norwich*, by which means the power of presenting to it was *pro ea vice* in the Queen; and she presented *Richard Hooker*, whom she loved well, to this good living of *Borne* the 7th of *July* 1595. in which living he continued till his Death, without any addition of Dignity or Profit. [. . .]

And I am next to declare, that his fifth Book (which is larger than his first four) was first also printed by it self *Anno* 1597. and dedicated to his Patron (for till then he chose none) the Archbishop. These Books were read with an admiration of their excellency in This, and their just fame spread it self also into foreign Nations. And I have been told more than forty years past, that either Cardinal *Allen*, or learned Doctor *Stapleton* (both English men, and in *Italy* about the time when *Hookers* four Books were first printed:) meeting with this general fame of them, were desirous to read an Author that both the Reformed and the learned of their own *Romish* Church did so much magnifie, and therefore caused them to be sent for to *Rome*; and after reading them, boasted to the Pope (which then was *Clement* the eighth) *that though he had lately said he never met with an English Book whose Writer deserved the name of Author*; yet there now appear'd a wonder to them, and it would be so to his Holiness, if it were in Latin, for *a poor obscure English Priest had writ four such Books of Laws, and Church Polity, and in a Style that exprest such a Grave, and so Humble Majesty, with such clear demonstration of Reason, that in all their readings they had not met with any that exceeded him*; and this begot in the Pope an earnest desire that Doctor *Stapleton* should bring the said four Books, and looking on the English read a part of them to him in Latin; which Doctor *Stapleton* did, to the end of the first Book; at the conclusion of which, the Pope spake to this purpose; *There is no Learning that this man hath not searcht into; nothing too hard for his understanding: this man indeed deserves the name of an Author; his Books will get reverence by Age, for there is in them such seeds of Eternity, that if the rest be like this, they shall last till the last fire shall consume all Learning.*

Nor was this high, the only testimony and commendations given to his Books; for at the first coming of King *James* into this Kingdom, he inquired of the Archbishop *Whitgift* for his friend Mr. *Hooker* that writ the Books of Church Polity; to which the answer was, that he dyed a year before Queen *Elizabeth*, who received the sad news of his Death with very much Sorrow; to which the King replied, *and I receive it with no less, that I shall want the desired happiness of seeing and discoursing with that man, from whose Books I have received such satisfaction: Indeed, my Lord, I have received more satisfaction in reading a leaf, or paragraph in* Mr. *Hooker,* though it were but about the *fashion* of *Churches*, or *Church musick,* or the like, but especially *of the Sacraments, than I have had in the reading particular large Treatises written but of one of those Subjects by others, though very learned men*; and, I observe *there is in Mr.* Hooker *no affected language, but a grave, comprehensive, clear manifestation of Reason, and that back't with the Authority of the* Scripture, *the* Fathers and School-men, *and with all* Law *both* Sacred and Civil. *And, though many others write well, yet in the next Age they will be forgotten; but doubtless there is in every page of* Mr. Hookers Book *the picture of a Divine Soul, such Pictures of* Truth *and* Reason, *and drawn in so sacred Colours, that they shall never fade, but give an immortal memory to the Author.* And it is so truly true, that the King thought what he spake, that as the most learned of the Nation have and still do mention Mr. *Hooker* with reverence, so he also did never mention him but with the Epithite of *Learned,* or *Judicious,* or *Reverend,* or *Venerable Mr.* Hooker. [. . .]

¶ At Borne

This Parsonage of *Borne* is from *Canterbury* three miles, and near to the common Road that leads from that City to *Dover*: in which Parsonage Mr. *Hooker* had not been Twelve months, but his Books, and the innocency and sanctity of his life became so remarkable, that many turn'd out of the Road, and others (Scholars especially) went purposely to see the man, whose life and learning were so much admired; and alas, as our Saviour said of St. *John Baptist, What went they out to see? a man cloathed in purple and fine linnen?*[1] no indeed, but an *obscure, harmless man, a man in poor Cloaths, his Loyns usually girt in a course Gown, or Canonical Coat; of a mean stature, and stooping, and yet more lowly in the thoughts of his Soul; his Body worn out, not with Age, but Study, and Holy Mortifications; his Face full of Heat-pimples, begot by his unactivity and sedentary life.* And to this true character of his person, let me add this of his dis-position and behaviour; God and Nature blest him with so blessed a bashfulness, that as in his younger days his Pupils might easily look him out of countenance; so neither then, nor in his age, *did he ever willingly look any man in the face; and was of so mild and hum-ble a nature, that his poor Parish Clerk and he did never talk but with both their Hats on, or both off, at the same time*: And to this may be added, that though he was not pur-blind, yet he was short or weak-sighted; and where he fixt his eyes at the beginning of his Sermon, there they continued till it was ended; and the Reader has a liberty to believe, that his modesty and dim sight, were some of the reasons why he trusted Mrs. *Churchman* to choose his Wife.

This Parish-Clerk lived till the third or fourth year of the late Long Parliament: betwixt which time and Mr. *Hookers* death, there had come many to see the place of his Burial, and the Monument dedicated to his memory by Sir *William Cooper* (who still lives) and the poor Clerk had many rewards for shewing Mr. *Hookers* Grave-place, and his said Monument, and did always hear Mr. *Hooker* mentioned with commendations and reverence: to all which, he added his own knowledge and observations of his humility and holiness; and in all which Discourses, the poor man was still more confirm'd in his opinion of Mr. *Hookers* vertues and learning; but it so fell out, that about the said third or fourth year of the Long Parliament, the then present Parson of *Borne* was Sequestred (you may guess why) and a *Genevian* Minister put into his good Living; this, and other like Sequestrations, made the Clerk express himself in a wonder, and say, *They had Sequestred so many good men, that he doubted if his good Master Mr.* Hooker *had lived till now, they would have Sequestred him too.*

[1] Matthew 11:8-10

It was not long, before this intruding Minister had made a Party in and about the said Parish, that were desirous to receive the Sacrament as in *Geneva*; to which end, the day was appointed for a select Company, and Forms and Stools set about the Altar or Communion-Table, for them to sit and eat, and drink; but when they went about this work, there was a want of some Joint-stools, which the Minister sent the Clerk to fetch, and then to fetch Cushions (but not to kneel upon); when the Clerk saw them begin to sit down, he began to wonder; but the Minister bad him *cease wondring, and lock the Church-door*; to whom he replied, *Pray take you the Keys, and lock me out, I will never come into this Church; for all men will say, my Master* Hooker *was a good Man, and a good Scholar, and I am sure it was not used to be thus in his days*. And, report says, the old man went presently home, and died; I do not say died immediately, but within a few days after.

But let us leave this grateful Clerk in his quiet Grave, and return to Mr. *Hooker* himself, continuing our observations of his Christian behaviour in this place, where he gave a holy Valediction to all the pleasures and allurements of Earth, possessing his Soul in a ver-tuous quietness, which he maintained by constant Study, Prayers, and Meditations; his use was to preach once every *Sunday*, and he or his Curate to Catechise after the second Lesson in the Evening Prayer; his Sermons were neither long nor earnest, but uttered with a grave zeal, and an humble voice; his eyes always fixt on one place to prevent his imagination from wandring, insomuch, that he seem'd to study as he spake; the design of his Sermons (as indeed of all his Discourses) was to shew Reasons for what he spake; and with these Reasons, such a kind of Rhetorick, as did rather convince and perswade, than frighten men into piety; studying not so much for matter (which he never wanted) as for apt illus-trations to inform and teach his unlearned Hearers by familiar Examples, and them make them better by convincing Applica-tions; never labouring by hard words, and then by needless dis-tinctions and sub-distinctions, to *amuse* his Hearers, and get glory to himself; but glory only to God. Which intention, he would often say, was as discernable in a Preacher, *as a Natural from an Artificial Beauty*. [. . .]

He was diligent to inquire who of his Parish were sick, or any ways distrest, and would often visit them, unsent for; supposing, that the fittest time to discover to them those Errors to which health and prosperity had blinded them; and having by pious reasons and prayers, moulded them into holy resolutions for the time to come, he would incline them to confession, and bewailing their sins, with purpose to forsake them, and then to receive the Communion, both as a strengthning of those holy resolutions, and as a seal betwixt God and them of his Mercies to their Souls, in case that present sickness did put a period to their lives.

And as he was thus watchful and charitable to the sick, so he was as diligent to prevent Law-suits, still urging his Parishioners and Neighbours, to bear with each others infirmities, and live in love, because (as St. *John* says) *he that lives in love, lives in God, for God is love.* And to maintain this holy fire of love constantly burning on the Altar of a pure heart, his advice was to watch and pray, and always keep themselves fit to receive the Communion; and then to receive it often, for it was both a confirming and strengthning of their graces; this was his advice: And at his entrance or departure out of any house, he would usually speak to the whole Family, and bless them by name; insomuch, that as he seem'd in his youth to be taught of God, so he seem'd in this place to teach his precepts, as *Enoch* did by walking with him, in all holiness and humility, making each day a step towards a blessed Eternity. And though in this weak and declining Age of the World, such Examples are become barren, and almost incredible, yet let his memory be blest with this true Recordation, because he that praises *Richard Hooker*, praised God, who hath given such gifts to men; and let this humble and affectionate Relation of him, become such a pattern, as may invite Posterity to imitate these his vertues.

¶ *His sickness and death*

About the Year 1600, and of his Age 46, he fell into a long and sharp sickness, occasioned by a cold taken in his passage by water betwixt *London* and *Gravesend*; from the malignity of which he was never recovered; for after that time till his death he was not free from thoughtful Days, and restless Nights; but a submission to his Will that makes the sick mans Bed easie by giving rest to his Soul, made his very languishment comfortable: and yet all this time he was sollicitous in his Study, and said often to Dr. *Saravia* (who saw him daily, and was the chief comfort of his life) *That he did not beg a long life of God, for any other reason, but to live to finish his three remaining Books of POLITY; and then, Lord, let thy servant depart in peace*, which was his usual expression. And God heard his prayers, though he denied the Church the benefit of them, as compleated by himself; and 'tis thought he hastened his own death, by hastening to give life to his Books: But this is certain, that the nearer he was to death, the more he grew in *Humility*, in *Holy Thoughts* and *Resolutions*.

About a month before his death, this good man, that never knew, or at least never consider'd, the pleasures of the Palate, became first to lose his appetite, and then, to have an aversness to all food; insomuch, that he seem'd to live some intermitted weeks by the smell of meat only, and yet still studied and writ. And now his guardian Angel seem'd to foretell him, that the day of his dissolution drew near; for which his vigorous Soul appear'd to thirst. In this time of his sickness, and not many days before his death, his Question was, *Are my Books and written Papers safe?* And being answered, *That they were*; his Reply was, *then it matters not; for no other loss can trouble me*.

About one day before his Death, Dr. *Saravia*, who knew the very secrets of his Soul, (for they were supposed to be Confessors to each other) came to him, and after a Conference of the Benefit, the Necessity, and Safety of the Churches Absolution, it was resolved the Doctor should give him both that and the Sacrament the day following. To which end, the Doctor came, and after a short retirement and privacy, they two return'd to the company, and then the Doctor gave him, and some of those friends which were with him, the blessed Sacrament of the body and blood of our Jesus. Which being performed, the Doctor thought he saw a reverend gaiety and joy in his face; but it lasted not long: for his bodily Infirmities did return suddenly, and became more visible, in so much that the Doctor apprehended death ready to seize him; yet, after some amendment, left him at Night, with a promise to return early the day following, which he did, and then found him better in appearance, deep in Contemplation, and not inclinable to Discourse; which gave the Doctor occasion to require his present Thoughts? to which he replied, *That he was meditating the number and nature of Angels, and their blessed obedience and order, without which peace could not be in Heaven; and oh that it might be so on Earth!* After which words he said, *I have lived to see this world is made up of perturbations, and I have been long preparing to leave it, and gathering comfort for the dreadful hour of making my account with God, which I now apprehend to be near; and though I have by his grace lov'd him in my youth, and fear'd him in mine age, and labour'd to have a conscience void of offence to him, and to all men; yet, if thou, O Lord, be extream to mark what I have done amiss, who can abide it? and therefore, where I have failed, Lord, shew mercy to me for I plead not my righteousness, but the forgiveness of my unrighteousness, for his merits who died to purchase pardon for penitent sinners; and since I owe thee a death, Lord let it not be terrible, and then take thine own time, I submit to it; let not mine, O Lord, but let thy Will be done*; with which expression he fell into a dangerous slumber; dangerous, as to his recovery; yet recover he did, but it was to speak only these few words, *Good Doctor, God hath heard my daily petitions, for I am at peace with all men, and he is at peace with me; and from that blessed assurance I feel that inward joy, which this world can neither give nor take from me: my Conscience beareth me this witness, and this witness makes the thoughts of death joyful. I could wish to live to do the Church more service, but cannot hope it, for my dayes are past as a shadow that returnes not:*[1] More he would have spoken, but his spirits failed him; and after a short conflict betwixt Nature and Death, a quiet Sigh put a period to his last breath, and so he fell asleep. And now he seems to rest like *Lazarus* in *Abrahams* bosom;[2] let me here draw his Curtain, till with the most glorious company of the *Patriarchs and Apostles*, the most Noble Army of *Martyrs* and *Confessors*, this most learned, most humble, holy man, shall also

[1] I Chronicles 29:15; Job 8:9   [2] Luke 16:19-51

awake to receive an eternal Tranquillity: and with it, a greater degree of Glory than common Christians shall be made partakers of.

In the mean time, bless O Lord! Lord bless his Brethren, the Clergy of this Nation, *with effectual endeavours to attain, if not to his great learning, yet to his* remarkable meekness, *his* godly simplicity, *and his* Christian moderation; *for these will bring peace at the last: And, Lord! let his most excellent Writings be blest with what he design'd, when he undertook them: which was,* Glory to Thee O God on High, Peace in thy Church, and Good Will to Mankind. *Amen, Amen.*

Izaak Walton.

THE
LIFE
OF
Mr. GEORGE HERBERT

¶ *The Introduction*

In a late retreat from the business of this World, and those many little cares with which I have too often cumbred my self, I fell into a Contemplation of some of those Historical passages that are recorded in Sacred Story; *and, more particularly, of what had past betwixt our* Blessed Saviour, *and that wonder of Women, and Sinners, and Mourners,* Saint Mary Magdalen.[1] *I call her Saint, because I did not then, nor do now consider her, as when she was possest with seven Devils; not as when her wanton Eyes, and dissheveld Hair, were designed and manag'd, to charm and insnare amorous Beholders: But I did then, and do now consider her, as after she had exprest a visible and sacred sorrow for her sensualities; as after those Eyes had wept such a flood of penitential tears as did wash, and that hair had wip't, and she most passionately kist the feet of hers, and our blessed* Jesus. *And I do now consider, that because she lov'd much, not only much was forgiven her: but that, beside that blessed blessing of having her sins pardoned, and the joy of knowing her happy Condition, she also had from him a testimony, that her* Alabaster box *of precious oyntment poured on his head and feet, and that* Spike-nard, *and those Spices that were by her dedicated to embalm and preserve his sacred body from putrefaction, should so far preserve her own memory, that these demonstrations of her sanctified love, and of her officious, and generous gratitude, should be recorded and mentioned wheresoever his Gospel should be read: intending thereby, that as his, so her name should also live to succeeding generations, even till time it self shall be no more.*

Upon occasion of which fair example, I did lately look back, and not without some content (at least to my self) that I have endeavour'd to deserve the love, and preserve the memory of my two deceased friends, Dr. Donne, *and Sir* Henry Wotton, *by declaring the several employ-*

[1] Mark 16:1-2; Luke 23:55 – 24:10

ments and various accidents of their Lives: And though Mr. George Herbert (whose Life I now intend to write) *were to me a stranger as to his person, for I have only seen him: yet since he was, and was worthy to be their friend, and very many of his have been mine; I judge it may not be unacceptable to those that knew any of them in their lives, or do now know them by mine, or their own Writings, to see this Conjunction of them after their deaths; without which, many things that concern'd them, and some things that concern'd the Age in which they liv'd, would be less perfect, and lost to posterity.*

For these Reasons I have undertaken it, and if I have prevented any abler person, I beg pardon of him, and my Reader.

¶ *His birth and education*

George Herbert was born the third day of *April*, in the Year of our Redemption 1593. The place of his Birth was near to the Town of *Montgomery*, and in that *Castle* that did then bear the name of that Town and County; that *Castle* was then a place of state and strength, and had been successively happy in the Family of the *Herberts*, who had long possest it: and, with it, a plentiful Estate, and hearts as liberal to their poor Neighbours. A Family, that hath been blest with men of remarkable wisdom, and a willingness to serve their Country, and indeed, to do good to all Mankind; for which they are eminent: But alas! this Family did in the late Rebellion suffer extreamly in their Estates; and the Heirs of that *Castle* saw it laid level with that earth that was too good to bury those Wretches that were the cause of it. [. . .]

This mother of *George Herbert* (of whose person and wisdom, and vertue, I intend to give a true account in a seasonable place) was the happy Mother of seven Sons, and three Daughters, which she would often say, was *Job's number*, and *Job's distribution*;[1] and as often bless God, that they were neither defective in their shapes, or in their reason; and very often reprove them that did not praise God for so great a blessing. [. . .]

I now come to give my intended account of *George*, who was the fifth of those seven Brothers.

[1] Job 1:2

George Herbert spent much of his Childhood in a sweet content under the eye and care of his prudent mother, and the tuition of a Chaplain or Tutor to him, and two of his Brothers, in her own Family (for she was then a Widow) where he continued, till about the age of twelve years; and being at that time well instructed in the Rules of Grammar, he was not long after commended to the care of Dr. *Neale*, who was then Dean of *Westminster*; and by him to the care of Mr. *Ireland*, who was then chief Master of that School; where the beauties of his pretty behaviour and wit, shin'd and became so eminent and lovely in this his innocent age, that he seem'd to be marked out for piety, and to become the care of Heaven, and of a particular good Angel to guard and guide him. And thus, he continued in that School, till he came to be perfect in the learned Languages, and especially in the Greek Tongue, in which he after prov'd an excellent Critick.

About the age of Fifteen, he, being then a Kings Scholar, was elected out of that School for *Trinity Colledge* in *Cambridge*, to which place he was transplanted about the year 1608. and his prudent mother well knowing, that he might easily lose, or lessen that virtue and innocence which her advice and example had planted in his mind; did therefore procure the generous and liberal Dr. *Nevil*, who was then Dean of *Canterbury*, and Master of that Colledge, to take him into his particular care, and provide him a Tutor; which he did most gladly undertake, for he knew the excellencies of his Mother, and how to value such a friendship.

This was the method of his Education, till he was setled in *Cambridge*, where we will leave him in his Study, till I have paid my promis'd account of his excellent Mother, and I will endeavour to make it short.

I have told her birth, her Marriage, and the Number of her Children, and have given some short account of them: I shall next tell the Reader, that her husband dyed when our *George* was about the Age of four years: I am next to tell that she continued twelve years a Widow: that she then married happily to a Noble Gentleman, the Brother and Heir of the Lord *Danvers* Earl of *Derby*, who did highly value both her person and the most excellent endowments of her mind.

In this time of her Widowhood, she being desirous to give

Edward her eldest son, such advantages of Learning, and other education as might suit his birth and fortune: and thereby make him the more fit for the service of his Country: did at his being of a fit age, remove from *Montgomery Castle* with him, and some of her younger sons to *Oxford*; and having entred *Edward* into *Queens Colledge*, and provided him a fit *Tutor*, she commended him to his Care; yet she continued there with him, and still kept him in a moderate awe of her self: and so much under her own eye, as to see and converse with him daily; but she managed this power over him without any such rigid sourness, as might make her company a torment to her Child; but with such a sweetness and complyance with the recreations and pleasures of youth, as did incline him willingly to spend much of his time in the company of his dear and careful Mother: which was to her great content: for, she would often say, 'That as our bodies take a nourishment sutable to the meat on which we feed: so, our souls do as insensibly take in vice by the example or Conversation with wicked Company': and would therefore as often say, 'That ignorance of Vice was the best preservation of Vertue: and, that the very knowledge of wickedness was as tinder to inflame and kindle sin, and to keep it burning.' For these reasons she indeared him to her own Company: and continued with him in *Oxford* four years: in which time, her *great* and *harmless wit*, her *chearful gravity*, and her *obliging behaviour*, gain'd her an acquaintance and friendship with most of any eminent worth or learning, that were at that time in or near that University; and particularly, with Mr. *John Donne*, who then came accidentally to that place, in this time of her being there: it was that *John Donne* who was after *Doctor Donne*, and Dean of *Saint Pauls London*: and he at his leaving *Oxford*, writ and left there in verse a Character of the Beauties of her body, and mind; of the first, he saies,

> *No* Spring nor Summer-Beauty, *has such grace*
> *As I have seen in an* Autumnal *face.*

Of the latter he sayes,

> *In all her words to every hearer fit*
> *You may at* Revels, *or at* Council sit.

The rest of her Character may be read in his printed Poems, in that Elegy which bears the name of the *Autumnal Beauty*. For both he and she were then past the meridian of mans life.

This Amity, begun at this time, and place, was not an *Amity* that polluted their Souls; but an *Amity* made up of a chain of sutable inclinations and vertues; an *Amity*, like that of St. *Chrysostoms* to his dear and vertuous *Olimpias*; whom, in his Letters, he calls his *Saint*: Or, an *Amity* indeed more like that of St. *Hierom* to his *Paula*; whose affection to her was such, that he turn'd Poet in his old Age, and then made her *Epitaph; wishing all his Body were turn'd into Tongues, that he might declare her just praises to posterity.* —— And this *Amity* betwixt her and Mr. *Donne*, was begun in a happy time for him, he being then near to the Fortieth year of his Age (which was some years before he entred into Sacred Orders;) A time, when his necessities needed a daily supply for the support of his Wife, seven Children, and a Family: And in this time she prov'd one of his most bountiful Benefactors; and he, as grateful an acknowledger of it. You may take one testimony for what I have said of these two worthy persons, from this following *Letter*, and *Sonnet*.

MADAM,
Your Favours to me are every where; I use them, and have them. I enjoy them at *London*, and leave them there; and yet find them at *Micham*: such Riddles as these become things unexpressible; and such is your goodness. I was almost sorry to find your Servant here this day, because I was loth to have any witness of my not coming home last Night, and indeed of my coming this Morning: But my not coming was excusable, because earnest business detein'd me; and my coming this day, is by the example of your St. *Mary Magdalen*, who rose early upon *Sunday*, to seek that which she lov'd most;[1] and so did I. And from her and my self, I return such thanks as are due to one to whom we owe all the good opinion, that they whom we need most, have of us —— by this Messenger, and on this good day, I commit the inclosed *Holy Hymns* and *Sonnets*

[1] Mark 16:1-2; Luke 24:1-10

(which for the matter, not the workmanship, have yet escap'd the fire) to your judgment, and to your protection too, if you think them worthy of it; and I have appointed this inclosed *Sonnet* to usher them to your happy hand.

Your unworthiest Servant,

Micham,   *unless your accepting him to be so,*

July 11.   *have mended him.*

1607   JO. DONNE.

To the Lady *Magdalen Herbert*; of St. *Mary Magdalen.*

Her of your name, whose fair inheritance
  Bethina *was, and jointure* Magdalo:
An active faith so highly did advance,
  That she once knew, more than the Church did know,
The Resurrection; *so much good there is*
  Deliver'd of her, that some Fathers be
Loth to believe one Woman could do this;
  But think these Magdalens *were two or three.*
Increase their number, Lady, *and their fame:*
  To their Devotion, *add your* Innocence:
Take so much of th' example, as of the name;
  The latter half; and in some recompence
That they did harbour Christ *himself, a Guest,*
  Harbour these Hymns, *to his dear name addrest.*

J.D.

These *Hymns* are now lost to us; but doubtless they were such, as they two now sing in *Heaven*.

There might be more demonstrations of the Friendship, and the many sacred Indearments betwixt these two excellent persons (for I have many of their Letters in my hand) and much more might be said of her great prudence and piety: but my design was not to write hers, but the Life of her Son; and therefore I shall only tell my Reader, that about that very day twenty years that this Letter was dated, and sent her, I saw and heard this Mr. *John*

Donne (who was then Dean of *St. Pauls*) weep, and preach her Funeral Sermon, in the Parish-Church of *Chelsey* near *London*, where she now rests in her quiet Grave: and where we must now leave her, and return to her Son *George*, whom we left in his Study in *Cambridge*.

And in *Cambridge* we may find our *George Herberts* behaviour to be such, that we may conclude, he consecrated the first-fruits of his early age to vertue, and a serious study of learning. And that he did so, this following Letter and Sonnet which were in the first year of his going to *Cambridge* sent his dear Mother for a New-years gift, may appear to be some testimony.

—— 'But I fear the heat of my late *Ague* hath dried up those springs, by which Scholars say, the Muses use to take up their habitations. However, I need not their help, to reprove the vanity of those many Love-poems, that are daily writ and consecrated to *Venus*; nor to bewail that so few are writ, that look towards *God* and *Heaven*. For my own part, my meaning (*dear Mother*) is in these Sonnets, to declare my resolution to be, that my poor Abilities in *Poetry* shall be all, and ever consecrated to Gods glory; and I beg you to receive this one as testimony.

> *My God, where is that ancient heat towards thee,*
> > *Wherewith whole showls of* Martyrs *once did burn,*
> > *Besides their other flames? Doth Poetry*
> *Wear* Venus *Livery? only serve her turn?*
> *Why are not* Sonnets *made of thee? and layes*
> > *Vpon thine Altar burnt? Cannot thy love*
> > *Heighten a spirit to sound out thy praise*
> *As well as any she? Cannot thy* Dove
> *Out-strip their* Cupid *easily in flight?*
> > *Or, since thy ways are deep, and still the same,*
> > *Will not a verse run smooth that bears thy name!*
> *Why doth that fire, which by thy power and might*
> > *Each breast does feel, no braver fuel choose*
> > *Than that, which one day,* Worms *may chance refuse.*
> *Sure Lord, there is enough in thee to dry*
> > *Oceans of* Ink; *for, as the Deluge did*

Cover the Earth, so doth thy Majesty:
Each cloud distils thy praise, and doth forbid
Poets *to turn it to another use.*

   Roses *and* Lillies *speak thee; and to make*
   A pair of Cheeks of them, is thy abuse.
Why should I Womens eyes *for Chrystal take?*
Such poor invention burns in their low mind
   Whose fire is wild, and doth not upward go
   To praise, and, on thee Lord, some Ink *bestow.*
Open the bones, and you shall nothing find
   In the best face *but* filth; *when Lord, in thee*
   The beauty *lies in the* discovery.

G.H.'

This was his resolution at the sending this Letter to his dear Mother; about which time, he was in the Seventeenth year of his Age; and, as he grew older, so he grew in learning, and more and more in favour both with God and man: insomuch, that in this morning of that short day of his life, he seem'd to be mark'd out for vertue, and to become the care of Heaven; for God still kept his soul in so holy a frame, that he may, and ought to be a pattern of vertue to all posterity; and especially, to his Brethren of the Clergy, of which the Reader may expect a more exact account in what will follow.

I need not declare that he was a strict Student, because, that he was so, there will be many testimonies in the future part of his life. I shall therefore only tell, that he was made *Bachelor of Art* in the year 1611. *Major Fellow* of the *Colledge, March* 15. 1615. And that in that year, he was also made *Master of Arts*, he being then in the 22*d* year of his Age; during all which time, all, or the greatest diversion from his Study, was the practice of Musick, in which he became a great Master; and of which, he would say, 'That it did relieve his drooping spirits, compose his distracted thoughts, and raised his weary soul so far above Earth, that it gave him an earnest of the joys of Heaven, before he possest them.' And it may be noted, that from his first entrance into the Colledge, the generous Dr. *Nevil* was a cherisher of his Studies, and such a lover of his person, his behaviour, and the excellent endowments of his mind, that he took him often into his own company; by which he confirm'd his native gentileness; and, if during this time he exprest any Error, it was, that he kept himself too much retir'd, and at too great a distance with all his inferiours: and his cloaths seem'd to prove, that he put too great a value on his parts and Parentage. [. . .]

¶ *His entrance into Sacred Orders*

I may not omit to tell, that he had often design'd to leave the University, and decline all Study, which he thought did impair his health; for he had a body apt to a *Consumption*, and to *Fevers*, and other infirmities which he judg'd were increas'd by his Studies; for he would often say, 'He had too thoughtful a Wit: a Wit, like a Pen-knife in too narrow a sheath, too sharp for his Body': But his Mother would by no means allow him to leave the University, or to travel; and, though he inclin'd very much to both, yet he would by no means satisfie his own desires at so dear a rate, as to prove an undutiful Son to so affectionate a Mother; but did always submit to her wisdom. And what I have now said, may partly appear in a Copy of Verses in his printed Poems; 'tis one of those that bears the title of *Affliction*: And it appears to be a pious reflection on Gods providence, and some passages of his life, in which he saies,

> *Whereas my birth and spirit rather took*
> *The way that takes the Town:*
> *Thou didst betray me to a lingring Book,*
> *And wrap me in a Gown:*
> *I was intangled in a World of strife,*
> *Before I had the power to change my life.*
>
> *Yet, for I threatned oft the Siege to raise,*
> *Not simpring all mine age:*
> *Thou often didst with* Academick *praise,*
> *Melt, and dissolve my rage:*

I took the sweetned Pill, till I came where
I could not go away, nor persevere.

Yet, least perchance, I should too happy be
        In my unhappiness;
Turning my purge to food, thou throwest me
        Into more sicknesses.
Thus doth thy power Cross-byass me, not making
Thine own gifts good; yet me from my ways taking.

Now I am here, what thou wilt do with me
        None of my Books will shew:
I read, and sigh, and wish I were a Tree,
        For then sure I should grow
To fruit or shade, at least, some Bird would trust
Her Houshold with me, and I would be just.

Yet, though thou troublest me, I must be meek;
        In weakness must be stout:
Well, I will change my service, and go seek
        Some other Master out:
Ah my dear God! though I am clean forgot,
Let me not love thee, if I love thee not.

                                        G.H.

In this time of Mr. *Herberts* attendance and expectation of some good occasion to remove from *Cambridge*, to Court; God, in whom there is an unseen Chain of Causes, did in a short time put an end to the lives of two of his most obliging and powerful friends, *Lodowick* Duke of *Richmond*, and *James* Marquess of *Hamilton*; and not long after him, King *James* died also, and with them, all Mr. *Herbert's* Court-hopes: So that he presently betook himself to a Retreat from *London*, to a Friend in *Kent*, where he liv'd very privately, and was such a lover of solitariness, as was judg'd to impair his health, more then his Study had done. In this time of Retirement, he had many Conflicts with himself, Whether he should return to the painted pleasures of a Court-life, or betake himself to a study of Divinity, and enter into Sacred Orders? (to which his dear Mother had often persuaded him.) These were such conflicts, as they only can know, that have endur'd them; for ambitious Desires, and the outward Glory of this World, are not easily laid aside; but, at last, God inclin'd him to put on a resolution to serve at his Altar.

He did at his return to *London*, acquaint a Court-friend with his resolution to enter into *Sacred Orders*, who persuaded him to alter it, as too mean an employment, and too much below his birth, and the excellent abilities and endowments of his mind. To whom he replied, 'It hath been formerly judged that the Domestick Servants of the King of Heaven, should be of the noblest Families on Earth: and, though the Iniquity of the late Times have made Clergy-men meanly valued, and the sacred name of *Priest* contemptible; yet I will labour to make it honourable, by consecrating all my learning, and all my poor abilities, to advance the glory of that God that gave them; knowing, that I can never do too much for him, that hath done so much for me, as to make me a Christian. And I will labour to be like my Saviour, by making Humility lovely in the eyes of all men, and by following the merciful and meek example of my *dear Jesus*.'

This was then his resolution, and the God of Constancy, who intended him for a great example of vertue, continued him in it; for within that year he was made Deacon, but the day when, or by whom, I cannot learn; but that he was about that time made Deacon, is most certain; for I find by the Records of *Lincoln*, that he was made Prebend of *Layton Ecclesia*, in the Diocess of *Lincoln*, *July* 15. 1626. and that this Prebend was given him, by *John*, then *Lord Bishop of that See*. And now, he had a fit occasion to shew that Piety and Bounty that was deriv'd from his generous Mother, and his other memorable Ancestors, and the occasion was this.

This *Layton Ecclesia*, is a Village near to *Spalden* in the County of *Huntington*, and the greatest part of the Parish Church was fallen down, and that of it which stood, was so decayed, so little, and so useless, that the Parishioners could not meet to perform their Duty to God in publick prayer and praises; and thus it had been for almost 20 years, in which time there had been some faint endeavours for a publick Collection, to enable the Parishioners to rebuild it, but with no success, till Mr. *Herbert* undertook it; and he, by his own, and the contribution of many of his Kindred, and other noble Friends, undertook the Re-edification of it; and made it so much his whole business, that he became restless, till he saw it finisht as it now stands; being, for the workmanship, a costly *Mosaick:* for the form, an *exact Cross*; and for the decency and beauty, I am assur'd it is the most remarkable Parish-Church, that this Nation affords. He lived to see it so wainscoted, as to be exceeded by none; and, by his order, the Reading Pew, and Pulpit, were a little distant from each other, and both of an equal height; for he would often say, 'They should neither have a precedency or priority of the other: but that *Prayer* and *Preaching* being equally useful, might agree like Brethren, and have an equal honour and estimation.' [. . .]

¶ *His marriage: and induction into the parish of Bemerton*

I shall now proceed to his Marriage; in order to which, it will be convenient, that I first give the Reader a short view of his person, and then an account of his Wife, and of some circumstances concerning both. – *He was for his person of a stature inclining towards Tallness; his Body was very strait, and so far from being cumbred with too much flesh, that he was lean to an extremity. His aspect was chearful, and his speech and motion did both declare him a Gentleman; for they were all so meek and obliging, that they purchased love and respect from all that knew him.*

These, and his other visible vertues, begot him much love from a Gentleman, of a Noble fortune, and a near kinsman to his friend the Earl of *Danby*; namely, from Mr. *Charles Danvers* of *Bainton*, in the County of *Wilts* Esq; this Mr. *Danvers* having known him long, and familiarly, did so much affect him, that he often and publickly declar'd a desire that Mr. *Herbert* would marry any of his Nine Daughters (for he had so many) but rather his Daughter *Jane*, than any other, because *Jane was his beloved Daughter*: And he had often said the same to Mr. *Herbert* himself; and that if he could like her for a Wife, and she him for a Husband, *Jane* should have a *double blessing*: and Mr. *Danvers* had so often said the like to *Jane*, and so much commended Mr. *Herbert* to her, that *Jane* became so much a Platonick, as to fall in love with Mr. *Herbert* unseen.

This was a fair preparation for a Marriage; but alas, her father died before Mr. *Herberts* retirement to *Dantsey*; yet some friends to both parties, procur'd their meeting; at which time a mutual affection entred into both their hearts, as a Conqueror enters into a surprized City, and Love having got such possession govern'd, and made there such Laws and Resolutions, as neither party was able to resist; insomuch, that she chang'd her name into *Herbert*, the third day after this first interview.

This haste might in others be thought a *Love-phrensie*, or worse: but it was not; for they had wooed so like Princes, as to have select Proxies: such, as were true friends to both parties; such as well understood Mr. *Herberts*, and her temper of mind; and also their Estates so well, before this Interview, that, the suddenness was justifiable, by the strictest Rules of prudence: And the more, because it prov'd so happy to both parties; for the eternal lover of Mankind, made them happy in each others mutual and equal affections, and compliance; indeed, so happy, that there never was any opposition betwixt them, unless it were a Contest which should most incline to a compliance with the others desires. And though this begot, and continued in them, such a mutual *love* and *joy*, and *content*, as was no way defective: yet this mutual *content* and *love*, and *joy*, did receive a daily augmentation, by such daily obligingness to each other, as still added such new affluences to the former fulness of these divine Souls, as was only improvable in Heaven, where they now enjoy it.

About three months after his Marriage, Dr. *Curle*, who was then Rector of *Bemerton* in *Wiltshire*, was made Bishop of *Bath* and *Wells* (and not long after translated to *Winchester*, and by that means the presentation of a Clerk to *Bemerton*, did not fall to the Earl of *Pembroke* (who was the undoubted Patron of it) but to the King, by reason of Dr. *Curles* advancement: but *Philip*, then Earl of *Pembroke* (for *William* was lately dead) requested the King to bestow it upon his kinsman *George Herbert*; and the King said, *Most willingly to Mr.* Herbert, *if it be worth his acceptance*: and the Earl as willingly and suddenly sent it him, without seeking; but though Mr. *Herbert* had formerly put on a resolution for the Clergy:

112

yet, at receiving this presentation, the apprehension of the last great Account that he was to make for the Cure of so many souls, made him fast and pray often, and consider, for not less that a month: in which time he had some resolutions to decline both the Priesthood, and that Living. And in this time of considering, *He endur'd* (as he would often say) *such spiritual Conflicts, as none can think, but only those that have endur'd them.*

In the midst of these Conflicts, his old and dear friend Mr. *Arthur Woodnot*, took a journey to salute him at *Bainton* (where he then was with his Wives Friends and Relations) and was joyful to be an Eye-witness of his Health and happy Marriage. And after they had rejoyc'd together some few days, they took a Journey to *Wilton*, the famous Seat of the Earls of *Pembroke*; at which time, the King, the Earl, and the whole Court were there, or at *Salisbury*, which is near to it. And at this time Mr. *Herbert* presented his Thanks to the Earl, for his presentation to *Bemerton*, but had not yet resolv'd to accept it, and told him the reason why; but that Night, the Earl acquainted Dr. *Laud*, then Bishop of *London*, and after Archbishop of *Canterbury*, with his Kinsmans irresolution. And the Bishop did the next day so convince Mr. *Herbert, That the refusal of it was a sin*; that a Taylor was sent for to come speedily from *Salisbury* to *Wilton*, to take measure, and make him Canonical Cloaths, against next day: which the Taylor did; and Mr. *Herbert* being so habited, went with his presentation to the learned Dr. *Davenant*, who was then Bishop of *Salisbury*, and he gave him Institution immediately (for Mr. *Herbert* had been made Deacon some years before) and he was also the same day (which was *April* 26. 1630) inducted into the good, and more pleasant, than healthful Parsonage of *Bemerton*: which is a Mile from *Salisbury*.

I have now Brought him to the Parsonage of Bemerton, *and to the thirty sixth Year of his Age, and must stop here, and bespeak the Reader to prepare for an almost incredible story, of the great sanctity of the short remainder of his holy life; a life so full of* Charity, Humility, *and all Christian vertues, that it deserves the eloquence of St.* Chrysostom *to commend and declare it! A life, that if it were related by a Pen like his, there would then be no need for this Age to look back into times past for the examples of primitive piety: for they might be all found in the life of* George Herbert. *But now, alas! who is fit to undertake it! I confess I am not: and am not pleas'd with my self that I must; and profess my self amaz'd, when I consider how few of the Clergy liv'd like him then, and how many live so unlike him now: But, it becomes not me to censure: my design is rather to assure the Reader, that I have used very great diligence to inform my self, that I might inform him of the truth of what follows; and though I cannot adorn it with eloquence, yet I will do it with sincerity.*

When at his Induction he was shut into *Bemerton* Church, being left there alone to Toll the Bell, (as the Law requires him:) he staid so much longer than an ordinary time, before he return'd to those Friends that staid expecting him at the Church-door, that his Friend, Mr. *Woodnot*, look'd in at the Church-window, and saw him lie prostrate on the ground before the Altar: at which time and place (as he after told Mr. *Woodnot*) he set some Rules to himself, for the future manage of his life; and then and there made a vow, to labour to keep them.

And the same night that he had his Induction, he said to Mr. *Woodnot, I now look back upon my aspiring thoughts, and think my self more happy than if I had attain'd what then I so ambitiously thirsted for: And, I can now behold the Court with an impartial Eye, and see plainly, that it is made up of* Fraud, *and* Titles, *and* Flattery, *and many other such empty, imaginary painted Pleasures: Pleasures, that are so empty, as not to satisfy when they are enjoy'd; but in God and his service, is a fulness of all* joy *and* pleasure, *and no satiety: And I will now use all my endeavours to bring my Relations and Dependants to a love and relyance* on him, who never fails those that trust him. *But above all, I will be sure to live well, because the vertuous life of a Clergyman, is the most powerful eloquence to perswade all that see it, to reverence and love, and at least, to desire to live like him. And this I will do, because I know* we live in an Age that hath more need of good examples, than precepts. *And I beseech that God, who hath honour'd me so much as to call me to serve him at his Altar: that as by his special grace he hath put into my heart these good desires, and resolutions: so, he will by his assisting grace give me ghostly strength to bring the same to good effect: and I beseech him that my humble and charitable life may so win upon others, as to bring glory to my* JESUS, *whom I have this day taken to be my Master and Governour; and I am so proud of his service, that I will alwaies observe, and obey, and do his Will; and alwaies call*

114

him Jesus my Master, *and I will alwayes contemn my birth, or any title or dignity that can be conferr'd upon me, when I shall compare them with my title of being a* Priest, *and serving at the* Altar *of* Jesus my Master.

And that he did so, may appear in many parts of his Book of *Sacred Poems;* especially, in that which he calls *the Odour.* In which he seems to rejoyce in the thoughts of that word *Jesus,* and say that the adding these words *my Master* to it, and the often repetition of them, seem'd to perfume his mind, and leave an oriental fragrancy in his very breath. And for his unforc'd choice to serve at Gods Altar, he seems in another place of his Poems (*the Pearl,* Matth. 13.) to rejoyce and say —— *He knew the waies of Learning: knew, what nature does willingly; and what, when 'tis forc'd by fire: knew the waies of honour, and when glory inclines the Soul to noble expressions: knew the Court: knew the waies of pleasure, of love, of wit, of musick,* and upon what terms he declined all these for the service of *his* Master JESUS, and then concludes, saying,

> *That, through these Labyrinths, not my groveling Wit,*
> *But thy Silk-twist, let down from Heaven to me;*
> *Did both conduct, and teach me, how by it,*
> > *To climb to thee.*

The third day after he was made Rector of *Bemerton,* and had chang'd his sword and silk Cloaths into a Canonical Coat; he return'd so habited with his friend Mr. *Woodnot* to *Bainton:* And immediately after he had seen and saluted his Wife, he said to her —— *You are now a Ministers Wife, and must now so far forget your fathers house, as not to claim a precedence of any of your Parishioners; for you are to know, that a Priests Wife can challenge no precedence or place, but that which she purchases by her obliging humility; and, I am sure, places so purchased, do best become them.* And let me tell you, *That I am so good a Herald, as to assure you that this is truth.* And she was so meek a Wife, *as to assure him it was no vexing News to her, and that he should see her observe it with a chearful willingness.* And indeed her unforc'd humility, that humility that was in her so original, as to be born with her, made her so happy as to do so; and her doing so, begot her an unfeigned love, and a serviceable

115

respect from all that convert with her; and this love followed her in all places, as inseparably, as shadows follow substances in Sunshine.

It was not many days before he return'd back to *Bemerton*, to view the Church, and repair the Chancel; and indeed, to rebuild almost three parts of his house which was fall'n down, or decayed by reason of his Predecessors living at a better Parsonage-house; namely, at *Minal*, 16 or 20 miles from this place. At which time of Mr. *Herberts* coming alone to *Bemerton*, there came to him a poor old Woman, with an intent to acquaint him with her necessitous condition, as also, with some troubles of her mind; but after she had spoke some few words to him, she was surpriz'd with a fear, and that begot a shortness of breath, so that her spirits and speech fail'd her; which he perceiving, did so compassionate her, and was so humble, that he took her by the hand, and said, *Speak, good Mother, be not afraid to speak to me; for I am a man that will hear you with patience; and will relieve your necessities too, if I be able: and this I will do willingly, and therefore,* Mother, *be not afraid to acquaint me with what you desire.* After which comfortable speech, he again took her by the hand, made her sit down by him, & understanding she was of his Parish, he told her, *He would be acquainted with her, and take her into his care*: And having with patience heard and understood her wants (and it is some relief for a poor body to be but hear'd with patience) he like a Christian Clergyman comforted her by his meek behaviour and counsel; but because that cost him nothing, he reliev'd her with money too, and so sent her home with a chearful heart, praising God, and praying for him. *Thus worthy, and* (like *Davids* blessed man) *thus lowly, was Mr.* George Herbert *in his own eyes*: and thus lovely in the eyes of others.[1]

At his return that Night to his Wife at *Bainton*, he gave her an account of the passages 'twixt him and the poor Woman: with which she was so affected, that she went next day to *Salisbury*, and there bought a pair of Blankets and sent them as a Token of her love to the poor Woman: and with them a Message, *That she would see and be acquainted with her, when her house was built at* Bemerton.

[1] See 1 Samuel 16:1-12

There be many such passages both of him and his Wife, of which some few will be related; but I shall first tell, that he hasted to get the Parish-Church repair'd; then, to beautifie the Chappel (which stands near his House) and that at his own great charge. He then proceeded to re-build the greatest part of the Parsonage-house, which he did also very compleatly, and at his own charge; and having done this good work, he caus'd these Verses to be writ upon, or ingraven in the Mantle of the Chimney in his Hall.

> To my Successor.
> *If thou chance for to find*
> *A new House to thy mind,*
> *And built without thy Cost:*
> *Be good to the Poor,*
> *As God gives thee store,*
> *And then my Labour's not lost.*

We will now by the Readers favour suppose him fixt at *Bemerton*, and grant him to have seen the Church repair'd, and the Chappel belonging to it very decently adorn'd, at his own great charge (which is a real Truth) and having now fixt him there, I shall proceed to give an account of the rest of his behaviour both to his Parishioners, and those many others that knew and convers'd with him.

Doubtless Mr. *Herbert* had consider'd and given Rules to himself for his Christian carriage both to God and man before he enter'd into *Holy Orders*, And 'tis not unlike, but that he renewed those resolutions at his prostration before the *Holy Altar*, at his Induction into the Church of *Bemerton*; but as yet he was but a *Deacon*, and therefore long'd for the next *Ember-week*,[1] that he might be ordain'd *Priest*, and made capable of Administring both the Sacraments. At which time, the Reverend Dr. *Humphrey Hinchman*, now Lord Bishop of *London* (who does not mention him, but with some veneration for his life and excellent learning) tells me, *He laid his hand on Mr.* Herberts *Head, and (alas!) within less then three Years, lent his Shoulder to carry his dear Friend to his Grave.*

---

[1] Four weeks in the year, roughly corresponding to the four seasons, in which Ember- or fast-days were appointed by the Church.

And that Mr. *Herbert* might the better preserve those holy Rules which such a *Priest* as he intended to be, ought to observe; and that time might not insensibly blot them out of his memory, but that the next year might shew him his variations from this years resolutions; he therefore did set down his Rules, then resolv'd upon, in that order, as the World now sees them printed in a little Book, call'd, *The Country Parson*, in which some of his Rules are:

The Parsons Knowledge.	*The Parson Condescend-*
The Parson on Sundays.	*ing.*
The Parson Praying.	*The Parson in his Journey.*
The Parson Preaching.	*The Parson in his Mirth.*
The Parsons Charity.	*The Parson with his Church-*
The Parson comforting	*wardens.*
the Sick.	*The Parson Blessing the*
The Parson Arguing.	*People.*

And his behaviour toward God and man, may be said to be a practical Comment on these, and the other holy Rules set down in that useful Book. A Book, so full of plain, prudent and useful Rules, that that *Country Parson*, that can spare 12 *d*. and yet wants it, is scarce excusable; because it will both direct him what he ought to do, and convince him for not having done it.

At the Death of Mr. *Herbert*, this Book fell into the hands of his friend Mr. *Woodnot*; and he commended it into the trusty hands of Mr. *Barnabas Oly*, who publisht it with a most conscientious, and excellent Preface; from which I have had some of those Truths, that are related in this life of Mr. *Herbert*. The Text for his first Sermon was taken out of *Solomons Proverbs*, and the words were, *Keep thy heart with all diligence.*[1] In which first Sermon, he gave his Parishioners many necessary, holy, safe Rules for the discharge of a good Conscience, both to God and man. And deliver'd his Sermon after a most florid manner; both with great learning and eloquence. But at the close of this Sermon, told them, *That should not be his constant way of Preaching, for, since Almighty God does not intend to lead men to heaven by hard Questions, he would not therefore*

[1] Proverbs 4:23

118

fill their heads with unnecessary Notions; but that for their sakes, his language and his expressions should be more plain and practical in his future Sermons. And he then made it his humble request, *That they would be constant to the Afternoons Service, and Catechising.* And shewed them convincing reasons why he desire'd it; and his obliging example and perswasions brought them to a willing conformity to his desires. [. . .]

¶ At Bemerton

And by this account of his diligence, to make his Parishioners understand what they pray'd, and why they prais'd, and ador'd their Creator: I hope I shall the more easily obtain the Readers belief to the following account of Mr. *Herberts* own practice; which was, to appear constantly with his Wife, and three Neeces (the daughters of a deceased Sister) and his whole Family, twice every day at the Church-prayers, in the Chappel which does almost joyn to his Parsonage-house. And for the time of his appearing, it was strictly at the Canonical hours of 10 and 4;[1] and then and there, he lifted up pure and charitable hand to God in the midst of the Congregation. And he would joy to have spent that time in that place, where the honour of his *Master Jesus* dwelleth; and there, by that inward devotion which he testified constantly by an humble behaviour, and visible adoration, he, like *Josua* brought not only *his own Houshold thus to serve the Lord*;[2] but brought most of his Parishioners, and many Gentlemen in the Neighourhood, constantly to make a part of his Congregation twice a day; and some of the meaner sort of his Parish, did so love and reverence Mr. *Herbert*, that they would let their Plow rest when Mr. *Herberts Saints-Bell* rung to Prayers, that they might also offer their devotions to God with him: and would then return back to their Plow.

---

[1] Herbert is publicly observing Matins and Evensong as an example to his flock. Walton is boldly linking his observance with two of the six pre-Reformation 'hours' of daily devotion, Terce and Vespers.
[2] Joshua 7:16-18

And his most holy life was such, that it begot such reverence to God, and to him, that they thought themselves the happier, when they carried Mr. *Herberts* blessing back with them to their labour. —— Thus powerful was his reason, and example, to perswade others to a practical piety, and devotion.

And his constant publick prayers did never make him to neglect his own private devotions, nor those prayers that he thought himself bound to perform with his Family, which alwaies were a Set-form, and not long; and he did alwaies conclude them with that Collect which the Church hath appointed for the day or week. —— *Thus he made every days sanctity a step towards that Kingdom where Impurity cannot enter.*

His chiefest recreation was Musick, in which heavenly Art he was a most excellent Master, and did himself compose many *divine Hymns* and *Anthems*, which he set and sung to his *Lute* or *Viol*; and, though he was a lover of retiredness, yet his love to *Musick* was such, that he went usually twice every week on certain appointed days, to the *Cathedral Church* in *Salisbury*; and at his return would say, *That his time spent in Prayer, and Cathedral Musick, elevated his Soul, and was his Heaven upon Earth*: But before his return thence to *Bemerton*, he would usually sing and play his part, at an appointed private Musick-meeting; and, to justifie this practice, he would often say, *Religion does not banish mirth, but only moderates, and sets rules to it.*

And as his desire to enjoy *his Heaven upon Earth*, drew him twice every week to *Salisbury*, so his walks thither, were the occasion of many happy accidents to others: of which, I will mention some few.

In one of his walks to *Salisbury*, he overtook a Gentleman that is still living in that City, and in their walk together, Mr. *Herbert* took a fair occasion to talk with him, and humbly begg'd to be excus'd, if he ask'd him some account of his faith, and said, *I do this the rather, because though you are not of my Parish, yet I receive Tythe from you by the hand of your Tenant; and, Sir, I am the bolder to do it, because I know there be some Sermon-hearers, that be like those Fishes, that always live in salt water, and yet are always Fresh.*

After which expression, Mr. *Herbert* asked him some needful Questions, and having received his answer, gave him such Rules for the trial of his sincerity, and for a practical piety, and in so loving and meek a manner, that the Gentleman did so fall in love with him, and his discourse, that he would often contrive to meet him in his walk to *Salisbury*, or to attend him back to *Bemerton*; and still mentions the name of Mr. *George Herbert* with veneration, and still praiseth God for the occasion of knowing him. [. . .]

In another walk to *Salisbury*, he saw a poor man, with a poorer horse, that was fall'n under his Load; they were both in distress, and needed present help; which Mr. *Herbert* perceiving, put off his Canonical Coat, and help'd the poor man to unload, and after, to load his horse: The poor man blest him for it: and he blest the poor man; and was so like the *good Samaritan*,[1] that he gave him money to refresh both himself and his horse; and told him, *That if he lov'd himself, he should be merciful to his Beast.* —— Thus he left the poor man, and at his coming to his musical friends at *Salisbury*, they began to wonder that Mr. *George Herbert* which us'd to be so trim and clean, came into that company so soyl'd and discompos'd; but he told them the occasion: And when one of the company told him, *He had disparag'd himself by so dirty an employment*; his answer was, *That the thought of what he had done, would prove Musick to him at Midnight; and that the omission of it, would have upbraided and made discord in his Conscience, whensoever he should pass by that place; for, if I be bound to pray for all that be in distress, I am sure that I am bound so far as it is in my power to practise what I pray for. And though I do not wish for the like occasion every day, yet let me tell you, I would not willingly pass one day of my life without comforting a sad soul, or shewing mercy; and I praise God for this occasion*: And now let's tune our Instruments. [. . .]

¶ *Nicholas Ferrar and Little Gidding*

About one month before his death, his friend Mr. *Farrer* (for an account of whom I am by promise indebted to the Reader, and intend to make him sudden payment) hearing of Mr. *Herberts* sickness, sent Mr. *Edmund Duncon* (who is now Rector of *Fryer Barnet*

[1] For the parable, see Luke 10:30-37

in the County of *Middlesex*) from his House of *Gidden Hall*, which is near to *Huntington*, to see Mr. *Herbert*, and to assure him, he wanted not his daily prayers for his recovery; and Mr. *Duncon* was to return back to *Gidden*, with an account of Mr. *Herberts* condition. Mr. *Duncon* found him weak, and at that time lying on his Bed, or on a Pallat; but at his seeing Mr. *Duncon*, he rais'd himself vigorously, saluted him, and with some earnestness *inquir'd the health of his brother* Farrer? of which Mr. *Duncon* satisfied him; and after some discourse of Mr. *Farrers* holy life, and the manner of his constant serving God, he said to Mr. *Duncon* —— *Sir, I see by your habit that you are a Priest, and I desire you to pray with me;* which being granted, Mr. *Duncon* ask'd him, *what Prayers?* to which, Mr *Herberts* answer was, *O sir, the Prayers of my Mother, the Church of* England, *no other Prayers are equal to them! but, at this time, I beg of you to pray only the* Litany, *for I am weak and faint;* and Mr. *Duncon* did so. After which, and some other discourse of Mr. *Farrer*, Mrs. *Herbert* provided Mr. *Duncon* a plain Supper, and a clean Lodging, and he betook himself to rest. – *This* Mr. Duncon *tells me;* and tells me, that at his first view of Mr. *Herbert*, he saw *majesty* and *humility* so reconcil'd in his looks and behaviour, as begot in him an awful reverence for his person: and saies, *his discourse was so pious, and his motion so gentile and meek, that after almost forty years, yet they remain still fresh in his memory.*

The next morning Mr. *Duncon* left him, and betook himself to a Journey to *Bath*, but with a promise to return back to him within five days, and he did so; but before I shall say any thing of what discourse then fell betwixt them two, I will pay my promis'd account of Mr. *Farrer*.

Mr. *Nicholas Farrer* (who got the reputation of being call'd Saint *Nicholas*, at the age of six years) was born in *London*: and doubtless had good education in his youth; but certainly was at an early age made Fellow of *Clare-Hall* in *Cambridge*, where he continued to be eminent for his *piety, temperance,* and *learning.* —— About the 26*th* year of his Age, he betook himself to Travel: in which he added to his *Latin* and *Greek*, a perfect knowledge of all the Languages spoken in the Western parts of our Christian world; and understood well the principles of their Religion, and of their manner, and the reasons of their worship. —— In this his

Travel he met with many perswasions to come into a communion with that Church which calls it self *Catholick*: but he return'd from his Travels as he went, eminent for his obedience to his Mother, *the Church of England*. In his absence from *England*, Mr. *Farrers* father (who was a Merchant) allow'd him a liberal maintenance; and, not long after his return into *England*, Mr. *Farrer* had by the death of his father, or an elder brother, or both, an Estate left him, that enabled him to purchase Land to the value of 4 or 500 *l.* a year; the greatest part of which Land was at *Little Gidden*, 4 or 6 miles from *Huntington*, and about 18 from *Cambridge*: which place, he chose for the privacy of it, and for the Hall, which had the Parish-Church, or Chappel belonging, and adjoining near to it; for Mr. *Farrer* having seen the manners and vanities of the World, and found them to be, as Mr. *Herbert* says, *A nothing between two Dishes*; did so contemn it, that he resolv'd to spend the remainder of his life in mortifications, and in devotion, and charity, and to be alwaies prepar'd for Death: —— And his life was spent thus.

He, and his Family, which were like a little Colledge, and about Thirty in number, did most of them keep *Lent*, and all *Ember-weeks* strictly, both in fasting, and using all those mortifications and prayers that the Church hath appointed to be then used: and, he and they, did the like constantly on *Fridays*, and on the *Vigils*, or Eves appointed to be fasted before the Saints-days; and this frugality and abstinence, turn'd to the relief of the Poor: but this was but a part of his charity, none but God and he knew the rest.

This Family, which I have said to be in number about Thirty, were a part of them his Kindred, and the rest chosen to be of a temper fit to be moulded into a devout life; and all of them were for their dispositions *serviceable* and *quiet*, and *humble*, and *free from scandal*. Having thus fitted himself for his Family, he did about the year 1630. betake himself to a constant and methodical service of God, and it was in this manner. —— He being accompanied with most of his Family, did himself use to read the Common prayers (for he was a Deacon) every day, at the appointed hours of Ten and Four, in the Parish Church which was very near his House, and which he had both repair'd and adorn'd; for it was fallen into a great ruine, by reason of a depopulation of the Village before Mr. *Farrer* bought the Mannor: And he did also constantly read the *Mattins* every Morning at the hour of six, either in the Church, or in an Oratory, which was within his own House: And many of the Family did there continue with him after the Prayers were ended, and there they spent some hours in singing *Hymns*, or *Anthems*, sometimes in the Church, and often to an Organ in the Oratory. And there they sometimes betook themselves to meditate, or to pray privately, or to read a part of the New Testament to themselves, or to continue their praying or reading the Psalms: and, in case the Psalms were not alwaies read in the day, then Mr. *Farrer*, and others of the Congregation, did at Night, at the ring of a Watch-bell, repair to the Church or Oratory, and there betake themselves to prayers, and lauding God, and reading the Psalms that had not been read in the day; and, when these, or any part of the Congregation grew weary, or faint, the Watch-bell was Rung, sometimes before, and sometimes after Midnight: and then another part of the Family rose, and maintain'd the Watch, sometimes by praying, or singing Lauds to God, or reading the Psalms: and when after some hours they also grew weary or faint, then they rung the Watch-bell, and were also reliev'd by some of the former, or by a new part of the Society, which continued their devotions (as hath been mentioned) until morning. —— And it is to be noted, that in this continued serving of God, the Psalter, or whole Book of Psalms, was in every four and twenty hours, sung or read over, from the first to the last verse: and this was done as constantly, as the Sun runs his Circle every day about the World, and then begins again the same instant that it ended.

Thus did Mr. *Farrer*, and his happy Family, serve God day and night: Thus did they alwaies behave themselves, as in his presence. And they did alwaies eat and drink by the strictest rules of Temperance; eat and drink so, as to be ready to rise at Midnight, or at the call of a Watch-bell, and perform their devotions to God. —— And 'tis fit to tell the Reader, that many of the Clergy that were more inclin'd to *practical piety*, and *devotion*, then to doubtful and needless Disputations, did often come to *Gidden Hall*, and make themselves part of that happy Society, and stay a week or more, and then join with Mr. *Farrer* and the Family in these Devotions, and assist and ease him or them in their Watch by Night;

124

and these various devotions, had never less than two of the Domestick Family in the Night; and the Watch was alwaies kept in the Church or Oratory, unless in extream cold Winter nights, and then it was maintain'd in a Parlour which had a fire in it: and the Parlour was fitted for that purpose; and this course of Piety, and great liberality to his poor Neighbours, Mr. *Farrer* maintain'd till his death, which was in the year 1639. [. . .]

¶ *His death; and* The Temple

I proceed to my account of Mr. *Herbert*, and Mr. *Duncon*, who, according to his promise, return'd from the Bath the fifth day, and then found Mr. *Herbert* much weaker than he left him: and therefore their Discourse could not be long; but at Mr. *Duncons* parting with him, Mr. *Herbert* spoke to this purpose —— *Sir, I pray give my brother* Farrer *an account of the decaying condition of my body, and tell him, I beg him to continue his daily prayers for me: and let him know, that I have consider'd,* That God only is what he would bee; *and that I am by his grace become now so like him, as to be pleas'd with what pleaseth him; and tell him, that I do not repine but am pleas'd with my want of health; and tell him, my heart is fixed on that place where true joy is only to be found; and that I long to be there, and do wait for my appointed change with* hope *and* patience. Having said this, he did with so sweet a humility as seem'd to exalt him, bow down to Mr *Duncon*, and with a thoughtful and contented look, say to him, —— *Sir, I pray deliver this little Book to my dear brother* Farrer, *and tell him, he shall find in it a picture of the many spiritual Conflicts that have past betwixt God and my Soul, before I could subject mine to the will of* Jesus my Master: *in whose service I have now found perfect freedom; desire him to read it: and then, if he can think it may turn to the advantage of any dejected poor Soul, let it be made publick: if not, let him burn it: for* I and it, *are less than the least of God's mercies.* —— Thus meanly did this humble man think of this excellent Book, which now bears the name of *The TEMPLE: Or, Sacred Poems*, and *Private Ejaculations*; of which, Mr. *Farrer* would say, *There was in it the picture of a divine Soul in every page; and that the whole Book was such a harmony of holy passions, as would enrich the World with pleasure and piety.* And it appears to have done so: for there have been more than Twenty thousand of them sold since the first Impression.

And this ought to be noted, that when Mr. *Farrer* sent this Book to *Cambridge* to be Licensed for the Press, the *Vice-Chancellor* would by no means allow the two so much noted Verses,

> *Religion stands a Tip-toe in our Land,*
> *Ready to pass to the* American *Strand.*

to be printed; and Mr. *Farrer* would by no means allow the Book to be printed, and want them: But after some time, and some arguments, for and against their being made publick, the *Vice-Chancellor* said, *I knew Mr.* Herbert *well, and know that he had many heavenly Speculations, and was a Divine Poet; but I hope the World will not take him to be an inspired Prophet, and therefore I Licence the whole Book*: So that it came to be printed, without the diminution or addition of a syllable, since it was deliver'd into the hands of Mr. *Duncon*, save only, that Mr. *Farrer* hath added that excellent Preface that is printed before it.

At the time of Mr. *Duncons* leaving Mr. *Herbert*, (which was about three weeks before his death) his old and dear friend Mr. *Woodnot*, came from *London* to *Bemerton*, and never left him, till he had seen him draw his last breath, and clos'd his Eyes on his Death-bed. In this time of his decay, he was often visited and pray'd for by all the Clergy that liv'd near to him, especially by his friends the Bishop and Prebends of the Cathedral Church in *Salisbury*; but by none more devoutly, than his Wife, his three Neeces (then a part of his Family) and Mr. *Woodnot*, who were the sad Witnesses of his daily decay; to whom he would often speak to this purpose. —— *I now look back upon the pleasures of my life past, and see the content I have taken in* beauty, *in* wit, *in* musick, *and* pleasant Conversation, *are now all past by me, like a dream, or as a shadow that returns not,*[1] *and are now all become dead to me, or I to them; and I see that as my father and generation hath done before me, so I also shall now suddenly (with* Job*) make my Bed also in the dark;*[2]

---

[1] I Chronicles 29:15; Job 8:9   [2] Job 17:13

and I praise God I am prepared for it; and I praise him, that I am not to learn patience, now I stand in such need of it; and that I have practised Mortification, and endeavour'd to dye daily, that I might not dye eternally; and my hope is, that I shall shortly leave this valley of tears, and be free from all fevers and pain: and which will be a more happy condition, I shall be free from sin, and all the temptations and anxieties that attend it; and this being past, I shall dwell in the new Jerusalem, dwell there with men made perfect; dwell, where these eyes shall see my Master and Saviour Jesus; and with him see my dear Mother, and all my Relations and Friends: —— But I must dye, or not come to that happy place: And this is my content, that I am going daily towards it; and that every day which I have liv'd, hath taken a part of my appointed time from me; and that I shall live the less time, for having liv'd this, and the day past. —— These, and the like expressions, which he utter'd often, may be said to *be his* enjoyment of Heaven, before he enjoy'd it. —— The *Sunday* before his death, he rose suddenly from his Bed or Couch, call'd for one of his Instruments, took it into hand, and said ——

> *My God, My God,*
> *My Musick shall find thee*
> *And every string*
> *Shall have his attribute to sing.*

And having tun'd it, he play'd and sung:

> *The Sundays of Mans life,*
> *Thredded together on times string,*
> *Make Bracelets, to adorn the Wife*
> *Of the eternal glorious King:*
> *On Sundays, Heavens dore stands ope;*
> *Blessings are plentiful and rife,*
> *More plentiful than hope.*

Thus he sung on Earth such Hymns and Anthems, as the Angels and he, and Mr. *Farrer*, now sing in Heaven.

Thus he continued meditating and praying, and rejoicing, till the day of his death; and on that day, said to Mr. *Woodnot, My dear*

Friend, I am sorry I have nothing to present to my merciful God but sin and misery; but the first is pardoned: and a few hours will now put a period to the latter; for I shall suddenly go hence and be no more seen.[1] Upon which expression, Mr. *Woodnot* took occasion to remember him of the Re-edifying *Layton* Church, and his many Acts of mercy; to which he made answer, saying, *They be good works, if they be sprinkled with the blood of Christ, and not otherwise.* After this Discourse he became more restless, and his Soul seem'd to be weary of her earthly Tabernacle; and this uneasiness became so visible, that his Wife, his three Neeces, and Mr. *Woodnot*, stood constantly about his bed, beholding him with sorrow, and an unwillingness to lose the sight of him whom they could not hope to see much longer. —— As they stood thus beholding him, his Wife observ'd him to breath faintly, and with much trouble: and observ'd him to fall into a sudden Agony; which so surpriz'd her, that she fell into a sudden passion, and requir'd of him to know, *how he did?* to which his answer was, *That he had past a Conflict with his last Enemy, and had overcome him, by the merits of his Master Jesus.* After which answer, he look'd up, and saw his Wife and Neeces weeping to an extremity, and charg'd them, *If they lov'd him, to withdraw into the next Room, and there pray every one alone for him, for nothing but their lamentations could make his death uncomfortable.* To which request, their sighs and tears would not suffer them to make any reply: but they yielded him a sad obedience, leaving only with him Mr. *Woodnot*, and Mr. *Bostock*. Immediately after they had left him, he said to Mr. *Bostock*, *Pray Sir open that door, then look into that Cabinet, in which you may easily find my last Will, and give it into my hand*; which having been done Mr. *Herbert* deliver'd it into the hand of Mr. *Woodnot*, and said, *My old Friend, I here deliver you my last Will, in which you will find that I have made you my sole Executor for the good of my Wife and Neeces; and I desire you to shew kindness to them, as they shall need it; I do not desire you to be just: for I know you will be so for your own sake; but I charge you, by the Religion of our friendship, to be careful of them.* And having obtained Mr. *Woodnots* promise to be so; he said, *I am now ready to dye*: after which words he said, *Lord, forsake me not now my strength*

[1] Psalm 39:13

faileth me: but grant me mercy for the merits of my Jesus; and now Lord, Lord now receive my Soul. And, with those words he breath'd forth his Divine Soul, without any apparent disturbance: Mr. *Woodnot*, and Mr. *Bostock*, attending his last breath, and closing his eyes.

Thus he liv'd, and thus he dy'd like a Saint, unspotted of the World, full of Alms-deeds, full of Humility, and all the examples of a vertuous life; which I cannot conclude better, than with this borrowed observation:

> —— *All must to their cold Graves;*
> *But the religious actions of the just,*
> *Smell sweet in death, and blossom in the dust.*

Mr. *George Herberts* have done so to this, and will doubtless do so to succeeding Generations. —— I have but this to say more of him: That if *Andrew Melvin*[1] dyed before him, then *George Herbert* dyed without an enemy. —— I wish (if God shall be so pleased) that I may be so happy as to dye like him.

Jz. Wa.

[1] Andrew Melvin (or Melville) was a Scottish theologian with whom Herbert had disputed.

THE
LIFE
OF
Dr. *ROBERT SANDERSON*,
Late
Lord Bishop of *Lincoln*.

Doctor *Robert Sanderson*, the late learned Bishop of *Lincoln*, whose Life I intend to write with all truth and equal plainness, was born the nineteenth day of *September*, in the year of our Redemption 1587. The place of his birth was *Rotheram* in the County of *York*; a Town of good note, and the more for that *Thomas Rotheram*, sometime *Archbishop* of that See was born in it; a man, whose great wisdom, and bounty, and sanctity of life, have made it the more memorable; as indeed it ought also to be, for being the birth place of our *Robert Sanderson*. And the Reader will be of my belief, if this humble Relation of his Life can hold any proportion with his great Piety, his useful Learning, and his many other extraordinary endowments. [. . .]

¶ *Dr. Sanderson resigns his Fellowship, and becomes a Parson*

[A]bout this time of his resignation he was presented to the Rectory of *Boothby Pannel* in the same County of *Lincoln*; a Town which has been made famous, and must continue to be famous, because *Dr. Sanderson*, the humble and learned *Dr. Sanderson*, was more than 40 years Parson of *Boothby Pannel*, and from thence dated all, or most of his matchless Writings.

To this Living (which was of less value, but a purer Air than *Wibberton*) he was presented by *Thomas Harrington* of the same County and Parish, Esq.; who was a Gentleman of a very ancient Family, and of great use and esteem in his Countrey during his whole life. And in this *Boothby Pannel* the meek and charitable *Dr.*

Sanderson and his Patron liv'd with an endearing, mutual, and comfortable friendship, till the death of the last put a period to it.

About the time that he was made Parson of *Boothby Pannel*, he resign'd his Fellowship of *Lincoln Colledge* unto the then Rector and Fellows: And his resignation is recorded in these words:

Ego Robertus Sanderson *per, &c.*

I Robert Sanderson, *Fellow of the Colledge of* St. Maries *and* All-Saints, *commonly call'd* Lincoln Colledge, *in the University of* Oxford, *do freely and willingly resign into the hands of the Rector and fellows, all the Right and Title that I have in the said Colledge, wishing to them and their Successors, all peace, and piety, and happiness, in the Name of the Father, and of the Son, and of the Holy Ghost.* Amen.

May 6. 1619.

Robert Sanderson.

And not long after this resignation, he was by the then Bishop of *York*, or the King, *Sede vacante*, made Prebend of the Collegiate Church of *Southwell* in that Diocese; and shortly after of *Lincoln* by the Bishop of that See.

And being now resolv'd to set down his rest in a quiet privacy at *Boothby Pannel*, and looking back with some sadness upon his removal from his general Acquaintance left in *Oxford*, and the peculiar pleasures of a University life; he could not but think the want of Society would render this of a Countrey Parson the more uncomfortable, by reason of that want of conversation; and therefore he did put on some faint purposes to marry. For he had considered, that though marriage be cumbred with more worldly care than a single life; yet a complying and prudent Wife changes those very cares into so mutual a content, as makes them become like the Sufferings of St. *Paul, Colos.* i. 24, which he would not have wanted, because *they occasioned his rejoycing in them.* And he having well considered this, and observ'd the secret unutterable joys that Children beget in Parents, and the mutual pleasures and contented trouble of their daily care and constant endeavours to bring up those little Images of themselves so, as to make them as happy as all those cares and endeavours can make them: He having considered all this, the hopes of such happiness turn'd his faint purpose into a positive resolution to marry. And he was so happy as to obtain *Anne*, the daughter of *Henry Nelson* Batchelor in Divinity, then Rector of *Haugham* in the County of *Lincoln* (a man of noted worth and learning.) And the Giver of all good things was so good to him, as to give him such a Wife as was suitable to his own desires; a Wife, that made his life happy by being always content when he was chearful; that divided her joys with him, and abated of his sorrow, by bearing a part of that burthen; a Wife, that demonstrated her affection by a chearful obedience to all his desires, during the whole course of his life; and at his death too, for she outliv'd him.

And in this *Boothby Pannel* he either found or made his Parishioners peaceable, and complying with him in the decent and regular service of God. And thus his Parish, his Patron, and he liv'd together in a religious love, and a contented quietness. He not troubling their thoughts by preaching high and useless notions, but such plain truths as were necessary to be known, believed, and practised, in order to their salvation. And their assent to what he taught was testified by such a conformity to his Doctrine, as declared they believ'd and lov'd him. For he would often say, *That without the last, the most evident truths (heard as from an enemy, or an evil liver) either are not, or are at least the less effectual; and do usually rather harden, than convince the hearer.*

And this excellent man did not think his duty discharged by only reading the Church Prayers, Catechizing, Preaching, and administring the Sacraments seasonably; but thought (if the Law or the Canons may seem to injoyn no more, yet) that God would require more than the defective Laws of man's making, can or does injoyn; the performance of that inward Law, which Almighty God hath imprinted in the Conscience of all good Christians, and inclines those whom he loves to perform. He considering this, did therefore become a law to himself, practising what his Conscience told him was his duty, in reconciling differences, and preventing Law-suits, both in his Parish and in the Neighbourhood. To which may be added his often visiting sick and disconsolate Families, perswading them to patience, and raising them from dejection by his advice and chearful discourse, and by adding his own Alms, if there were any so poor as to need it; considering how acceptable it is to Almighty God, when we do as we are advis'd by St. *Paul, Gal* 6. 2, *help to bear one anothers burthen,* either of *sorrow* or *want*: and what a comfort it will be, when the Searcher of all hearts shall call us to a strict account for that evil we have done, and the good we have omitted, to remember we have comforted and been helpful to a dejected or distressed Family.

And that his practice was to do good, one Example may be, That he met with a poor dejected Neighbour that complain'd he had taken a Meadow, the Rent of which was 9 *l.* a year; and when the Hay was made ready to be carried into his Barn, several days constant rain had so raised the water, that a sudden Flood carried all away, and his rich Landlord would bate him no rent; and that unless he had half abated, he and seven children were utterly undone. It may be noted, That in this Age there are a sort of people so unlike the God of mercy, so void of the bowels of pity, that they love only themselves and children; love them so, as not to be concern'd, whether the rest of mankind waste their days in sorrow or shame; People that are curst with riches, and a mistake that nothing but riches can make them and theirs happy. But 'twas not so with Dr. *Sanderson*; for he was concern'd, and spoke comfortably to the poor dejected man; bade him go home and pray, and not load himself with sorrow, for he would go to his Landlord next morning, and if his Landlord would not abate what he desired, he and a Friend would pay it for him.

To the Landlord he went the next day; and in a conference, the Doctor presented to him the sad condition of his poor dejected Tenant; telling him how much God is pleas'd when men compassionate the poor: and told him, That though God loves Sacrifice, yet he loves Mercy so much better, that he is pleas'd when call'd *the God of mercy.* And told him, the riches he was possest of were given him by that *God of mercy,* who would not be pleas'd, if he that had so much given, yea, and forgiven him too, should prove like the rich Steward in the Gospel, *that took his fellow servant by the throat to make him pay the utmost farthing.*[1] This he told him. And

---

[1] The story Walton is thinking of is Matthew 18:23-35, but he is quoting from the Sermon on the Mount (Matthew 5:26) and remembering a similar 'rich Steward' story which he quotes from later in the passage (Luke 16:1-13).

told him, That the Law of this Nation (by which Law he claims his Rent) does not undertake to make men *honest* or *merciful*; but does what it can to restrain men from being *dishonest* or *unmerciful*, and yet was defective in both: and that taking any Rent from his poor Tenant, for what God suffered him not to enjoy, though the Law allowed him to do so, yet if he did so, he was too like that rich Steward which he had mentioned to him; and told him that riches so gotten, and added to his great Estate, would, as *Job* says, *prove like gravel in his teeth,*[1] would in time so corrode his Conscience, or become so nauseous when he lay upon his Death-bed, that he would then labour to vomit it up, and not be able: and therefore advis'd him, being very rich, to make Friends of his *unrighteous Mammon,*[2] before that evil day come upon him: But however, neither for his own sake, nor for God's sake, to take any Rent of his poor dejected sad Tenant, for that were to gain a temporal, and lose his eternal happiness. These and other such reasons, were urg'd with so grave and so compassionate an earnestness, that the Landlord forgave his Tenant the whole Rent.

The Reader will easily believe that Dr. *Sanderson*, who was himself so meek & merciful, did suddenly and gladly carry this comfortable news to the dejected Tenant; and will believe, that at the telling of it there was a mutual rejoycing. 'Twas one of *Job*'s boasts, *That he had seen none perish for want of clothing: and that he had often made the heart of the widow to rejoyce. Job* 31. And doubtless Dr. *Sanderson* might have made the same religious boast of this, and very many like occasions. But since he did not, I rejoyce that I have this just occasion to do it for him; and that I can tell the Reader, I might tire my self and him in telling how like the whole course of Dr. *Sanderson*'s life was to this which I have now related. [. . .]

[1] Actually Lamentations 3:16
[2] See Luke 16: 9-11

¶ *The King's Chaplain in Ordinary*

In this contented obscurity he continued, till the learned and good Archbishop *Laud*, who knew him well in *Oxford* (for he was his contemporary there) told the King ('twas the knowing and conscientious King *Charles* the I.) that there was one Mr. *Sanderson*, an obscure Countrey Minister, that was of such sincerity, and so excellent in all Casuistical learning, that he desir'd his Majesty would make him his Chaplain. The King granted it most willingly, & gave the Bishop charge to hasten it, for he long'd, to discourse with a man that had dedicated his Studies to that useful part of learning. The Bishop forgot not the King's desire, and Mr. *Sanderson* was made his Chaplain in Ordinary in *November* following, 1631. And when they became known to each other, the King did put many Cases of Conscience to him, and receiv'd from him such deliberate, safe, and clear solutions, as gave him great content in conversing with him: so that at the end of his months attendance, the King told him, *He should long for the next* November; *for he resolv'd to have a more inward acquaintance with him, when that month and he return'd.* And when the month and he did return, the good King was never absent from his Sermons, and would usually say, *I carry my ears to hear other Preachers, but I carry my conscience to hear Mr.* Sanderson, and to act accordingly. And this ought not to be conceal'd from Posterity, That the King thought what he spake: For he took him to be his Adviser in that quiet part of his life, and he prov'd to be his Comforter in those days of his affliction, when he apprehended himself to be in danger of Death or Deposing. [. . .]

And let me here take occasion to tell the Reader this truth, not commonly known, that in one of these Conferences this conscientious King told Dr. *Sanderson*, or one of them that then waited with him, *That the remembrance of two Errors did much afflict him,* which were, *his assent to the Earl of* Strafford's *death, and the abolishing Episcopacy in* Scotland; *and that if God ever restored him to be in a peaceable possession of his Crown, he would demonstrate his Repentance by a publick Confession and a voluntary penance* (I think barefoot) *from the* Tower *of* London, *or* Whitehall, *to St.* Paul's *Church, and desire the people to intercede with God for his pardon.* I am sure one of them told it me, lives still, and will witness it. [. . .]

I now return to Dr. *Sanderson* in the Chair in *Oxford*, where they that comply'd not in taking the *Covenant, Negative Oath*, and *Parliament Ordinance* for Church Discipline and Worship, were under a sad and daily apprehension of Expulsion; for the Visiters were daily expected, and both City and University full of Souldiers, and a party of Presbyterian Divines, that were as greedy and ready to possess, as the ignorant and ill-natur'd Visiters were to eject the dissenters out of their Colledges and Livelyhoods: But notwithstanding *Dr. Sanderson* did still continue to read his Lecture, and did to the very faces of those Presbyterian Divines and Souldiers, read with so much reason, and with a calm fortitude make such applications, as if they were not, they ought to have been asham'd, and beg'd pardon of God and him, and forborn to do what follow'd. But these thriving sinners were hardned; and as the Visiters expel'd the Orthodox, they, without scruple or shame, possest themselves of their Colledges; so that with the rest, *Dr. Sanderson* was (in *June* 1648.) forc'd to pack up and be gone, and thank God he was not imprison'd, as *Dr. Sheldon, Dr. Hammond*, and others then were. [. . .]

And in *London* all the Bishops Houses were turn'd to be Prisons, and they fill'd with Divines, that would not take the Covenant, or forbear reading Common Prayer, or that were accus'd for some faults like these. For it may be noted, That about this time the Parliament set out a Proclamation to incourage all Lay-men that had occasion to complain of their Ministers for being troublesome or scandalous, or that conformed not to Orders of Parliament, to make their complaint to a Committee for that purpose; and the Minister, though 100 miles from *London*, should appear there and give satisfaction, or be sequestred; (and you may be sure no Parish could want a covetous, or malicious, or crossgrain'd complainant:) by which means all Prisons in *London*, and in some other places, became the sad habitations of Conforming Divines.

And about this time the Bishop of *Canterbury* having been by an unknown Law condemned to die, and the execution suspended for some days, many of the malicious Citizens fearing his pardon, shut up their Shops, professing not to open them till Justice was executed. This malice and madness is scarce credible, but I saw it. [. . .]

We have now overtaken Dr. *Sanderson* at *Boothby* Parish, where he hop'd to have enjoy'd himself, though in a poor, yet in a quiet and desir'd privacy; but it prov'd otherwise: For all corners of the Nation were fill'd with Covenanters, Confusion, Committee-men and Soldiers, serving each other to their several ends, of revenge, or power, or profit; and these Committee-men and Soldiers were most of them so possest with this Covenant, that they became like those that were infected with that dreadful Plague of *Athens*; the Plague of which Plague was, that they by it became maliciously restless to get into company, and to joy (so the Historian[1] saith) when they had infected others, even those of their most beloved or nearest Friends or Relations; and though there might be some of these Covenanters that were beguil'd, and meant well; yet such were the generality of them, and temper of the times, that you may be sure Dr. *Sanderson*, who though quiet and harmless, yet an eminent dissenter from them, could not live peaceably; nor did he: For the Soldiers would appear, and visibly disturb him in the Church when he read Prayers, pretending to advise him how God was to be serv'd most acceptably: which he not approving, but continuing to observe order and decent behaviour in reading the Church Service, they forc'd his Book from him, and tore it, expecting extemporary Prayers.

At this time he was advis'd by a Parliament man of power and note, that lov'd and valued him much, not to be strict in reading all the *Common Prayer*, but make some little variation, especially if the Soldiers came to watch him; for then it might not be in the power of him and his other Friends to secure him from taking the Covenant, or Sequestration: for which Reasons he did vary somewhat from the strict Rules of the Rubrick. I will set down the very words of Confession which he us'd, as I have it under his own hand; and tell the Reader that all his other variations were as little, & much like to this.

---

[1] *Theucidides* [– I.W.]. Thucydides (*c.* 460/455 – *c.* 399 BC) wrote the *History of the Peloponnesian War*.

¶ *His Confession*

O Almighty God and merciful Father, we thy unworthy Servants do with shame and sorrow confess, that we have all our life long gone astray out of thy ways like lost sheep; and that by following too much the vain devices and desires of our own hearts, we have grievously offended against thy holy Laws both in thought, word and deed; we have many times left undone those good duties, which we might and ought to have done; and we have many times done those evils, when we might have avoided them, which we ought not to have done. We confess, O Lord, that there is no health at all, nor help in any Creature to relieve us; but all our hope is in thy mercy, whose justice we have by our sins so far provoked: Have mercy therefore upon us, O Lord, have mercy upon us miserable offenders: spare us good God, who confess our faults, that we perish not; but according to thy gracious promises declared unto mankind in Christ Jesus our Lord, restore us upon our true Repentance into thy grace and favour. And grant, O most merciful Father, for his sake, that we henceforth study to serve and please thee by leading a godly, righteous, and a sober life, to the glory of thy holy Name, and the eternal comfort of our own souls, through Jesus Christ our Lord.   Amen.

In these disturbances of tearing his Service Book, a Neighbour came on a Sunday, after the Evening Service was ended, to visit and condole with him for the affront offered by the Soldiers. To whom he spake with a composed patience, and said; *God hath restored me to my desir'd privacy, with my wife and children, where I hop'd to have met with quietness, and it proves not so; but I will labour to be pleas'd, because God, on whom I depend, sees 'tis not fit for me to be quiet. I praise him, that he hath by his grace prevented me from making shipwrack of a good Conscience to maintain me in a place of great reputation and profit: and though my condition be such, that I need the last; yet I submit, for God did not send me into this world to do my own, but suffer his will, and I will obey it.* Thus by a sublime depending on his wise, and powerful, and pitiful Creator, he did chearfully submit to what God had appointed, justifying the truth of that Doctrine which he had preach'd.

About this time that excellent Book of the *King's Meditations in his Solitude* was printed, and made publick: and Dr. *Sanderson* was such a lover of the Author, and so desirous that the whole world should see the character of him in that Book, and something of the cause for which they suffer'd, that he design'd to turn it into Latin: but when he had done half of it most excellently, his friend Dr. *Earle* prevented him, by appearing to have done the whole very well before him.

About this time his dear and most intimate Friend, the learned Dr. *Hammond*, came to enjoy a conversation and rest with him for a few days, and did so. And having formerly perswaded him to trust his excellent memory, and not read, but try to speak a Sermon as he had writ it, Dr. *Sanderson* became so complyant as to promise he would. And to that end they two went early the Sunday following to a Neighbour Minister, and requested to exchange a Sermon; and they did so. And at Dr. *Sanderson*'s going into the Pulpit, he gave his Sermon (which was a very short one) into the hand of Dr. *Hammond*, intending to preach it as 'twas writ; but before he had preach'd a third part, Dr. *Hammond* (looking on his Sermon as written) observed him to be out, and so lost as to the matter, that he also became afraid for him; for 'twas discernable to many of the plain Auditory: But when he had ended this short Sermon, as they two walk'd homeward, Dr. *Sanderson* said with much earnestness, *Good Doctor give me my Sermon, and know, that neither you, nor any man living, shall ever perswade me to preach again without my Books.* To which the reply was, *Good Doctor be not angry; for if I ever perswade you to preach again without Book, I will give you leave to burn all those that I am Master of.* [. . .]

I met him accidentally in *London* in sad-coloured clothes, and God knows, far from being costly: the place of our meeting was near to *little Britain*, where he had been to buy a Book, which he then had in his hand: we had no inclination to part presently; and therefore turn'd to stand in a corner under a Penthouse (for it began to rain) and immediately the wind rose, and the rain increased so much, that both became so inconvenient, as to force us into a cleanly house, where we had *Bread, Cheese, Ale, &* a *Fire* for our money. This rain and wind were so obliging to me, as to force our stay there for at least an hour, to my great content and advantage; for in that time he made to me many useful observations with much clearness and conscientious freedom. I shall relate a part of them, in hope they may also turn to the advantage of my Reader. He seem'd to lament, that the Parliament had taken upon them to abolish our Liturgy, to the scandal of so many devout and learned men, and the disgrace of those many Martyrs, who had seal'd the truth and use of it with their blood: and that no Minister was now thought godly that did not decry it; and, at least, pretend to make better Prayers *ex tempore*: and that they, and only they that could do so, prayed by the Spirit, and were godly; though in their Sermons they disputed, and evidently contradicted each other in their Prayers. And as he did dislike this, so he did most highly commend the *Common Prayer* of the Church, saying, *The Collects were the most passionate, proper, and most elegant expressions that any language ever afforded; and that there was in them such* piety, *and that so interwoven with* instructions, *that they taught us to know the power, the wisdom, the majesty, and mercy of God, and much of our duty both to him and our Neighbour; and that a Congregation behaving themselves reverently, & putting up to God these joynt and known desires for pardon of sins, and praises for mercies receiv'd, could not but be more pleasing to God, than those raw, unpremeditated expressions, to which many of the hearers could not say* Amen.

And he then commended to me the frequent use of the *Psalter* or *Psalms of David*; speaking to this purpose, *That they were the Treasury of Christian Comfort, fitted for all persons and all necessities; able to raise the soul from dejection by the frequent mention of God's mercies to repentant sinners; to stir up holy desires; to increase joy; to moderate sorrow; to nourish hope, and teach us patience, by waiting God's leasure; to beget a trust in the mercy, power, & providence of our Creator; & to cause a resignation of our selves to his will; & then (and not till then) to believe our selves happy.* This he said the *Liturgy* and *Psalms* taught us; and that by the frequent use of the last they would not only prove to be our souls comfort, but would become so habitual, as to transform them into the image of his soul that composed them. After this manner he express'd himself concerning the Liturgy & Psalms; & seem'd to lament that this, which was the Devotion of the more Primitive times, should in common Pulpits be turn'd into needless debates about *Free-will, Election,* and *Reprobation,* of which, and many like Questions, we may be safely ignorant, because Almighty God intends not to lead us to

Heaven by hard Questions, but by meekness and charity, and a frequent practice of Devotion. [. . .]

¶ *Character of Dr. Sanderson*

I hope I shall not disoblige my Reader, if I here inlarge into a further Character of his person and temper. As first, That he was moderately tall; his behaviour had in it much of a plain comliness, and very little (yet enough) of ceremony or courtship; his looks and motion manifested affability and mildness, and yet he had with these a calm, but so matchless a fortitude, as secur'd him from complying with any of those many Parliament injunctions, that interfer'd with a doubtful conscience. His Learning was methodical and exact; his wisdome useful; his integrity visible; and his whole life so unspotted, that all ought to be preserved as Copies for Posterity to write after; the Clergy especially, who with impure hands ought not to offer Sacrifice to that God, whose pure eyes abhorr iniquity.

There was in his Sermons no improper Rhetorick, nor such perplex'd divisions, as may be said to be like too much light, that so dazles the eyes that the sight becomes less perfect: But there was therein no want of useful matter, nor waste of words; and yet such clear distinctions as dispel'd all confus'd Notions, and made his hearers depart both wiser, and more confirm'd in vertuous resolutions.

His memory was so matchless and firm, as 'twas only overcome by his bashfulness; for he alone, or to a friend, could repeat all the *Odes of Horace*, all *Tully's Offices*, and much of *Juvenal* and *Persius* without Book; and would say, *The repetition of one of the* Odes *of* Horace *to himself was to him such musick, as a Lesson on the* Viol *was to others, when they play'd it to themselves or friends.* And though he was blest with a clearer Judgment than other men, yet he was so distrustful of it, that he did over-consider of consequences, and would so delay and reconsider what to determine, that though none ever determin'd better, yet, when the Bell toll'd for him to appear and read his Divinity Lectures in *Oxford*, and all the Scholars attended to hear him, he had not then, or not till then, resolv'd and writ what he meant to determine; so that that appear'd to be a truth, which his old dear Friend Dr. *Sheldon* would often say, namely, *That his judgment was so much superiour to his phancy, that whatsoever this suggested, that dislik'd and controul'd; still considering and reconsidering, till his time was so wasted, that he was forc'd to write, not (probably) what was best, but what he thought last.* And yet what he did then read, appear'd to all hearers to be so useful, clear, and satisfactory, as none ever determin'd with greater applause. [. . .]

¶ Dr. Sanderson is made Bishop of Lincoln at the Restoration

[A]t the King's return *Dr. Sheldon*, the late prudent Bishop of *Canterbury* (than whom none knew, valued, or lov'd *Dr. Sanderson* more or better) was by his Majesty made a chief Trustee to commend to him fit men to supply the then vacant Bishopricks. And *Dr. Sheldon* knew none fitter than *Dr. Sanderson*, and therefore humbly desired the King that he would nominate him: and that done, he did as humbly desire *Dr. Sanderson* that he would for Gods and the Churches sake, take that charge and care upon him. *Dr. Sanderson* had, if not an unwillingness, certainly no forwardness to undertake it; and would often say, *He had not led himself, but his Friend would now lead him into a temptation, which he had daily pray'd against; and besought God, if he did undertake it, so to assist him with his grace, that the example of his life, his cares and endeavours, might promote his glory, and help forward the salvation of others.*

This I have mentioned as a happy preparation to his Bishoprick; and am next to tell that he was consecrated Bishop of *Lincoln* at *Westminster* the 28*th* of *October*, 1660. [. . .]

¶ *He beautifies the Bishop's House*

The Bishops chief House at *Buckden*, in the County of *Huntington*, the usual Residence of his Predecessors (for it stands about the midst of his Diocese) having been at his Consecration a great part of it demolish'd, and what was left standing under a visible decay, was by him undertaken to be erected and repair'd; and it was perform'd with great speed, care, and charge. And to this may be added, That the King having by an *Injunction* commended to the care of the Bishops, Deans, and Prebends of all Cathedral Churches, *the repair of them, their Houses, and augmentation of small Vicarages*; He, when he was repairing *Bugden*, did also augment the last, as fast as Fines were paid for renewing Leases: so fast, that a Friend taking notice of his bounty, was so bold as to advise him to remember; *he was under his first fruits, and that he was old, and had a wife and children yet but meanly provided for, especially if his dignity were considered.* To whom he made a mild and thankful answer, saying, *It would not become a Christian Bishop to suffer those houses built by his Predecessors, to be ruin'd for want of repair; and less justifiable to suffer any of those that were call'd to so high a calling as* to sacrifice at God's altar, *to eat the bread of sorrow constantly, when he had a power by a small augmentation to turn it into the bread of cheerfulness: and wish'd, that as this was, so it were also in his power to make all mankind happy, for he desired nothing more. And for his wife and children, he hop'd to leave them a competence; and in the hands of God, that would provide for all that kept innocence, and trusted his providence and protection, which he had always found enough to make and keep him happy.* [. . .]

¶ *His sickness and death*

Before I give an account of Dr. *Sanderson*'s last sickness, I desire to tell the Reader that he was of a healthful constitution, chearful and mild, of an even temper, very moderate in his diet, and had had little sickness, till some few years before his death; but was then every Winter punish'd with a *Diarrhea*, which left him not till

143

warm weather return'd and remov'd it: And this distemper did, as he grew elder, seize him oftner, and continue longer with him. But though it weakned him, yet it made him rather indispos'd than sick; and did no way disable him from studying (indeed too much.) In this decay of his strength, but not of his memory or reason (for this distemper works not upon the understanding), he made his last Will, of which I shall give some account for confirmation of what hath been said, and what I think convenient to be known, before I declare his death and burial. [. . .]

As for my corruptible Body, I bequeath it to the Earth whence it was taken, to be decently buried in the Parish Church of Bugden, towards the upper end of the Chancel, upon the second, or (at the farthest) the third day after my decease; and that with as little noise, pomp, and charge as may be, without the invitation of any person how near soever related unto me, other than the Inhabitants of Bugden; without the unnecessary expence of Escocheons, Gloves, Ribbons, &c. and without any Blacks to be hung any where in or about the House or Church, other than a Pulpit Cloth, a Hearse Cloth, and a Mourning Gown for the Preacher; whereof the former (after my Body shall be interred) to be given to the Preacher of the Funeral Sermon, and the latter to the Curat of the Parish for the time being. And my will further is, That the Funeral Sermon be preached by my own Houshold Chaplain, containing some wholesome discourse concerning Mortality, the Resurrection of the Dead, and the Last Judgment; and that he shall have for his pains 5l. upon condition, that he speak nothing at all concerning my person, either good or ill, other than I my self shall direct; only signifying to the Auditory that it was my express will to have it so. And it is my will, that no costly Monument be erected for my memory, but only a fair flat Marble stone to be laid over me, with this Inscription in legible Roman characters, Depositum Roberti Sanderson nuper Lincolniensis Episcopi, qui obiit Anno Domini MDCLXII. & ætatis suæ septuagesimo sexto, Hic requiescit in spe beatæ resurrectionis. *This manner of burial, although I cannot but foresee it will prove unsatisfactory to sundry my nearest Friends and Relations, and be apt to be censured by others, as an evidence of my too much parsimony and narrowness of mind, as being altogether unusual, and not according to the mode of these times; yet it is agreeable to the sense of my heart, and I do very much desire my Will may be carefully observed herein, hoping it may become exemplary to some or other: at least howsoever testifying at my death (what I have so often and earnestly professed in my life time (my utter dislike of the flatteries commonly used in Funeral Sermons, and of the vast Expences otherwise laid out in Funeral Solemnities and Entertainments, with very little benefit to any, which (if bestowed in pious and charitable works) might redound to the publick or private benefit of many persons.*

I am next to tell, that he died the 29*th* of *January*, 1662. and that his Body was buried in *Bugden* the third day after his death; and for the manner, that 'twas as far from ostentation as he desir'd it; and all the rest of his Will was as punctually performed. And when I have (to his just praise) told this truth, *That he died far from being rich*, I shall return back to visit, and give a further account of him on his last Sick-bed.

His last Will (of which I have mentioned a part) was made about three weeks before his death, about which time finding his strength to decay by reason of his constant infirmity, and a consumptive cough added to it, he retir'd to his Chamber, expressing a desire to enjoy his last thoughts to himself in private, without disturbance or care, especially of what might concern this world. [. . .]

He in this retirement had the Church Prayers read in his Chamber twice every day; and at nine at night some Prayers read to him and a part of his Family out of the *Whole Duty of Man*. As he was remarkably punctual and regular in all his studies and actions; so he used himself to be for his Meals. And his dinner being appointed to be constantly ready at the ending of Prayers, and he expecting and calling for it, was answered, *It would be ready in a quarter of an hour*. To which his reply was, *A quarter of an hour? Is a quarter of an hour nothing to a man that probably has not many hours to live*. And though he did live many hours after this, yet he liv'd not many days; for the day after (which was three days before his death) he was become so weak and weary of either motion or sitting, that he was content, or forc'd to keep his bed. In which I desire he may rest, till I have given some account of his behaviour there, and immediately before it.

The day before he took his bed (which was three days before his death) he, that he might receive a new assurance for the pardon of his sins past, and be strengthned in his way to the *new Jerusa-lem*, took the blessed Sacrament of the Body and Blood of his, and our blessed *Jesus*, from the hands of his Chaplain Mr. *Pullin*, accompanied with his Wife, Children, and a Friend, in as awful, humble, and ardent a manner, as outward reverence could express. After the praise and thanksgiving for it was ended, he spake to this purpose; *Thou, O God, took'st me out of my mothers womb, and hast been the powerful Protector of me to this present moment of my life; thou hast neither forsaken me now I am become grey-headed, nor suf-fered me to forsake thee in the late days of temptation, and sacrifice my Conscience for the preservation of my liberty or estate. 'Twas by grace that I have stood, when others have fallen under my trials: and these mercies I now remember with joy and thankfulness; and my hope and desire is, that I may die praising thee.*

The frequent repetition of the *Psalms of David* hath been noted to be a great part of the Devotion of the Primitive Christians: The Psalms having in them not only Prayers and holy Instructions, but such Commemorations of God's Mercies, as may preserve comfort, and confirm our dependence on the power, and provi-dence, and mercy of our Creator. And this is mention'd in order to telling, that as the holy Psalmist said, that *his eyes should prevent both the dawning of the day and the night watches, by meditating on God's word:*[1] so 'twas Dr. *Sanderson*'s constant practice every morning to entertain his first waking thoughts with a repetition of those very Psalms, that the Church hath appointed to be con-stantly read in the daily Morning Service; and having at night laid him in his bed, he as constantly clos'd his eyes with a repeti-tion of those appointed for the Service of the Evening, remem-bring & repeating the very Psalms appointed for every day; and as the month had formerly ended and began again, so did this Exercise of his Devotion. And if his first waking thoughts were of the World, or what concern'd it, he would arraign and condemn himself for it. Thus he began that work on earth, which is now his imployment in heaven.

After his taking his Bed, and about a day before his death, he desir'd his Chaplain, Mr. *Pullin*, to give him Absolution: And at

---

[1] Psalm 119:147 [– I.W.]

his performing that Office, he pull'd off his Cap, that Mr. *Pullin* might lay his hand upon his bare head. After this desire of his was satisfied, his Body seem'd to be at more ease, and his mind more chearful; and he said, *Lord, forsake me not now my strength faileth me, but continue thy mercy, and let my mouth be filled with thy praise.*[1] He continued the remaining night and day very patient, and thankful for any of the little Offices that were perform'd for his ease and refreshment: and during that time, did often say the 103 *Psalm* to himself, and very often these words, *My heart is fixed, O God, my heart is fixed where true joy is to be found.*[2] His thoughts seem'd now to be wholly of death, for which he was so prepar'd, that that *King of Terrors* could not surprise him *as a thief in the night;*[3] for he had often said, *he was prepar'd, and long'd for it.* And as this desire seem'd to come from Heaven; so it left him not, till his Soul ascended to that Region of blessed Spirits, whose Imployments are to joyn in consort with him, and sing *praise* and *glory* to that God, who hath brought them to that place, *into which sin and sorrow cannot enter.*[4]

Thus this pattern of *meekness* and primitive *innocence* chang'd this for a better life. 'Tis now too late to wish that my life may be like his; for I am in the eighty fifth year of my Age; but I humbly beseech Almighty God, that my death may; and do as earnestly beg of every Reader to say Amen.

Blessed is the man in whose Spirit
there is no guile.   Psal. 32. 2.

[1] Incorporating Psalm 38:10 and Psalm 51:15, which is also a response usually made at Matins and Evensong in the Book of Common Prayer

[2] Not Psalm 103 but an embellishment of Psalm 57:7

[3] The 'King of Terrors' possibly refers to Psalm 55:4 and/or Job 24:17; Job 24:14, 1Thessalonians 5:2

[4] Revelations 21:1-4

LIFE
OF
JOHN HALES.

¶ *Memoranda respecting John Hales*[1]

John Hales, the fourth sonne of John Hales of High Church, neer Bath, in Somersetshire, by Brigide his wife, one of the Goldsburghs of Knahill, in Wiltshire, was born in the city of Bath, where his Father then dwelt, (his Grandfather yet living at Highchurch). His parents being of Gentile quality, kept him to school at Wells and Killmaston in that countrey, till he was fit for the universitie which was about the thirteenth yeare of his age.

He was admitted Scholar of Corpus Christi in Oxford, 1597, Ap. 16.

But being under age, not then sworn, till Aug. 17, 1599.

There he continued till he was Bachelor of Arts. Admitt. Jul. 9, 1603. Determ. Lent following.

1605. But then by the perswasion of Sir Henry Saville much taken with his excellent parts, he removed to Merton College, where he was chosen Prob. Sept. 2. Admitted Oct. 9. Admitted Fellow, Oct. 13, 1606.

He proceeded to his Master's Degree. Admitted Jan. 20, 1609. At the Act 1609, July 10.

Regius Professor of Greek, 1612, (potuis 1613 or 15.) Left it 1619.

He left his Fellowship at Merton College. Admitted Fellow of Eton College, May 24, 1613.

Chaplain to Sir Dudley Carleton, Ambassador to the States; and by that means present at the Synod of Dort. Perhaps for that end.

---

[1] This intelligence I had from a sister of his, being a widow, antient, and in want, named Brigide Gulliford, who came to Oxford to desire reliefe, Jan. 20, 1663. But the register of C.C.C. Oxf, diff. 1597, Ap. 16: Johannem Hales natum in villa vocat. Highchurch in com. Somerset Bathon et Wellens. Dioces. aetatis suae annum agentem decimum tertium circiter festum sive diem Paschales ult. præterit. (uti asseruit) in Discip. dict. Coll. admis. [– I.W.]

Came to Dort, Nov. 13, 1618. Went away about Feb. 8. V. Lett. pp.93, 100, 97.

In his being there appeares no ground for the story of Episcopius urging Joh. 3, 16.

Qu. Whether it were not rather Martinius. V. Lett. pp. 87, 92.

Insignia. Johannes Halesius Hujus Coll. Socius et Canonicus de Windsor.

Vide Heyl. Life of A. B. Laud, p.362, and Parker's Reproof, p.135, etc.

Prob. of Windsor, May (end) 1639.

Turned out of his Fellowship upon the engagement, 1649.

Musarum et Charitum Amor
Johannes Halesius
(Nomen non tam Hominis quam Scientiæ)
Hic non jacet
At Lutum quod assumsit optimum
Infra ponitur
Nam certe supra mortales emicuit
Moribus Suavissimis
Ingenio subtilissimo pectore pleno sapuit
Mundo sublimior
Adeoque aptior Angelorum Choro
Aetatis suæ 72.
Impensis Pet. Curweni olim hujus Coll.
Alumni 72.

Hales was born, 1584. Bapt. in St. James' Church, Bath, 5 May. King's Professor of Greek, by grant dated 15 Sept, 1612, which took effect shortly after Doctor Perin dying May 3, 1615.

[1673.]

¶ *Letter respecting John Hales*

I have told you that he satisfied many scruples, and in order to
what followes, I must tell you that a yeare or two after the beginning of the long parliament, the citizens and many yong lecturers
(scollers of their zeale and pich for Learning, and precedence)
had got Mr. Brightman's booke or Coment on the Revelations to
be reprinted and greatly magnified: in which was so many gros
Errors and absurd conclusions about government by Bishops,
and other explications to the humors and the present ringleaders
of the then Parliament (all whereof Brightman is now proved
false, and that party not yet ashamed) with which the lecturers
and their followers were so transported with Brightman's opinions, that they swallowed them without chawing, and all thought
simple that approved him not.

About this time comes a friend to Mr. Hales (being a neighbour
gentleman,) and requests that a kinsman of his that was trobled
with some sad thoughts and scruples might obtain a conference
with him, in order to the quieting of his minde: which was redyly
granted by Mr. Hales. When the perplext partie came to him at
the howre apoynted, Mr. Ha. having taken him into his study,
and shut the dore in order to a private and larg discourse with
him, the perplext partie being set down takes out of his pocket a
bible, turnes to the profit Daniell, reades a part of one of the chap-
ters, askes the meaning of that, and how it was to be reconciled
with a part of the revelation of St. John. When Mr. Ha. had heard
him reade, and heard him make his queries or scruples, he told
him, he was mistaken in taking him for a fit man to satisfie his
conscience, and that if he wood be satisfied he must goe to some
of the young devines now about London, and not come to so old
a devine as he was, but they wood doe it readily.

About the time he was forc't from the Lady Saltrs, that family
or college broke up, or desolv'd, a little before which time, they
were resolv'd to have Mr. Ha. picture taken, and to that end, a
picture maker had promis'd to attend at Ricking to take it, but
fail'd of his time, and Mr. Ha. being gone thence, dyed not long
after. The not having his picture was lamented very much by the
societie, in wch number the Bish^s Sister (once M^{ris} Anne King,

now the Lady How) undertooke boeth for theirs and her owne satisfaction to draw it, and did so, in black and white, boeth excellently well as to the curiousness and as well as to the likenes. But before she wood shew it to any that know either him or herselfe, she writ underneth it, this which she ment to be an Apologie for her undertaking it.

> Though by a sudden and unfeard surprize,
> Thou lately taken wast from thy friends' eies:
> Even in that instant, when they had design'd
> To keipe thee by thy picture still in minde:
> Least thou like others lost in deth's dark night
> Shouldst stealing hence vanish quite out of sight;
> I did contend with greater zeale then art,
> This shadow of my phansie to impart:
> Which all shood pardon, when they understand
> The lines were figur'd by a woman's hand,
> Who had noe copy to be guided by
> But Hales imprinted in her memory.
> Thus ill cut Brasses serve uppon a grave,
> Which less resemblance of the persons have.

You may take notice that she is a most generous and ingenious Lady. Greater friendship 'twixt her and Mr. Ha. she has told me he told her he had liv'd 14 days with bere and bred and tosts, in order to try how litell would keepe him if he were sequestered. She told me he would eate very fully at a diner, and of the strongest or coarsest of the mete rather than the finest.

She told me he was never out of Humour but always even, and humble, and quiet, never disturbed by any news, or any losse or any thing that concerned the world, but much affected if his friends were in want or sick.

At his being at Rickkings towards his later end when he was alone he was usually reading Tho. à Kempis, which of a small print he read without specktacels.

He kept his opinions to himself especially towards his later part of his life and would often say there was plainness in all necessary trewths.

He was Bowser [Bursar] about that time when in the contest began betwixt the King and Parliament [and] boeth armies had sequestered the College rents: so that he could not get money to pay wages to the servants, or for victuals for the schollers. But after 9 weekes hiding himselfe to preserve the college writings and keyes, he was forc'd to appere, at the end of which time, the old woman that conceal'd him demanded but 6d. a weeke for his browne bread and bere, which was all his meate, and he wood give her 12d. His concealment was so nere the Cottage or Highway, that he said after, pleasantly, those that searched for him might have smelt him if he had eaten garlick.

This was told me by Mrs. Powny from whome Mr. Montague it may be, had [it] more perfectly.

He lived 5 yeares after he was sequestered. He dyeth the 19th of May, Anno /q/, Mrs. Powny, and was by his owne comand buried next day in the Church yeard. He had a monument made for him (by some friend) wch is now in Eaton church yard.

He was not good at any continuance to get or save money for himselfe; yet he undertooke to do it for Sir H. Wotton, who was a neglector of mony, and Mr. Ha. told me had had got £300 together at the time of his deth, a some to which Sir H. had long been a stranger, and would ever have been if he had managed his owne money-business. It was happily got together to bury him, and inable him to doe some offices of honor, and justice, and gratitude, and charitie.

Mrs Powny told me Sir Fra. Bacon and the Lord Falkland came one day purposely from London to sup and discourse with him, and return'd early next morning.

Mr. Ha. like Paule at Damascus, eate not in 3 dayes.

I thinke he bought and gave the howse in which he dyed to Mrs. Powny's husband, who had beine his honest servant of which /q/.

I have heard that Mr. Ha. being suppos'd to hold some hethrodox opinions, he, to testifie the contrary, did in his sickness (which was not long,) declare his beleife to his pupell, the Lady Salter's son, which he tooke in his writing from his owne mouth. This, Mr. Salter (who is now dead,) told me long since, and promised me a Copie of it.

Mr. Mountague, formerly the scolem^r of that college and now fellow 'tis like has it, and he hath promised me to write and give me what materiall passages he can rem^r concerning him, and he will give them to Mr. Marryot if the be cal'd for.

He or Mrs. Powny will answere all the q as to the yeare of his deth, and who was at the charge of his monument, how long he lay sick, his behaviour then, and what ells is defective in theise collections gathered by me. Mrs. Powny dwells nere the college, and Mr. Montague is constantly in it being now sickly.

As you reade this make y^r que. and let them be given to me or Mr. Marryot who may get a resolution for you. J.W. Octo. 20, 73.

I think the Lady Salter did many yeares since tell me she had the profession of the beliefe taken by her son, . . . Salter, from Mr. Hales' mouth. If she have it, I will endeavour to get it of her. Her Husband's name was Sir William, her son's name, Emund.

Then was told this by Mr. Anthony Faringdon, and have heard it discourst by others, that Mr. Thomas Cary, a poet of note, and a great libertine in his life and talke, and one that had in his youth bein acquainted with Mr. Ha. sent for Mr. Hales to come to him in a dangerous fit of sickness, and desired his advice and absolution, which Mr. Hales, uppon a promise of amendment, gave him, (this was I think in the country.) But Mr. Cary came to London, fell to his old company, and into a more visable scandalous life, and especially in his Discourse, and be [being] taken very sick, that which proved his last, and being much trowbled in mind procured Mr. Ha. to come to him in this his sickness and agony of minde, desyring earnestly, after a confession of many of his sins to have his Prayers, but wood by noe means give him either the sacrament or absolution.

FROM

Love and Truth,
in Two Modest and Peaceable Letters,
Written from a Quiet and Conformable Citizen
of London,
to Two Busie and Factious Shop-keepers in Coventry
(1680)

And now, after so long seriousness, give me liberty to be so pleasant as to tell you a Tale, by which I intend not to provoke you, but to explain my meaning.

"There was a North-Country man, that came young and poor to *London*, to seek that which he call'd his fortune, and it proved to be an Hostler in an Inn of good note in that city, in which condition he continued some years, and by diligence and frugality got and save so much money, that in time he became the Master of that Inn. And not long after his arrival to that happiness, he sent for three of his Neeces, one to serve him in his Kitchin; and the other two did serve for some years in a like condition in other houses, 'till mine *Host* their Unkle died; who, at his death, left to each of them a hundred pound, to buy each of them a North-Country Husband; and also to each of them ten pound to buy new Cloaths, and bear their charges into the North, to see their Mother.

"The three Sisters resolved to go together; and the day being appointed, two of them bought very fantastical Cloaths, and as gaudy Ribbands, intending thereby to be noted and admired; but the third was of a more frugal humour, (yet aimed at admiration too) and said she would save her money, wear her old Cloaths, and yet be noted and get reputation at a cheaper rate: For she would hold some singular new fantastical opinion in Religion, and thereby get admirers, and as many as they should; and it proved so."

And doubtless this is the Ambition of many Women, Shop-keepers, and other of the Common People of very mean parts, who would not be admired or noted if they did not trouble themselves and others, by holding some odd, impertinent, singular opinions. And tell me freely, do you not think that silence would become our Cosin Mrs. B.— than to talk so much and so boldly, against those Clergy-men, and others that bow *at* the Altar (she says *to* the Altar) and use other like reverence in Churches, where she and her Party are so familiar with God as to use none?

Notes on Ben Jonson:
Letter to John Aubrey, 1680
For your Friends quaere *this*

I only knew Ben Jonson: But my Lord of Winton knew him very well; and says, he was in the 6th., that is, the uppermost forme in Westminster scole, at which time his father dyed, and his mother married a brickelayer, who made him (much against his will) help him in his trade; but in a short time, his scolemaister, Mr. Camden, got him a better imployment, which was to attend or accompany a son of Sir Walter Rauley's in his travills. Within a short time after their return, they parted (I think not in cole blood) and with a love sutable to what they had in their travills (not to be commended). And then Ben began to set up for himself in the trade by which he got his subsistance and fame, of which I need not give any account. He got in time to have £100 a yeare from the king, also a pension from the cittie, and the like from many of the nobilitie and some of the gentry, which was well pay'd, for love or fere of his railing in verse, or prose, or boeth. My lord told me, he told him he was (in his long retyrement and sickness, when he saw him, which was often) much afflickted, that hee had profaned the scripture in his playes, and lamented it with horror: yet that, at that time of his long retyrement, his pension (so much as came in) was given to a woman that govern'd him (with whome he liv'd and dyed near the Abie in Westminster); and that neither he nor she tooke too much care for next weike: and wood be sure not to want wine: of which he usually tooke too much before he went to bed, if not oftener and soner. My lord tells me, he knowes not, but thinks he was born in Westminster. The question may be put to Mr. Wood very easily upon what grounds he is positive as to his being born their; he is a friendly man, and will resolve it. So much for brave Ben. You will not think the rest so tedyous as I doe this.

For your 2nd and 3rd *quaere* of Mr. Hill, and Bilingsley, I do neither know nor can learn any thing worth teling you.

For your two remaining *quaere* of Mr. Warner, and Mr. Harriott this:

Mr. Warner[1] did long and constantly lodg nere the water-stares, or market, in Woolstable. Woolstable is a place not far from Charing-Crosse, and nerer to Northumberland-house. My lord of Winchester tells me, he knew him, and that he sayde, he first found out the cerculation of the blood, and discover'd it to Dr. Harvie (who said that 'twas he (himselfe) that found it) for which he is memorally famose. Warner had a pension of £40 a yeare from that Earle of Northumberland that lay so long a prisner in the Towre, and som allowance from Sir. Tho. Aylesbury, and with whom he usually spent his sumer in Windsor Park, and was welcom, for he was harmless and quiet. His winter was spent at the Woolstable, where he dyed in the time of the parlement of 1640, of which or whom, he was no lover.

Mr. Herriott,[2] my lord tells me, he knew also: That he was a more gentile man than Warner. That he had £120 a yeare pension from the said Earle (who was a lover of their studyes), and he lodgings in Syon-house, where he thinks, or believes, he dyed.

This is all I know or can learne for your friend; which I wish may be worth the time and trouble of reading it.

I.W.

November 22, 80.

---

[1] Walter Warner (d. 1640), mathematician and philosopher. His treatise on the circulation of the blood may have been seen by Harvey, but does not anticipate Harvey's conclusions.

[2] Thomas Hariot (1560-1621), mathematician and tutor to Sir Walter Ralegh, for whom he surveyed Virginia in 1585. He influenced the development of modern algebra, and used a telescope to observe the sun-spots and comets of 1607 and 1618.

Inscription on his Marriage Chest

IZAAK WALTON.   RACHEL FLOUD

Joyned Together in the Holie Bond of Wedlocke
On the 27th Daie of Decembere.   A. 1626 D.

WE ONCE WERE TWO, WE TWO MADE ONE
WE NO MORE TWO, THROUGH LIFE BEE ONE.

An Elegie Upon Dr. Donne

Is *Donne*, great *Donne* deceas'd? then England say
Thou hast lost a man where language chose to stay
And shew it's gracefull power. I would not praise
That and his vast wit (which in these vaine dayes
Make many proud) but as they serv'd to unlock
That Cabinet, his mind: where such stock
Of knowledge was repos'd, as all lament
(Or should) this generall cause of discontent.
    And I rejoyce I am not so severe,
But (as I write a line) to weepe a teare
For his decease; Such sad extremities
May make such men as I write *Elegies*.
    And wonder not; for, when a generall losse
Falls on a nation, and they slight the crosse,
God hath rais'd *Prophets* to awaken them
From stupifaction; witnesse my milde pen,
Not us'd to upbraid the world, though now it must
Freely and boldly, for, the cause is just.
    Dull age, Oh I would spare thee, but th'art worse,
Thou art not onely dull, but hast a curse
Of black ingratitude; if not, couldst thou
Part with miraculous *Donne*, and make no vow
For thee and thine, successively to pay
A sad remembrance to his dying day?

Did his youth scatter *Poetrie*, wherein
Was all Philosophie? Was every sinne,
Character'd in his *Satyres*? made so foule
That some have fear'd their shapes, and kept their soule
Freer by reading verse? Did he give *dayes*
Past marble monuments, to those, whose praise
He would perpetuate? Did hee (I feare
The dull will doubt;) these at his twentieth yeare?
But, more matur'd: Did his full soule conceive,
And in harmonious-holy-numbers weave
A Crowne of sacred sonnets, fit to adorne
A dying Martyrs brow: or, to be worne
On that blest head of *Mary Magdalen*:
After she wip'd Christs feet, but not till then?
Did hee (fit for such penitents as shee
And hee to use) leave us a *Litany*?
Which all devout men love, and sure, it shall,
As times grow better, grow more classicall.
Did he write *Hymnes*, for piety and wit
Equall to those the great *Prudentius* writ?
Spake he all *Languages*? knew he all *Lawes*?
The grounds and use of *Physick*; but because
'Twas mercenary wav'd it? Went to see
That blessed place of *Christs nativity*?
Did he returne and preach him? preach him so
As none but hee could do? his hearers know
(Such as were blest to heare him) this is truth.
Did he confirme thy aged? convert thy youth?
Did he these wonders? And is this deare losse
Mourn'd by so few? (few for so great a crosse).
   But sure the silent are ambitious all
To be *Close Mourners* at his Funerall;
If not; In common pitty they forbare
By repetitions to renew our care;
Or, knowing, griefe conceiv'd, conceal'd, consumes
Man irreparably, (as poyson'd fumes
Do waste the braine) make silence a safe way
To inlarge the soule from these walls, mud and clay,

(Materialls of this body) to remaine
With *Donne* in heaven, where no promiscuous paine
Lessens the joy wee have, for, with *him,* all
Are satisfyed with *joyes essentiall.*

My thoughts, Dwell on this *Joy*, and do not call
Griefe backe, by thinking of his Funerall;
Forget he lov'd mee; Waste not my sad yeares;
(Which haste to *Davids* seventy, fill'd with feares
And sorrow for his death;) Forget his parts,
Which find a living grave in good mens hearts;
And (for, my first is daily paid for sinne)
Forget to pay my second sigh for him:
Forget his powerfull preaching; and forget
I am his *Convert*. Oh my frailtie! let
My flesh be no more heard, it will obtrude
This lethargie: so should my gratitude,
My vowes of gratitude should so be broke;
Which can no more be, then *Donnes* vertues spoke
By any but himselfe; for which cause, I
Write no *Encomium*, but an *Elegie.*
(1633)

On a Portrait of DONNE Taken in his Eighteenth Year.

This was for Youth, Strength, Mirth, and wit that Time
Most count their Golden Age; but t'was not thine.
Thine was thy later yeares, so much refind
From youthd Drosse, Mirth and wit; as thy pure mind
Thought (like the Angels) nothing but the Praise
Of thy Creator, in those last, best Dayes.
Witnes this Booke, (thy Embleme) which begins
With Love; but endes, with Sighes, and Teares for sinns.

160

Epitaph on David Hookham

SACRED TO THE MEMORY OF
DAVID HOOKHAM,
Who died A.D. 1647,
Aged 63 Years

Within this turfe, on which in life he trod,
Rests David Hookham, waiting for his God.
A peaceful, honest, faithful life he led;
And blessed as he break his daily bread,
Simple his manners, candid was his look,
His mirrour was the bright and purling brook;
And life's clear waters as they passed on,
Reminded him how soon he should be gone.
At last his rod and angle he laid by,
And humbly dyed. May all like David dye,
And serve their Lord and Master faithfully,
As David Hookham in this world served me.

Couplet on Dr. Richard Sibbes (1650)

Of this blest man, let this just praise be given,
Heaven was in him, before he was in heaven.

On the Death of my dear friend Mr. William Cartwright, relating to the foregoing Elegies.

I cannot keep my purpose, but must give
Sorrow and Verse their way; nor will I grieve
Longer in silence; no, that poor, poor part
Of nature's legacy, Verse void of Art,
An undissembled teares, CARTWRIGHT shall have
Fixt on his Hearse; and wept into his grave.

Muses I need you not; for, Grief and I
Can in your absence weave an Elegy:
Which we will do; and often inter-weave
Sad Looks, and Sighs; the ground-work must receive
Such Characters, or be adjudg'd unfit
For my Friends shroud; others have shewed their Wit,
Learning, and Language fitly; for these be
Debts due to his great Merits: but for me,
My aymes are like my self, humble and low,
Too mean to speak his praise, too mean to show
The World what it has lost in losing thee,
Whose Words and Deeds were perfect Harmony.

But now 'tis lost, lost in the silent Grave,
Lost to us Mortals, lost, 'till we shall have
Admission to that Kingdom, where He sings
Harmonious Anthems to the King of Kings.

Sing on blest Soul! be as thou wast below,
A more than common instrument to show
Thy Makers praise; sing on, whilst I lament
Thy loss, and court a holy discontent,
With such pure thoughts as thine, to dwell with me,
Then I may hope to live, and dye like thee,
To live belov'd, dye mourn'd, thus in my grave;
Blessings that Kings have wish'd, but cannot have.

To My Reverend Friend the Author of the Synagogue

Sir,
I lov'd you for your Synagogue,[1] before
I knew your person; but now love you more;
                                    Because I find
It is so true a picture of your mind:
                        Which tunes your sacred lyre
                        To that eternal quire;

[1] Walton is referring to Christopher Harvey.

162

Where holy *Herbert* sits
(O shame to prophane wits)
And sings his and your Anthems, to the praise
Of Him that is the first and last of daies.

These holy Hymns had an Ethereal birth:
For they can raise sad souls above the earth
And fix them there
Free from the worlds anxieties and fear.
Herbert and you have pow'r
To do this: ev'ry hour
I read you kills a sin,
Or lets a vertue in
To fight against it; and the Holy Ghost
Supports my frailties, lest the day be lost.

This holy war, taught by your happy pen,
The Prince of Peace approves. When we poor men
Neglect our arms,
W'are circumvented with a world of harms.
But I will watch, and ward,
And stand upon my guard,
And still consult with you,
And *Herbert*, and renew
My vows, and say, Well fare his, and your heart,
The fountains of such sacred wit and art.

Epitaph on his Second Wife, Anne Ken

Here lyeth buried so much as
could die of ANNE, the Wife of
Isaak Walton;
who was
a Woman of Remarkable Prudence,
and of the Primitive Piety; her great
and general knowledge being adorned

with such true humility, and blest
with so much Christian meekness, as
made her worthy of a more memorable
Monument.
She dyed! (Alas, that she is dead!)
the 17th of April, 1662, aged 52.
Study to be like her.

Commendatory Verses to Jeremiah Rich
in his 'Short-hand Improved'

TO HIS FRIEND THE AUTHER ON THIS HIS INGENIOUS WORKE
INTITULED RICH REDEVIVUS

Had I the happy Genius to Endite
In lofty Verse as fast as thou canst write,
I might not then perhaps dispair to raise
A worthy Monument unto thy Praise,
That might in Smooth and well Tun'd numbers tell
How much thy pen all others doth Excell.
But being dull I can proceed noe Higher
Then to approve thy Labours and Admire.
The Magicke of thy Industry Alarms
The silent Ghosts, who yeeld unto its Charms.
By honest Negromancy here wee have
Ingenious Rich raisd from his Slumbering Grave,
Who though surprizd is yet Content to see
His Art Refind, Improvd, out done by thee,
Whose pains make gratefull Brevity to Vye
In these few Leaves with perspicuity:
The whole soe short, and yet so plainely pend,
The dullest Brains thy Rules may Comprehend.
The use of such rare Art and Various worth
Deserves whole Volummes for to sett it forth.
It preserves secrets from the Curious Eye,
Saves tedious pains, Releives the Memory,

And Clipps Tymes wings, for thus transcribe we may
More in one hower, then others in a day,
The Heavenly Seed which powerfull Preachers sowe
By help of This is made more like to Growe;
For Manna gather'd thus, Lasts many a yeare,
Which elce is too oft lost by the treacherous Ear.
Then on my frind, Reguard not Criticks Rage,
But with thy Booke oblige our slothful Age.
Though Envy fret and bark and disapprove,
The Good and Just will pay Applause and Love.   (1676)

Izaak Walton's Will

August the 9th, 1683.

In the name of God Amen. I Izaak Walton the elder of Winchester being this present day in the neintyeth yeare of my age and in perfect memory for which praysed be God: but Considering how sodainly I may be deprived of boeth doe therfore make this my last will and testament as followeth. And first I doe [declare] my beleife to be that their is only one God who hath made the whole world and me and all mankinde to whome I shall give an acount of all my actions which are not to be justified, but I hope pardoned for the merits of my saviour Jesus. – And because [the profession] of Cristianity does at this time, seime to be subdevided into papist and protestant, I take it to be at least convenient to declare my beleife to be in all poynts of faith, as the Church of England now professeth. And this I doe the rather, because of a very long and very trew friendship with some of the Roman Church.

And for my worldly estate, (which I have nether got by falshood or flattery or the extreme crewelty of the law of this nation,) I doe hereby give and bequeth it as followeth. – First I give my son-in-law Doctor Hawkins and to his Wife, to them I give all my tytell and right of or in part of a howse and shop in Pater-noster-rowe in London: which I hold by lease from the Lord Bishop of London for about 50 years to come. And I doe also give to them all my right and tytell of or to a howse in Chansery-lane, London; where in Mrs. Greinwood now dwelleth, in which is now about 16 years to come. I give these two leases to them, they saving my executor from all damage concerning the same. (And I doe also give to my saide dafter all my books this day at Winchester and Droxford: and what ever ells I can call mine their, except a trunk of linen which I give my son Izaak Walton. But if he doe not marry, or use the saide linen himselfe, then I give the same to my grand-doughter Anne Hawkins).

And I give to my son Izaak, all my right and tytell to a lease of Norington farm, which I hold from the lord Bishop of Winton.

And I doe also give him all my right and tytell to a farme or land near to Stafford: which I bought of Mr. Walter Noell: I say, I give it to him and [his] heares for ever. But upon the condition following. Namely – if my sone shall not marry before he shall be the age of forty and one yeare; or being marryed shall dye before the saide age and leve noe son to inherit the saide farme or land: or if his sonn [or sonns] shall not live to attain the age of twentie and one yeare, to dispose otherwayes of it, then I give the saide farme or lande to the towne or corperation of Stafford (in which I was borne), for the good and benifit of some of the saide towne, as I shall direct and as followeth. But first note, that it is at this present time rented for £21 10s. a yeare. (and is like to hold the said rent, if care be taken to keipe the barne and howsing in repaire) and I wood have and doe give ten pownd of the saide rent, to binde out yearely two boyes, the sons of honest and pore parents to be apprentices to som tradesmen or handy-craftmen, to the intent the saide boyes [may] the better afterward get their owne living. – And I doe also give five pownd yearly, out of the said rent to be given to some meade-servant, that hath atain'd the age of twenty and [one] yeare (not les), and dwelt long in one servis, or to som honest pore man's daughter, that hath atain'd to that age, to [be] paide her, at or on the day of her marriage.

And this being done, my will is, that what rent shall remaine of the saide farme or lande, shall be disposed of as followeth.

First I doe give twenty shillings yearely, to be spent by the maior of Stafford and those that shall collect the said rent: and dispose of it as I have and shall hereafter direct. And that what mony or rent shall remain undisposed offe shall be imployed to buie coles for some pore people, that shall most neide them in the saide towne; the saide coles to be delivered in the last weike in Janewarye, or in the very first weike in Febrewary: I say then, because I take that time to be the hardest and most pinching times with pore people. And God reward those that shall doe this with out partialitie and with honestie and a good contience.

And if the saide maior and others of the saide towne of Stafford, shall prove so necligent or dishonest as not to imploy the rent by me given as intended and exprest in this my will, (which God forbid,) then I give the saide rents and profits, of the saide farme or land, to the towne and chiefe magistrats or governers of Ecles-

167

hall, to be disposed by them in such maner as I have ordered the disposall of it, by the towne of Stafford. The said farm or land being nere the towne of Ecles-hall.

And I give to my son-in-law Doctor Hawkins, (whome I love as my owne son) and to my dafter his wife, and my son Izaak to each of them a ring with these words or motto; – love my memory, I.W. obiet = to the Lord Bishop of Winton a ring with this motto – a mite for a million: I.W. obiet =" And to the friends hearafter named I give to each of them a ring with this motto A friends farewell. I.W. obiet" = And my will is, the said rings be delivered within forty dayes of my deth. And that the price or valew of all the saide rings shall be – 13s. 4d. a peice.

I give to Doctor Hawkins Doctor Donns Sermons; which I have hear'd preacht, and read with much content. To my son Izaak I give Doctor Sibbs his *Soules Conflict*, and to my doughter his *Brewsed Reide*; desiring them to reade them so, as to be well aquanted with them. And I also give to her all my bookes at Winchester and Droxford, and what ever in those two places are or I can call mine: except a trunk of linen, which I gave to my son Izaak, but if he doe not live to make use of it, then I give the same to my grand-dafter, Anne Hawkins. And I give my dafter Doctor Halls Works which be now at Farnham.

To my son Izaak I give all my books, (not yet given) at Farnham Castell and a deske of prints and pickters; also a cabinet nere my beds head, in which are som littell thngs that he will valew, tho of noe great worth.

And my will and desyre is, that he will be kind to his Ante Beacham and his ant Rose Ken: by alowing the first about fiftie shilling a yeare in or for bacon and cheise (not more), and paying £4 a yeare toward the bordin of her son's dyut to Mr. John Whitehead. For his ante Ken, I desyre him to be kinde to her according to her necessitie and his own abillitie. And I comend one of her children to breide up (as I have saide I intend to doe) if he shall be able to doe it. As I know he will; for, they be good folke.

I give to Mr. John Darbishire the Sermons of Mr. Anthony Faringdon, or of doctor Sanderson, which my executor thinks fit. To my servant, Thomas Edgehill I give five pownd in mony, and all my clothes linen and wollen except one sute of clothes, (which

I give to Mr. Holinshed, and forty shiling) if the saide Thomas be servant at my deth, if not my cloths only.

And I give my old friend Mr. Richard Marriott ten pownd in mony, to be paid him within 3 months after my deth. And I desyre my son to shew kindeness to him if he shall neide, and my son can spare it.

And I doe hereby will and declare my son Izaak to be my sole executor of this my last will and testament; and Doctor Hawkins, to see that he performs it, which I doubt not but he will.

I desyre my buriall may be nere the place of my deth; and free from any ostentation or charg, but privately: this I make to be my last will, (to which I only add the codicell for rings,) this 16. day of August, 1683.

Witnes to this will.

IZAAK WALTON.

The rings I give are as on the other side.

To my brother Jon Ken.
To my sister his wife.
To my brother Doctor Ken.
To my sister Pye.
To Mr. Francis Morley.
To Sir George Vernon.
To his wife.
To his 3 dafters.
To Mrs. Nelson.
To Mr. Rich. Walton.
To Mr. Palmer.
To Mr. Taylor.
To Mr. Tho. Garrard.
To the Lord Bishop of Sarum.
To Mr. Rede his Servant.
To my Coz. Dorothy Kenrick.
To my Coz. Lewin.
To Mr. Walter Higgs.
To Mr. Cha. Cotton.
To Mr. Rich. Marriott

To my brother Beacham.
To my sister his wife.
To the lady Anne How.
To Mrs. King Doctor Philips wife.
To Mr. Valantine Harecourt.
To Mrs. Elyza Johnson.
To Mrs. Mary Rogers.
To Mrs. Elyza Milward.
To Mrs. Doro. Wallop.
To Mr. Will. Milward of
       Christ-Church, Oxford.
To Mr. John Darbeshire.
To Mr. Veudvill.
To Mrs. Rock.
To Mr. Peter White.
To Mr. John Lloyde.
To my Coz. Greinfells
   – widow.
16 Mrs. Dalbin must not
   be forgotton.

22

Note that several lines are blotted
out of this will for they are twice repeted:
And, that this will is now signed & sealed,   IZAAK WALTON
this twenty and fourth day of October
1683 in the presence of us —
    Witnes, Abra. Markland.
        Jos: Taylor.
        Thomas Crawley.

The last part of *The Life of Dr. John Donne*, with revisions.

Four versions of the *Life of Donne* were published in Walton's life-time. The first, and shortest, appeared in 1640 as a biographical preface to Donne's *LXXX Sermons*. Walton revised the text for separate publication in 1658, and then again in 1670 and 1675 for its inclusion in his collected *Lives* of Donne, Wotton, Hooker and Herbert.

The famous last section of the *Life of Donne* is here given below in all its forms. On the left is the version of 1640, which is the shortest and most different of them. On the right the version of 1675, the final text to receive Walton's revisions, is printed, and variant readings from the texts of 1658 and 1670 appear in notes at the foot of the page.

<u>From the edition of 1640</u>

He was of stature moderately tall; of a straight and equally proportioned body, to which all his words and gave an unexpressible addition of comelinesse.

His aspect was cheerfull, and such as gave a silent testimony of a cleere knowing soule, and of a conscience at peace with it selfe.

<u>From the edition of 1675[1]</u>

He was of Stature moderately tall, of a strait and equally-proportioned body, to which all his words and actions gave an unexpressible addition of Comeliness.[2]

The melancholy and pleasant humor,[3] were in him so contempered, that each gave advantage to the other, and made his Company one of the delights of Mankind.[4]

His fancy was unimitably high, equalled only[5] by his great wit; both being made useful by a commanding judgment.[6]

[1] This RH column also represents the versions of 1658 and 1670. Differences are given in the notes below.

2 1658 *Comelinesse.*

3 1658 and 1670, no comma.

4 1658 *mankind.*

5 1658 and 1670 *onely.*

6 1658 and 1670 *judgement.*

His melting eye shewed he had a soft heart, full of noble pity, of too brave a spirit to offer injuries, and too much a Christian, not to pardon them in others.

His fancy was un-imitable high, equalled by his great wit, both being made usefull by a commanding judgement.

His mind was liberall, and unwearied in the search of knowledge, with which his vigorous soule is now satisfied, and employed in a continuall praise of that God that first breathed it into his active body, which once was a

His aspect *was chearful,*[7] *and such,*[8] *as gave a silent testimony of a clear knowing soul, and of a Conscience at peace with it self.*

His melting eye,[9] *shewed that he had a soft heart, full of noble compassion;*[10] *of too brave a soul to offer injuries, and too much a Christian not to pardon them in others.*

He did much contemplate (especially after he entred into his Sacred Calling) the mercies *of Almighty God, the* Immortality of the Soul, *and the* joyes of Heaven; *and would often say,* Blessed be God that he is God only, and divinely like himself.[11]

He was by nature highly passionate, but more apt to reluct at the excesses of it. A great lover of the offices of humanity, and of so merciful[12] *a spirit, that* he never beheld the miseries of Mankind[13] without pity and relief.

He was earnest and unwearied in the search of knowledge; *with which,*[14] *his vigorous soul is now satisfied, and employed in a continual praise of that God that first breathed it into his active body; that body, which*[15] *once*

---

[7] 1658 *cheerfull.*
[8] 1658 and 1670, no comma.
[9] 1658 and 1670, no comma.
[10] 1658, comma for semicolon.
[11] 1658 and 1670, Blessed be God that he is God divinely like himself.
[12] 1658 *mercifull.*
[13] 1658 mankind.
[14] 1658 and 1670, no comma.
[15] 1658 *active body; which once:* 1670, *active body; that body which once* (no comma)

Temple of the holy Ghost, and is now become a small quantity of Christian dust. But I shall see it re-animated.

IZ: WA..

was a Temple of the Holy Ghost, *and is now become a small quantity of* Christian dust:

But I shall see it reanimated.[16]

I.W.

Feb. 15. 1639.[17]

[16] 1658 *reinanimated* (no hyphen). This version of 'reanimated' is only otherwise found in Donne.

[17] Typically, Walton only gives this date for the version of 1675.